INSIDE A PARADISE

by
June Wilcoxon Brown
Edited by Julius M. Wilensky

All photos by the author unless otherwise indicated

Library of Congress Card No. 91-65345
ISBN No. 0-918752-14-0
SAN No. 210-5810

EDITOR'S PREFACE

June Wilcoxon Brown has written over 60 short stories, published in newspapers and magazines including Family Circle, Canadian Home Journal, Gent, Holland's, The Boston Globe and many others. Her non-fiction articles have appeared in Atlantic Monthly, American Mercury, Christian Science Monitor, Milwaukee Journal, Travel, and others.

June once won the Writer's Cup, presented annually for outstanding achievement in journalism by Theta Sigma Chi (now Women in Communications). During the 1950's she was listed as one of "2000 Women of Achievement in America." June has been listed in "Who's Who of American Women" for more than 15 years.

Ms. Brown was born in West Lafayette, Ohio. Her father was a U.S. Geological Survey topographer. As a child, June lived in 21 states and went to school in 12! She graduated from the University of Maryland at College Park with a B.A.

For six years June did promotion and publicity for Wilson Steamship Lines. At that time, she was also Vice-President of the Central Businessmen's Association of Washington, DC. She and her husband then moved to Madison, Wisconsin, where she began her writing career. She was Editor of Select Magazine, and wrote a syndicated radio show for The U.S. Electric Utilities spokesman.

After several trips to St. Thomas, the Browns relocated there in 1965, startling all their Madison friends. Al Brown chucked a good job, but he's lived to a ripe old age in St. Thomas, so it must have been a good move. Read this book and judge for yourself how well June liked it. The Browns both got into community service and social activities in St. Thomas just as they had done in Madison.

Wescott Cove has been publishing for 20 years, and knows good writing when it comes our way. Though this is a different genre than the cruising guides and nautical books we are known for, it was too good to pass up. It gives so much information about an island that has become a cruising destination, as well as a cruising jumping-off point, that we think it will fit into our nautical distribution.

I have fond memories of the Virgin Islands. In 1965, my wife, Dutch and I and the Cunninghams from Old Greenwich had a wonderful 17-day cruise on a bareboat charter out of Lagoon, Benner Bay. We visited every harbor in all of the British and American Virgins. The weather was perfect and winds were never less than 15 knots nor more than 25. This trip started my Caribbean writing career, and I've been back to the Caribbean 18 times since. Though we've found better sailing in the Leewards and Windwards and better snorkeling in Honduras, Belize and Mexico, I have a soft spot in my heart for St. Thomas.

We were shopping on Main Street in Charlotte Amalie, strolling towards the Post Office, just in time to catch the strains of a uniformed brass band.

They came down Garden Street and turned right into Main Street, creating a monumental traffic jam. We crossed the street and walked up the hill towards Government House for a better look. It turned out to be a funeral procession that took 15 minutes to pass. The band was playing something I'd never heard in slow cadence. The procession seemed to be classified by occupation, and the whole town was in it, afoot or in cars. Among them were weeping nurses (I thought he was a doctor), a girls' softball team (I thought he was a coach), then the Governor's car cut into the procession, flags flying from his antenna. I asked a lady, and she told me it was for an old revered black man whose children and grandchildren were community leaders. June says they don't do this anymore, but this tribute was most impressive.

Working with June to bring you this book has been our pleasure, and we are proud to present to you the work of this trained observer and prize-winning author.

Julius M. Wilensky
February, 1991

LIST OF MAPS IN THIS BOOK

HOW I CAME TO WRITE THIS BOOK

To satisfy the insatiable curiosity of friends about our lives in St. Thomas after we moved here in 1965, I began writing Christmas letters in 1966. I covered day-to-day living problems, amusing and heart-warming incidents, newspaper bloopers, and interesting facts that highlighted the differences of Stateside and island living.

Sixteen years later because I was ill, we did not send out the usual two hundred letters, and we received a deluge of mail asking why and wanting us to continue them. Many people had saved all the letters and dozens had preserved theirs in loose-leaf folders. The life of the Crazy Browns, who had become willing Robinson Crusoes and moved to a cozy little island in the Caribbean fascinated them. We dispelled the idea that tropical islands were idyllic paradises.

I began then to wonder if I should not write a book about "living," not "just vacationing" on a tropical island. Later, when I tried to end the letters after twenty years, the response made me decide that if a cross section of two hundred people from all over the United States and abroad wanted to know about our lives, it was time to put twenty-five years of our experiences into a book.

Thus "Inside American Paradise" was born and won a 1989 Honorable Mention in the International Literary Awards. Soon after, on first submission, Julius Wilensky, President of Westcott Publishing Company in Stamford, Connecticut promptly bought it.

Working with Julius has been a learning experience and a great pleasure. His twenty years in the publishing business has provided me editing knowledge from which I have greatly benefitted and made me realize the many advantages of dealing directly with a small publisher who is in a position to make immediate decisions.

Besides Julius Wilensky, I want to express my gratitude to Aimery Caron and Marti Giovan for their critiques of Cha-Cha Town; Publisher Ariel Melchior, Jr. and Managing Editor Penny Feuerzeig of the Daily News for their advice; Dolores Jowers for her help with photos and historical information; and Sir Carpenter Batchelder, Nat Norris, Gigner McConnell, Maxine Carter, and Ira Smith for background material on their unique homes.

Julius Wilensky and I hope you will find "Inside American Paradise" a pleasure to read.

June Wilcoxon Brown

TABLE OF CONTENTS

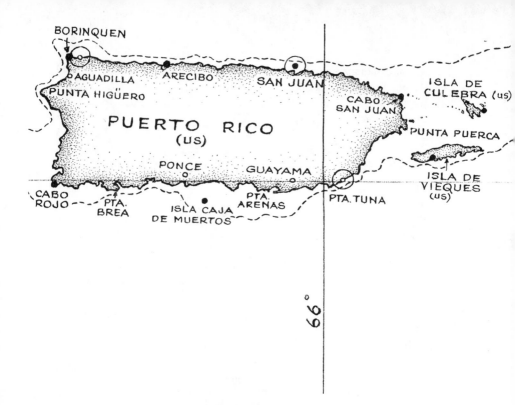

Taxi and tour bus stand at Cruz Bay Park in Cruz Bay Village, St. John. Almost the entire economy of both St. John and St. Thomas depends on tourism

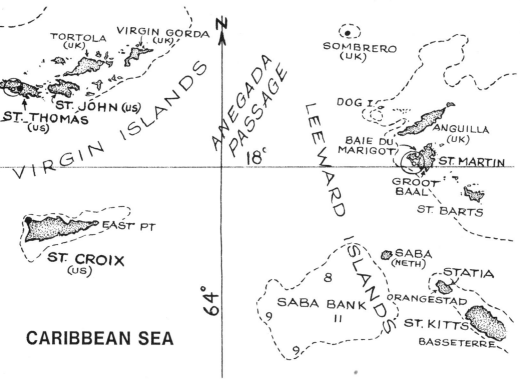

Puerto Rico to Leeward Islands
Showing Location of Virgin Islands
Scale: 1:1,800,000

Legend

• Lighthouse
○ Radio Direction
   Finding Station

Beach at Trunk Bay, St. John. There's an underwater marked trail for snorkelers

PART 1: INSIDE LOOKING BACK

CHAPTER 1

GENESIS

HOW WE CAME TO ST. THOMAS

Early Impressions

"Inside!"

The first time I heard someone shout that word outside our house in St. Thomas, U.S. Virgin Islands, I found a tall black man standing at the front door.

"Yes?" I said, peering out at him.

"Inside," he repeated.

My puzzlement showed, because he grinned. "You say, 'Outside, inside,' " he directed in a West Indian accent.

"Outside, inside," I parroted. He came inside.

That is the way I learned how St. Thomians "ring the doorbell," so to speak.

On that beautiful September morning in 1965, my teacher turned out to be an "egg man" who wanted to sell me eggs. Since I was a woman in need of eggs, I bought a dozen and made a weekly deal.

Through the grapevine, I learned of the "mushroom lady"; that Edith Feiner's Flower Shop sold whipping cream; and the Sea Chest, a paint store, carried S.S. Pierce canned goods. Shopping rivaled treasure hunting.

"Egg men" and "mushroom ladies" are, sadly, no more. But a few days ago I heard a man call "Inside!"

Delighted, I answered back, "Outside, inside!" and by magic palm frond returned to those idyllic days of the 60s when my husband Al and I discovered the U.S. Virgin Islands and, in particular, St. Thomas. Thirteen miles at its longest point, three at its widest, the island totals thirty-two square miles. Only a freckle on Mother Earth's face.

Aboard a rickety and ancient DC-3, we flew from San Juan to St. Thomas for the first time in the fall of 1960. We laughed at the roller-coaster feel of occasional air pockets and marvelled at the incredibly blue Caribbean. In a cloudless sky, sunbeams turned the sea's tranquil water into an endless field of shimmering diamonds. Our smiles to each other confirmed our belief that we **were** approaching Paradise.

Shortly, the plane landed on a Band-Aid-size runway. After digging in its heels, it came eyeball-to-eyeball with a spunky little mountain. Surrendering a moment later, it swung around and headed for the airport terminal, a huge camouflaged hangar left over from the days when the military was St. Thomas' Big Brother.

My knuckles regained color after I disembarked and felt solid ground beneath me. Note: The spunky little mountain was bull-dozed away for our new airport. Consequently, regular commuters no longer need a whiff of smelling salts before landing.

White surrey-fringed jeeps, striped in pink, green, or blue, rented for $10 a day were picked up inside the terminal—an inspired arrangement.

Driving away in our gala pink and white jeep, we saw "Keep Left" prominently displayed on the dashboard. A couple of close calls soon taught us and other right-hand-side drivers that if we wanted to live, we drove on the left.

The sprinkling of tourists in those days loved the sporty jeeps, and on the road we waved to each other like soul mates as we clattered and jolted over dirt trails searching for isolated beaches. Preferably, these sea-lapped hideaways were shaded by palms, seagrape trees with fruit that tastes like grapes, and manchineel trees. Eat one of the manchineel's poisonous "death apples" and like Adam, you have had it. Without a snake.

In the early 60s, St. Thomas was a laid-back island with two traffic lights. Donkeys and goats ambled leisurely as beachcombers along roadsides. Informal members of European nobility relaxed on cool, wide verandahs facing the sea.

Suntanned barefoot artists in shorts found new inspiration. And Herman Wouk wrote his novel "Don't Stop the Carnival" from a comfortable eyrie that overlooked Charlotte Amalie and its harbor.

Sometimes Alec Waugh, pursuing Caribbean research for his novels, stayed at Hotel 1829, a charming old Danish hillside mansion painted pink and tenderly embraced with tropical vegetation.

Once when Waugh planned an island visit, a friend of his informed a prominent St. Thomas hostess the author would be here and preferred "small, intimate black-tie dinners."

She responded with a one-liner: "Doesn't everyone?"

Even Marian Anderson and Shirley Chisholm succumbed to the island's charm and bought land. Riise Stevens built a showplace house on a cliff above the sea. Victor Borge considered legendary Contant Estate, but finally settled for a Danish mansion on St. Croix. Our loss.

The Jonathan Winters found Smith's Fancy, up a narrow, twisted Charlotte Amalie street, the perfect holiday retreat. Hosted by artist Ira Smith and his wife, Stevie, this popular guest house boasted a credible art gallery and foliaged terrace for harbor-viewing during cocktails and dinner.

Jim Tillett, well-known British textile designer and painter, had recently moved to St. Thomas from Mexico City. After restoring the crumbling stone buildings of a picturesque old Danish plantation at Tutu Village, he set up workshops for artists and craftspeople.

Set among tall trees and lush plants, a remodeled cowshed featured Jim's tropical designs being silkscreened on sea-island cotton and other fine fabrics—and still does. A high-ceilinged, stone-floored barn housed a boutique with clothes designed by Jim's wife, Rhoda. The boutique is

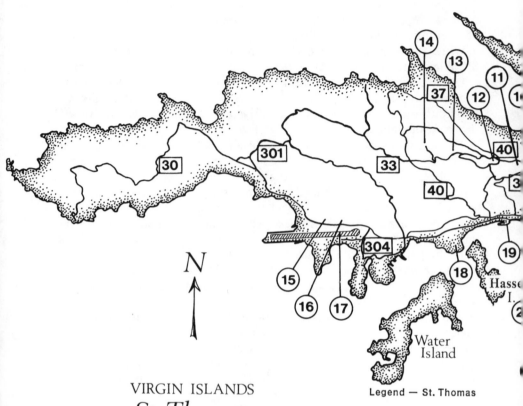

N

VIRGIN ISLANDS
St. Thomas

Water Island

Hasse I.

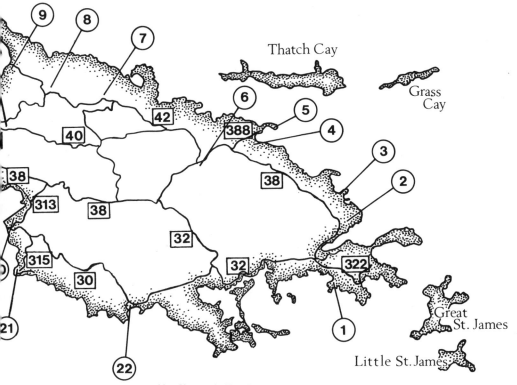

Thatch Cay

Grass Cay

Great St. James

Little St. James

14. Mountain Top Bar and Restaurant
    Home of the Banana Daiquiri
15. Raichhold Center for the Arts
16. University of the Virgin Islands
17. Airport
18. Frenchtown
19. Charlotte Amalie
20. West Indian Co. Dock and Havensight Mall
21. Frenchman's Reef and Mooring
22. Balongo Bay Beach Resorts

Numbers in squares are road route numbers

gone, but a tinkling fountain and outdoor Mexican Restaurant with a talkative macaw perched on a gnarly dead tree trunk add to the ambience.

This spacious complex, called "Tillett Gardens," began to sponsor arts and crafts shows in 1980 and ended up with three a year. Displaying artists, local and from abroad, sell their works and share in prizes. Style shows, acrobats, Mocko Jumbie stilt-dancers, and folk dancers enliven activities. "Arts Alive" and "Classics in the Garden" concerts now occupy Rhoda's time.

After numerous visits over the next few years, we could not resist the peaceful allure of the islands. We folded our igloo in Madison, Wisconsin in 1965 and headed for the sun, sand, and serenity of St. Thomas. After all, the license plates boasted: "American Paradise."

Our Happy Homes

We learned quickly that being a "tourist" in Paradise resembled living here about as much as a pampered Pekingese resembles a Prairie Dog.

Our first hillside home was a disaster.

If I mention "hillside" too often, it is because our island is **all** hillsides. A travel editor once wrote: "People build houses on St. Thomas where the terrain is too steep for mountain goats."

That describes our hillside to a T. Any sizable rain roared down from the mountain above us in Niagara Falls torrents and made a swimming pool of our living room. Since Al has the buoyancy of a sandbag in water, this presented problems. Consequently, in March 1966, we moved into a residence we called "Hidden Hill."

Arts & crafts exhibit at Tillet Gardens.
Rhoda Tillet (center) at showcase of jewelry craftsman

El Papagayo Restaurant at Tillet Gardens.
Talkative macaw perched at top is named "Chico"

One thousand feet above the sea, our rambling four-bedroom tropical house and swimming pool outside, not **inside**, reposed comfortably in two acres of botanical gardens shaded by huge trees: mahogany, flamboyant, mango, avocado. The French gardeners of the former owners labored five years fencing in the property with a ten-foot, red hibiscus hedge and constructing stone terraces filled with a Monet palette of flowers.

We posthaste purchased a fourteen-volume Encyclopedia of Gardening and became horticulture authorities. Quite a surprise to our Stateside friends who knew my past gardening activities centered around growing sweet-potato and avocado-seed vines in old jelly glasses. Still we meant it. With books in hand, we identified a hundred flowers, plants, and trees.

The northside mountain behind us protected rather than inundated **this** piece of land, thus preserving its rare old trees. African Tulip, Brazilian Rose, breadfruit (brought to the West Indies by Captain Bligh), lime, and a spreading Saman tree were among the survivors of island hurricanes.

A large Brazilian Rose tree graced the terrace below the gallery where we ate our meals. When the tree bloomed, the huge yellow rose-like, but scentless blossoms, always managed to fall flat on their faces. Each morning before breakfast, I trotted down and turned them over—dozens—so we and our house guests could enjoy their beauty all day.

One impressed house guest said, "I'm glad you a-**rose** to the occasion!"

Our most dazzling flowers were hybrid orange hibiscus and white crinkled paper ones with centers delicately tinted in pastels; the golden Rain of Gold blossoms that hedged the flagstone path from house to swimming pool; the terraces of flaming Poinsettias at Christmas, or purple Oleanders all year; and the non-stop blooming red Crown of Thorns everywhere. See why we needed that Encyclopedia?

We even had night-blooming Cereus. Late at night, when the tree frogs chirped and amphibian relatives unlimbered their bassoons in concert, we sometimes roamed the grounds to find a Cereus ready to bloom.

Transfixed, we watched its spectacular show. As if touched by Houdini's wand, the waxy white blossoms slowly unfolded in the perfumed and shadowy moonlight, wafting us to an exotic old Persian garden. At times, as many as seven blooms appeared on a cactus stem attached to a tree trunk or branch.

Occasionally we brought an unopened Cereus inside and floated it in a crystal bowl. As the night progressed, we watched it gradually display its lily-white petals. Times like this, we glimpsed Paradise.

Realtor Arthur Witty once said of Hidden Hill, "It's like living in a park."

So, since Hidden Hill was not in the way of a mountain run-off, we lived happily ever after. Well, more or less, for eight years.

Our first year, after correcting two sections of plumbing that inconsiderately drained uphill instead of down and flooded two bathrooms, we rejuvenated the swimming pool. Unused for several years, it required as much paint and plaster as a seventy-year-old female saloon keeper. Added to this sizable, costly job was five hundred dollars to fill the pool with **water**, not champagne.

One thing Paradise does not have is water. In olden days, rain collected in home cisterns provided most island needs. Hillside catchments of concrete or brick, looking like giant "earth bandages," supplied the rest.

St. Thomas began using desalination plants in the 60s and early 70s, but still barged water from Puerto Rico to meet our demands. Puerto Rico now uses all its available water. If our plants cannot furnish enough for us, people on public water suffer through rationing.

Cisterns of those living in the country are usually large enough to more than supply our requirements, so we only buy water during droughts—or to fill swimming pools.

When our refurbished pool was ready to be filled, the truck rumbled up and down the mountain from a supply tank in town until late afternoon.

After the trucker left, we jumped in the water and splashed around like midget porpoises, luxuriating in the pool and its pastoral setting. Even our birds twittered happily. At last our pool troubles were behind us. Not far behind. What fools ye mortals be!

Two days later, we discovered the pool leaked a quarter inch a day. This created stick-your-finger-in-the-dike panic.

We tried everything. Armed with a marine putty, Al, looking like a Cousteau skin diver, plopped over the side in scuba equipment to seal suspicious cracks. No luck. We hired a professional diver who crack-hunted inch-by-inch with the tenacity of a crab. No luck. Finally we decided we must swim—or sink, so we built a new pool inside the old one.

A few days after we completed the pool, an early morning earthquake, strong enough to drive us from our beds to stand in doorways, shook our house. After the tremor passed, we rushed to the pool, neither one uttering a sound. Water sloshed back and forth like a bowl of water carried by a small boy.

Silent, close scrutiny revealed no cracks. WHOOPEE!

No more pool trouble plagued us. The pool and its terrace with sun cots, outdoor tables and chairs under umbrellas, and whimsical, covered bar became our entertaining center and special joy to "snowbird" house guests.

Over the years we shared the beauty of Hidden Hill's gardens with any legitimate group: Garden Clubs from Panama and South America; Danish West Indies Society hosted by St. Thomas Friends of Denmark; Underwater Council Convention; Antilles School House and Garden Tours; and Nick and Maxine Carter's twenty-five Florida guests in St. Thomas for a weekend house party. For them, we created a special sign: "Wildlife Preserve."

Such occasions were Paradise plusses. We fudged a little to leave the impression with visitors we lived in a Garden of Eden *sans souci.*

Several tricks bewitched guests. As we first strolled the grounds identifying flora, Al suggested each person pick a lime. After we arrived back at the house, he created frothy daiquiris. With the first sip, our guests' faces lighted up like a tropical sunrise. Ambrosia.

Eating ripe papaya, avocados, grapefruit, and bananas from our trees in mid-winter mind-boggled our friends, who left home in heavy coats and galoshes. When our breadfruit was ripe, I concocted a breadfruit salad that resembles potato salad, but my Spanish Sabre tree salad was the favorite delicacy.

After tossing the tree's crisp white blossoms into the salad, along with other ingredients, I draped extra blossoms around the salad bowl's rim. For the "Brown Hibiscus Special" I poured hibiscus liqueur from Haiti over vanilla ice cream and tucked a fresh red hibiscus alongside.

Staging? Cheating? Of course. Before a dinner party doesn't every hostess shove clutter in the closet and get out the silver candlesticks? Same thing, and it works. Island visitors still remember Hidden Hill's house specialties.

Now, for the first time, our past guests will learn how we manipulate the mirrors in Paradise. Stay tuned.

ST. JOHN

On that first 1960 trip to St. Thomas, we took the twenty-minute ferry ride to St. John—the "baby sister" of the three U.S. Virgin Islands—which shares schools, hospital, and political affairs with nearby St. Thomas rather than distant St. Croix.

Looking ahead at the puff-clouded azure sky and the parade of mountainous emerald islands flanking Sir Francis Drake Channel was like glimpsing heaven (I think. Will report on that later.)

We were also briefed on its history. We learned that Arawak and Carib Indians inhabited St. John long before Danes settled around Coral Bay in 1718. Using slave labor, the Danes rapidly developed prosperous cotton and sugar plantations. A merciless slave code imposed September 5, 1733 incited a surprise slave attack on Coral Bay's Fort Berg, November 23, 1733. Rebel slave insurrections on each plantation followed and slaves held St. John six months. Their knowledge of the interior bush and back trails made them formidable foes. They repelled attacks by St. Thomas Danes and Tortola's British soldiers before the Martinque French recaptured St. John, April 1734.

Rather than endure captivity and horrible torture, the rebels fled to Mary Point and plunged to death on the rocks below, so says a legend that probably originated from cliffs there pock-marked red from the mineral hematite. Verified groups, however, did commit suicide: one near Ram Head, May, 1734, and the remaining rebel slaves gathered above Brown Bay north of Leinster Bay and shot themselves.

The sugar plantation era ended when the Virgin Islands abolished slavery in 1848. Still a few plantations remained until about 1919 when St. John's last sugar factory on Reef Bay's north shore ceased operation. The island then became an idyllic retreat until the Danish West Indian Company opened Caneel Bay Resort in 1935 and tourists discovered St. John's Arcadian charm in the 40's and 50's.

Photo by Daniel Gomez

Cruz Bay and Village, St. John, showing The Battery, built 1735 to defend against future slave revolts. Warfside Village (shopping center) and Gallows Point townhouses can also be seen beyond The Battery.

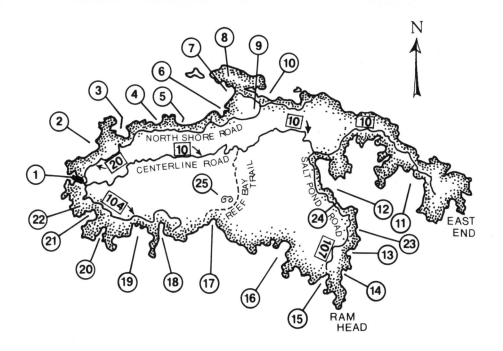

VIRGIN ISLANDS
St. John

St. John Legend
Numbers in squares are road route numbers
1. St. John Ferry, Dock, Park, and Village
2. Caneel Bay and Caneel Bay Plantation Resort
3. Hawksnest Bay and Beach, (and Canks)
4. Trunk Bay and Beach with marked
   Underwater Trail
5. Cinnamon Bay and Beach
6. Big and Little Maho Beaches
7. Francis Bay
8. Mary Point
9. Annaberg Sugar Mill
10. Leinster Bay
11. Hurricane Hole
12. Coral Bay and Village - site of St. John's first
   Danish sugar plantation in 1718, and Fort
   Berg ruins
13. John's Folly Bay
14. Trunk Bay
15. Salt Pond Bay
16. Laneshun Bay
17. Reef Bay
18. Fish Bay
19. Rendezvous Bay
20. Chocolate Hole
21. Great Cruz Bay
22. Hyatt Regency Resort Hotel
23. Lucy's Restaurant and Bar, Friis Bay
24. Shipwreck Landing Restaurant and Bar
25. Petroglyphs

Historians should visit the St. John Museum, since 1974 in the Cruz Bay Battery, but now moved to the restored Estate House of "Enighed" near St. John's ferry dock. Called the Elaine I. Sprauve Library and Museum, it features Danish West Indian and natural history, arts and crafts, and prehistoric exhibits.

Armed with all this history and knowledge, we set off for the twenty-minute ferry ride to St. John. From the boat's bow we saw the series of green mountainous islands flanking Sir Francis Drake Channel. Never before had we seen a combination of sea, sky, and islands to surpass it.

Our St. John guide was "Limejuice" Richards. When he was a baby, his mother called him "Sweet Limejuice" and part of the nickname stuck. Limejuice jeeped us first to beautiful Trunk Bay, an exquisite curve of gentle surf and pale sand edged with lacy green vegetation. Its well-labeled underwater snorkling trail has made Trunk Bay world famous today. On our first visit in 1960, facilities were practically nil, but now visitors find lifeguards, snack bar, showers, and snorkel gear rental along with tour groups and weekend beach buffs who sometimes crowd the area.

Cinnamon Bay, the National Park Campground's lengthy sandy beach runs Trunk a close second these days, notably with snorkelers who enjoy the fringing reefs of a small nearby island. Tents, one-room cottages, and campsites are for rent here, with reservations necessary, and facilities include shops, commissary, cafeteria, showers, and a small museum.

Big Maho and Little Maho Bay along with Francis Bay have calm waters all year, and Big Maho has lifeguards but no other facilities. Its usually peaceful, shaded beach attracts weekend organized beach parties and family picnics.

Hawksnest Beach, quiet and secluded, is a favorite of St. John residents, and is sometimes used for filming motion pictures. Its facilities are limited to barbecue grills under cover and portable toilets.

Trunk Bay, St. John

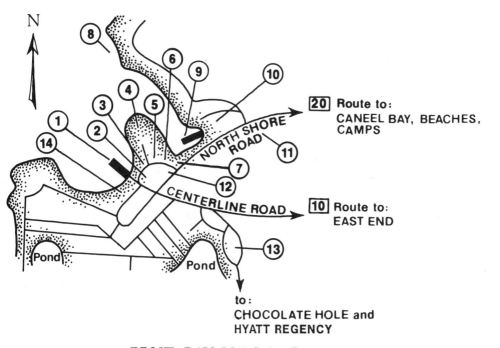

CRUZ BAY VILLAGE

Cruz Bay Village Legends

1. Dock for St. Thomas Ferries
2. Cruz Bay Park
3. Taxis and Shuttle Buses
4. Battery — Fort built in 1735
5. Immigration and U.S. Customs
   Public Rest Rooms
6. Public Parking
7. St. John Car Rentals
8. Airplane Shuttle Ramp
9. National Park Dock
10. V.I. National Park Visitor Center
11. Mongoose Junction — Unique Studio Shops
    and Restaurants
12. U.S. Post Office
13. St. John Museum — now Elaine I. Sprauve
    Library and Museum
14. Wharfside Village — Shopping Complex

If you really want to get away from it all, pack a picnic lunch, fill your gas tank in Cruz Bay—gas stations are rare on St. John—and search out your own hideaway beach. The island's interior will reward you with a never-ending panorama of breathtaking sea and land views even if you don't find a perfect piece of seashore.

Limejuice also took us to Caneel Bay Plantation—a former sugar plantation which at that time was being converted into a luxury resort by Laurance Rockefeller. Now it is the palm-shaded sandbox of political celebrities: Kissingers, Lady Bird Johnson, Carters, and the like, as well as movie stars.

Afterwards, Limejuice drove us through the heavily forested area of St. John's National Park. Mr. Rockefeller bought 5000 acres of St. John in the 50s and gave the land to the National Park Service, preserving forever for Virgin Islanders and visitors most of the island's untouched beauty. The aforementioned camping grounds and spectacular beaches, along with trails for hikers, now offer bird watchers, nature buffs, and Virgin Island families a Snow White-and-Seven-Dwarfs wooded wonderland.

Over-zealous Virgin Island senators sometimes present other uses for this National Park. One wanted to chop down the tall trees and undergrowth and convert the area into low-cost housing. Others have had equally ill-considered ideas. Thank goodness, more level heads prevailed. Even Paradise needs watchdogs.

Limejuice showed us the fernlike Sensitive Plant that curls up when touched. After he squeezed a bay leaf between his fingers, he held it under my nose. The fragrance was celestial.

A mixture of these bay leaves with spices and orange peel produces St. John Bay Rum. Made in St. Thomas, it is a favorite after-shave scent of men all over the world who want to smell as good as their wives.

At the Annaberg ruins, a former Danish sugar plantation, we learned about island herbs from a friendly lady costumed in a colorful long, full skirt and a bright bandana tied around her head. Limejuice also drove us

Caneel Bay and Caneel Bay Plantation Resort, St. John

Photo by Daniel Gomez

Historic Annaberg Sugar Mill ruins, St. John

past the home of Robert Oppenheimer. He looked after the house when Dr. Oppenheimer was not there.

A present-day beloved character on St. John is Miss Lucy. In the mid-60s when we could not find Limejuice for sightseeing guests, we found Miss Lucy, whose trademark bougainvillea bouquets rested in cattle-horn vases atop her taxi's radiator cap. Her good humor and knowledge of St. John history made her an entertaining guide. Besides, everyone on St. John knew Miss Lucy and vice versa. We sought her out several times afterward. Then we lost track of her.

I was delighted to discover her again recently. Still active in island sightseeing and perky as ever, Miss Lucy now has a spick-and-span sightseeing van with "Lucy's Tours" prominently painted on the sides and bougainvillea still fills cattle-horn vases on her radiator cap. She also has Lucy's Restaurant and Bar in St. John's Coral bay area between Calabash Boom and John's Folly at Friis Bay. You can't miss it. A large sign proclaims "Lucy's Restaurant and Bar" and attached underneath are cattle-horn vases filled with bougainvillea.

A relaxed, friendly place on a large open porch beside the sea, Lucy's serves lunch and dinner every day but Monday, starting at eleven o'clock. Sunday brunch is from 10:30 to 3:30. I enjoyed a thick, delicious "real" turkey sandwich on the best bread I have ever tasted. This much-loved lady is worth running down. For sightseeing and good homemade food, you will "love Lucy".

Another popular place for lunch and dinner in the Coral Bay vicinity is Shipwreck Landing Restaurant and Bar. Open seven days a week, it also offers seaside dining and cool breezes. St. John's East End appears to be coming into its own these days.

You'll know you've found St. John's Miss Lucy when you see her tour bus with her trademark cattle horns filled with bougainvillea

Editor's note: We've been to every harbor and walked every settlement and seen all the sights on land and sea on all of the British and American Virgins. Though there are fine harbors and great interest ashore in all these lovely isles, and marvelous snorkeling in Gorda Sound, my favorite is still St. John. It's more than a National Park—it's a national treasure! Don't leave St. Thomas without a visit to St. John.

Ferry dock, Cruz Bay, St. John. Frequent ferry service makes it easy to travel between St. Thomas and St. John

CHAPTER 2

WHAT DO YOU DO ALL DAY?

When friends and acquaintances first found out we were moving to St. Thomas, you would have thought we were going to a "space station."

It is different today, but in 1965, the majority of "Continentals"—the Virgin Island name for people from mainland United States—had no idea where St. Thomas was. Many did not even know where the Caribbean was.

"Do they have electricity there?" one woman asked.

Today I would answer that with, "Frequently."

Visitors sometimes say, "I collect stamps. I want to buy some of yours while I'm here."

"Why don't you wait until you get home?" we suggest. "You can get the same kind there and they won't stick together in your luggage."

"You use United States stamps?"

"We're a United States territory and we pay the same taxes you do. We even have a zip code."

"Well, what do you know . . ."

If we are around Market square (pronounced "Mahket") and visitors hear St. Thomians jabbering, they invariably ask, "What language do people speak here?"

"American English," I assure them, "but among themselves many speak a West Indian vernacular with an American or English accent, depending on the island where they were born. Their speech can be expressive and colorful, but it takes getting used to."

So you will understand what I mean, here is an example from Arona Petersen's weekly column in the Daily News lampooning government officials.

"Maybe if I wus you and you wus me, I cud see how you reasonin out dis ting but you can't put goat head in same pot wid sheep head, dey in diffrunt rank altogedder." Give it a calypso beat and you will get it.

Before I leave Arona Petersen, a witty and vivacious woman, I want to explain that she is a popular Caribbean author, artist, folklorist, storyteller, and an authority on our Virgin Island culture and cuisine. The Daily News praised her "vision, persistence, cajolerie and elbow work," as the driving force behind the 1986 debut concert of the Virgin Islands Folkloric Company at Reichold Center for the Arts.

Petersen's books "Kreole Ketch n' Keep" and "Herbs and Proverbs" are a delight for anyone interested in island folk sayings, customs, recipes, and in uses for Caribbean herbs. At present she is compiling a cookbook.

In 1971, Petersen participated in the "Man and His World" event held on the site of Montreal's Expo '67. The invitation came through James Morris, Director of the Smithsonian's Performing Arts Division.

During a visit to St. Thomas, he discovered her authentic West Indian cooking (Johnny Cakes, fish and fungi, Kallaloo and homemade ice cream) at her former open-air restaurant, Hillside Way. When plans for the fair were under way, he remembered Mrs. Petersen and West Indian cuisine found a warm reception in Montreal.

From our first days in St. Thomas until now, the question visitors ask most frequently is, "What do you do all day?"

The tone implies we beachcomb. If abroad and I meet someone unacquainted with the Virgin Islands, the question is the same, but the tone suggests we inhabit a South Sea atoll and lead a Robinson Crusoe-Friday existence. When we are without electricity, telephone, and water, the comparison is within jumping distance of the truth.

I explain that we have no milkman, laundryman, nor store deliveries. We go in town every day to pick up mail and buy The Daily News. Most days we take our trash and garbage to a roadside dumpster where it is picked up—or sometimes not picked up—by Public Works trucks. Otherwise, like everyone anyplace, we face mundane daily tasks. Once a week, we grocery shop and go to the bank. We run errands, and try to get things "fixed."

Getting Things Fixed

Getting things "fixed" is where our lives part from anything rational.

First, we do not have a formal directory of "fix-it" men. Be it housepainters, plumbers, electricians, woodworkers, masons, or handymen, we get them via the grapevine. Black or white, young or old, native or Continental, they are all alike. A fiercely independent, know-it-all lot.

Second, the U.S. Virgin Islands have 10 more holidays than the United States. Hurricane Thanksgiving Day is one; Organic Act Day another. Intriguing names, yes? Consequently, every week you have a 50–50 chance of running into a Monday holiday.

Reaching a "fixer" by phone can take a week. Starting on Tuesday (after the Monday holiday), you discover your man is not back from his long weekend. Wednesday his phone is out of order. Thursday yours is out of order.

This is not **always** the telephone company's fault. Recently a Power Authority crew boring for a pole, drilled through an underground cable, leaving 16,000 phones as dead as doornails for several days. Truck drivers also knock down utility poles with the precision of champion bowlers.

Anyhow, when you finally reach your "fix-it" man on Friday, he is overloaded with work and tells you to call next week. He sounds hungover. He probably is.

If you leave word for the "fixer" to call **you**, he probably will not. He will telephone a month or two later—when he runs out of work and needs a job.

Men have come, given us a price to repair a leaking roof, and set the day to start. We never heard from them again. Prices rarely make sense. Bids to paint our house once ranged from $1200 to $6000.

If workmen show up, imported supplies do not.

A task supposed to take two weeks, takes six. Costs keep escalating. Some project prices compare favorably with Donald Trump's spending money.

Everyone is an "expert" on whatever you want done. Recently, an "expert" on replacing ceilings started nailing new wallboard over soggy old wallboard. When we challenged this procedure, he confessed he had never done such work before.

Driver's License and Car Registration

Boring and annoying trivial chores are not taken care of as easily here as in the States. Getting your car inspected or renewing your driver's license can consume a half-day and any reserve of patience. Sometimes, simply filling out out a form has the challenge of an Army obstacle course.

Our first driver's license application form is a good example. It started out telling the applicant to see the reverse side for instructions. When you turned over the sheet of paper, it was blank.

Turning back to the other side to make sure you had read it correctly (you had), you saw, "Signature in your own handwriting" printed beneath the signature line. We learned by osmosis that despite what the one-year form said, we paid $9.00 for a three-year license.

Car inspection was, for a while, just short of playing Russian roulette. To test your brakes, you were instructed to head for a wall and stop. If you did not crash into the wall, you passed. If you crashed the wall, you passed on. (Oops! Too bad.)

Renewing your license wins the gold medal for driving you to the booby hatch. As the French say, *"La queue. Toujours la queue!"* Well, in St. Thomas, you will also find impatient lines—disgruntled applicants bunched together like corralled cattle—plus a few diabolical diversions.

The electricity sometimes goes off the moment before it is your turn to have your picture taken—with the super Polaroid instant camera—for your laminated license. You wait, or go home, which means you have to come back another day.

If you are white, your photograph comes out looking as if you have just come from a cake bake-off sponsored by Pillsbury flour. The lighting is never set properly for white faces. You cannot blame anyone when you consider the population percentages: in 1965, 5 percent white, 95 percent black. today it is about 15 percent to 85 percent.

If an electric outage does not occur while you are renewing your license, do not discount the camera breaking down.

One day when a man came by boat from St. John to renew his driver's license, the camera stopped functioning. Despite all efforts by license bureau employees to fix it, the camera remained on strike. When the man had to leave to catch his boat back to St. John, the time wasted and cost of not getting his license upset him enormously.

The sympathetic license bureau employee promised to send his license by mail as soon as the camera functioned. This placated the man until, on the boat, he began to wonder how this was possible since he would not be there to have his picture taken.

The mystery solved itself a few days later when the driver's license arrived with a picture of a vacant chair.

Soon after, the man grocery shopped at a St. Thomas Pueblo supermarket. Asked to produce his driver's license as identification in order to have his check accepted, he pulled out the new driver's license.

Puzzled, the Pueblo manager studied it, then said, "This isn't a picture of you, it's a picture of a chair."

After the man explained his license bureau troubles, the groceryman accepted his check without question. He had been here several years and knew it could happen in St. Thomas.

On with "what we do all day."

Our first few island years, Al helped several friends, part-time: one with a bottled gas company; another with a furniture store; and a real estate entrepreneur who needed a trouble shooter.

Finally he settled down to keepng Hidden Hill in running order. No small job. He painted window frames, repaired electrical and plumbing snafus, and kept two lawn mowers operating for Ivan, our four-star gardener from Anguilla. Ivan taught me how to brew bush tea and wield a machete.

Since buses did not serve our country area, Al also spent ten hours a week bringing in help.

Once, after having fixed a plumbing problem, an impressed house guest told Al, "I never knew you were handy with things like that."

"I feel as well equipped as the plumber who maintains he can find buried water pipes with a hibiscus branch," Al said, grinning.

This reminds me of the day we moved into Hidden Hill. The exterminator, after he showed us where termites had eaten the wood around one window, said he knew a man who could, in one day, take out the window, make a new casement, and put the window back in.

When we arrived before seven o'clock in the morning to prepare for the movers, our man awaited us, barefoot and with a saw. Al provided nails, hammer, and pieces of lumber.

While men moved furniture into our new home, and I directed placement of the pieces, Al went back and forth between the houses to make sure all went well. Although we had misgivings about the job the man working on the window would do, we were too occupied to pay attention to him.

Finally, near six o'clock, the movers left.

Exhausted, I went to check out the window man, who had just finished. I could not believe what I saw. The window was perfect—the work of a master craftsman.

Unable to conceal my pleasure, I said, "It's beautiful! You've really done a good day's work."

With a half-smile and eyes twinkling, he said, "So have you, Missy!"

That took place over twenty years ago. If only workmen today measured up to that window man.

Community Service

Al also affiliated with the St. Thomas Rotary Club as a Past Service member and, over a number a years, was active in setting up a Foundation and Scholarship Fund. In 1984 he received the first Neil Weiss Award for a Paul Harris Fellow. Neil Weiss, St. Thomas Rotarian, established the fund to honor Rotarians for distinguished community service. Rotary International Foundation receives $1000 for a Paul Harris Fellow in the awardee's name. This helps continue the Foundation's scholarship program throughout the world. Al won it, but I was proud.

In 1972, Al spearheaded a "Let's Keep It Clean" campaign to rid St. Thomas of litter. Unsuccessful. He also volunteered his services for our Tourist Hospitality Lounge and the League of Women Voters. I called the list of members he telephoned to remind of upcoming meetings his "call girls."

As for me, the first two years, I continued to write a syndicated radio show for Beverly Stark, television and radio spokeswoman in the 60s for Stateside Electric Utilities. In 1966, just before Christmas, I began to sit in for Mary Brooks Jackson, who started a local hour-long radio show for women. Called "Mary-Go-Round," it lasted ten years.

After Mary resigned, I sat in five years for Louise Noble's "Conversation" before resigning.

Population explosion came to the island and traffic resembled Hong Kong at rush hour. Getting to the studio meant battling bumper to bumper traffic, and the stress factor zoomed after franchise businesses from the States took over many Main Street tourist stores.

I have never understood why people come to St. Thomas for a relaxed life, but once here, drive like "Indy 500" racers and bring Stateside gung-ho hysteria with them. The time had come to fold up my mike and head for a hammock. The hilarious moments as well as the trials of those 15 years will be covered—or uncovered—in Chapter 7, "On the Air."

In 1967, I joined the St. Thomas Garden Club, and became a member of the St. Thomas Community Music Association's Board of Directors. Chapter 3, "We Shall Have Music," reveals the things that can go wrong on an island bent on bringing culture to its inhabitants.

In the late 70s, I wrote a "Caribbean Corner" column for "This Is Madison" magazine, and began again to write seriously. Unfortunately, the mid-80s brought crowds, cads, cocaine, and crime to St. Thomas. We felt invaded! Our era of tranquillity was gone forever; we had no choice. Move or adjust. We adjusted. Sort of.

From the beginning, Al and I wanted to be part of island life. We, along with many other Continentals and island natives, contributed to the late Kay Atcheson's St. Thomas School of Dance and Ballet Theatre of the Virgin Islands, St. Thomas Historical Trust, Conservation Society, Humane Society, St. Thomas Rescue, Inc. (a volunteer organization that saves untold lives), Boy Scouts, Girl Scouts, various school activities, public television, homes for orphans and the elderly.

When it comes to helping the community, this partial list of civic activities proves life on our island is not much different from that of the United States. If a baseball team, beauty queen, or Mocko Jumbi dance group needs money for Stateside competitions, everyone—black and white, school children and adults—comes to the rescue.

Speaking of black and white, it is as good a time as any to face that subject. We frequently answer questions about racial relations in St. Thomas.

In the 60s, any racial problems were minor, and the compatibility of blacks and whites could have been called "a showcase of democracy."

Gradually over the years, attitudes changed. Part of the change came from black Virgin Island veterans returning from Army service, where they first met racial prejudice. They were not old enough to realize white people could not be categorized any more than black people. A wide spectrum of attitudes toward blacks from whites prevailed just as it did toward whites from blacks.

When civic-minded blacks and whites became aware of the widening gap in 1974, they organized a "tromp" down Main Street. The event attracted 5,000 people, black and white, marching arm in arm to steel bands. A heart-warming spectacle. Some good resulted for awhile, then came a period when belligerent young blacks harassed whites.

Fortunately that tense period ended as quickly as it came. I still believe there is no place else in the world where blacks and whites live together in such close quarters and get along so well. This does not deny problems, but many people, black and white, care enough about the welfare of St. Thomas to strive constantly for racial harmony.

Back to what we do all day.

A big plus for living in a constant summer climate is the opportunity to participate in outdoor sports all year. Public and private tennis courts, an eighteen-hole golf course, horse shows and races, and dog shows, are a small part of available activities. The sea world around us offers swimming, boating and fishing. What do we do? As a native St. Thomian might say, "Mon, what don't we do?" That is, if we have time left over from chores and "fix-it" men.

So, when your thermometer in January hits 20 below, hop on a plane and pop down to St. Thomas for a week as a "pampered" tourist. We will envy you, because we will not be lolling under a palm tree waiting for a coconut to drop. We will be foot-shifting in line at the Post Office, waiting a half-hour to pick up a package. On second thought, maybe we should check in at the same hotel.

Yacht Haven Marina, Ramada Yacht Haven Hotel, West Indian Company's Cruise Ship Dock. Leftmost ship is *Soverign of the Seas,* one of the word's largest. Cruise ships are a fact of life in Charlotte Amalie, St. Thomas, the Caribbean's most popular port of call

CHAPTER 3

WE SHALL HAVE MUSIC

In the fall of 1966, Judi Witty changed my tranquil island life.

Former MGM dancer and friend of Ginger Rogers, Judi, who knew about my involvement with Madison, Wisconsin music groups, inveigled me into filling her expiring term on the Board of Directors of the Community Music Association of St. Thomas. It seemed a dignified civic endeavor. I went peacefully.

It did not take me long to learn that any resemblance to Stateside music associations, living or dead, could not be assumed.

First, selling tickets at $10 each for the yearly series of four concerts was a breeze. We printed 900, the number of bodies the Charlotte Amalie High School auditorium could seat. Since the Music Association's concerts provided our cultural highlights, tickets sold like banana hot cakes. Thyra Hodge Smith, a bundle of energy, habitually sold the most tickets, and habitually won Carnival's top prize for the best single entry in the Adult Parade. Scratch the usual Music Association's battle to raise funds.

Even securing top level talent for four concerts on a $9000 budget offered no great challenge.

Charlotte Paiewonsky, Chairman of the Artist Selection Committee and overlady of A.H. Riise tourist shops successfully played a sleight of hand magician's role. Dealing only with Hurok, Herbert Barrett Management, or the Columbia Management Artists of New York, she wheedled world-renowned artists out of these prestigious booking offices.

Consequently, the Music Association presented the best available in music, dance, and opera, even if our concert hall was not named Carnegie.

So what worried our Board of Directors? Let us pray.

First: "Please, dear God, let there be no electric outage the night of the concert." This meant no air-conditioning, no lights, no public address system in the high school's auditorium. Can you imagine a lovely soprano in an elegant Dior gown illuminated by a flaming pine knot torch?

Second: "Please, dear God, make our tubercular 12-year-old Steinway grand piano last through another concert season. (We kept it in a steel cage, like ones used for tigers, to keep aspiring young Horowitzes from debasing it.) Also, please make sure Mr. Gomez--piano tuner for the Casals Festival from San Juan, Puerto Rico--arrives without mishap on concert day."

Getting him here was the thankless responsibility of Leopold Benjamin, our most music knowledgeable Board member.

Third: "Please, dear God, make sure we have all the props we need for each concert **on the island**. Not in San Juan or New York. Amen."

From the beginning, the Board meeting discussions made it clear to me that I could be of little help in solving any dilemma. I had never faced their posers. Thank goodness, I had sense enough to keep quiet and listen. Anyhow, I remembered Will Rogers saying, "You can't learn nothin' if you're talking." That dear man with his cowboy hat, lasso—and no horse—had a lot of "horse sense." So I listened.

Eventually, before our 1966-67 concert series began, the Board elected me Co-Chairman of Reception in charge of Artists and Inez Harvey to take care of After-Concert Dinners. My duties included meeting the artists at the airport and taking them to their hotel. My committee transported performers to rehearsal, the concert, the after-concert dinner, and back to the hotel. During their St. Thomas sojourn, we took care of any requests, from shopping and beauty parlor appointments to sightseeing. On departure, we chauffeured them to the airport.

My obligations did not sound too daunting. Besides my committee would help. Little did I know what awaited me in the wings.

Adventure With the New York Brass Quintet

My initiation as airport greeter started with the New York Brass Quintet and should have warned me of forthcoming pitfalls. A last minute emergency cancelled out the other greeter, so I stuffed three Quintet members, their instruments and luggage into my VW bug. One piece of luggage had been lost or we could not have made it. Fortunately the other two members, unbeknownst to me, had arrived two days early for sun and surf.

Grateful for the VW's sun-top, we opened it to relieve the inside pressure. One instrument poked up through the hold like a periscope. Boun-

Ferries and excursion boats make the St. Thomas waterfront a busy place

cing along together through town, we all decided this was not the way we would want to cross a continent. We reached Bluebeard's Hotel intact. Before leaving them, I wrote my telephone number on a card in case they needed me before I called them in the morning to arrange for rehearsal.

I was hardly through the door before a Quintet member called. His white tie had been in the lost suitcase. Could I find one for him in time for tomorrow night's concert?

Of course.

Despite a telephone campaign that would have elected a president, no one—not even the Governor nor the Lieutenant-governor—had a real live white tie. We simply were not a tails-and-white-tie island. As I became more frantic, I thought of our friend, Harry Bonar, who pulled rabbits out of hats when we could not find a needed item on St. Thomas. He had lived here a long time and had connections.

Harry soothed me back to normalcy and swore on a Bach fugue he would have a white tie at Bluebeard's the next night when my committee picked up the Quintet to take them to the concert.

Arriving at the appointed time, I immediately spotted Harry running up the hotel's driveway. He cupped something in both hands as if it were the Hope Diamond. When I hurried from the car and reached out to take what looked like a white tie, he recoiled.

"Don't touch it!" he cried, out of breath. "I couldn't find a white tie," he added hasitly, "I made one out of a paper napkin. The glue is still drying."

Only a few of us "knew for sure" which Quintet member wore a paper napkin white tie. Although seemingly composed, he confessed afterward to uneasiness as he tooted away during the concert.

•

Coordinating concert activities around school activities on concert day was like trying to clean up a nursery for nap hour.

In late afternoon, potted palms arrived and put up a brave front to hide the fact that the stage belonged to a high school auditorium. The palms only partially succeeded. The piano was let out of its cage, and Mr. Gomez, the piano tuner from San Juan, God willing, tuned it.

Nina Corneiro attended to backstage and dressing room needs. Cyril Harrigan installed the public address system and flashed lights off and on for proper lighting effects. When air-conditioning finally blessed the auditorium, he checked that too. Our first air-conditioned concert was like spending three hours in a supermarket deep-freeze. Concert goers still shivered a week later.

Prop people came to deposit stage furnishings. Sometimes we set up extra chairs. If presenting a dance group, we swept the stage (even though swept earlier), because during a past performance, a barefoot dancer cut her foot on a sliver of glass. The late Kay Atcheson, founder of our Ballet School, once spent an entire afternoon on hands and knees scraping chewing gum off the stage floor. Some of us tried to help, but lasted only a half-hour. Kay's devotion to the art of dance had no limits.

School girls wear uniforms in St. Thomas

Many concert problems originated from New York booking agents, who waited until the last minute to make hard-to-come-by reservations for the artist during our top tourist season.

Adventure With Martha Schlamme

My most traumatic experience centered around Martha Schlamme, the talented international folk singer, who sang her "Songs of Many Lands" in concert, with Ronald Clairmont as her accompanist, in December 1968.

Three days before their arrival, her booking agent requested hotel reservations. After endless telephone calls which involved waiting for elusive dial-tones, retrieving lost connections, getting wrong numbers and busy signals, we finally secured rooms at the newly-opened Royal Mail Inn.

Now, the Royal Mail Inn (which is no more) was, in the late 60s, a charming, isolated inn on tiny Hassel Island in the Charlotte Amalie harbor, only a five-minute boat ride from the city's waterfront. However, unless you could walk on water, you could not get there any way except by boat.

The Inn was a perfect place for honeymooners wanting to get away from it all: swimming pool, pleasant rooms, beautiful view, excellent food. It was not the perfect place for performing artists who had deadlines. Deadlines like rehearsal and a concert.

Trouble began with Miss Schlamme's and Mr. Clairmont's arrival. Elaborate arrangements that would have done justice to a bank robbery had been worked out with the Inn management so eveything would run smoothly. I know now this is the time when there is sure to be trouble. It is the St. Thomas Law. I was new to the island then and innocent.

Still I did not overlook the vagaries of Hassel Island transportation. Although the Inn expected a second boat to transport guests back and forth to Charlotte Amalie, it had not arrived. That left us dependent on only one boat. To prevent any hitch, I arranged to call from the airport after Schlamme and Clairmont landed. This assured the boat's presence at the city dock and immediate transportation for the concert artists to Royal Mail Inn.

At that time, you could never count on a plane until it rolled down the runway. (Things really have not changed much.) I spent so much time at the airport waiting for house guests or performing artists, a woman I knew slightly once asked me if I worked there. I said I was considering it.

The foolproof arrangements did not cover the sky opening up and dumping a Big Dipper full of rain on St. Thomas as we left the airport. The downpour continued. We arrived at the designated dock. No Royal Mail boat. Only more rain. After 15 minutes cooped up in my valiant little VW with my guests, I braved the downpour to find a telephone. In those days, VWs swarmed over St. Thomas like ants. Along with the surrey-fringed jeeps, they made sense on the one-car-wide streets and narrow, bumpy roads. They did not make sense as entertainment centers for concert artists.

Thank goodness, I soon found a working telephone. The Royal Mail Inn management reported that the water-drenched engine of their boat would not start. They were working on it. It should be fixed in an hour. He suggested we go to a bar, or find a "friendly boat" to help out. After he gave me a description of the "friendly boat," I ran up and down the waterfront in the rain trying to find it. I never did. It had sense enough to come in out of the rain. I did not.

Soggy as a mop, I returned to the VW where we sat disconsolately. Even if we opened a window an inch, rain poured in. Inside our VW "sauna," we searched for a next move. No luck. My encouraging laughter and chit-chat grew strained along with theirs. It was one of the worst hours of my life.

Finally the rain lessened to a drizzle, and we saw a small outboard motor boat laboring out of the darkness from the Inn's direction. I scurried from the questionable sanctuary of the VW to ask the boat's operator if he came from the Inn. He did. He transported help back and forth. He confirmed my fears that the Inn's main boat was still out of order. I finally persuaded him to transport my celebrities. It would have been easier to hold him up and confiscate the boat, but I did not have a gun.

Miss Schlamme, in a beautiful milk-chocolate crepe dress with matching doeskin pumps and coat with a fox collar, staggered unceremoniously into the little bobbing boat. Mr. Clairmont, carrying his topcoat and wearing a brown wool suit of Byronic cut, a long-sleeved orange shirt, and brown and white striped tie, lurched after her. I closed my eyes. I could not bear to watch their luggage being tossed in after them. I was certain a piece would go overboard. No splash. I opened my eyes. The time was 8 p.m. and the temperature was over eighty degrees.

In the darkness and faint drizzle, I watched them chug away through choppy waters, headed for a destination none of us could discern. I waved and shouted encouragement. Huddled forlornly against rain and roll, luggage piled helter-skelter around them, they could neither hear nor see me.

As I got into my VW, I realized the whole set-up must appear to them like the beginning of a Dracula movie. Miss Schlamme confessed afterwards she had been certain something sinister awaited them.

The next day the Inn boat remained inoperative. The small outboard was again pressed into service for rehearsal. Even in casual clothes, our concert artists found getting in and out of the boat unnerving. They were not small people and the sea was still rough. We arrived forty minutes late for rehearsal, which meant rearranging a hair appointment for Miss Schlamme.

At least, the Inn finally arranged for the "friendly boat" to transport our concert artists. It was a good-sized covered vessel, not the greatest, but compared to the outboard, it looked like the Onassis yacht "Christina." Still, it reached the dock pick-up for the concert fifteen minutes late.

In all fairness to the Inn, Miss Schlamme told me in a telephone conversation, confirming concert pick-up time, flu had confined **everyone** at the Inn to bed and no food was being served. Oh, no! I greeted her at the

St. Thomas has beautiful white sand beaches. This one at Sapphire Beach Resort

dock with a brown paper bag containing a Thermos of coffee and turkey sandwiches. It was shortly after Thanksgiving.

No complaints. Martha and Ronald—shared adversities soon put people on a first-name basis—gratefully munched leftover turkey all the way to the auditorium. In Martha's classroom dressing room, not exactly star quality, I helped her into her gown and fastened her up. We had by now a concentration-camp-inmate relationship in order to survive our hardships.

As always, once the curtain went up, all went perfectly. Miss Schlamme gave a superb performance, and the after-concert dinner was a great success. Even the "friendly boat" stayed at the pier until after midnight to return the artists to the Inn. The Board of Directors of the Music Association could settle back to build up strength for the next concert. . .

Not yet.

Ronald Clairmont almost did not get back to New York in time for another concert. He neglected to reconfirm his airline tickets even though I had told him to. We haunted the airport for hours, running from desk to desk, pleading, cajoling—threatening will get you no place in the islands.

Finally we found a seat on a San Juan shuttle. Once there, he would be on stand-by to New York. No problem. A highly-talented pianist with a good sense of humor, Ronald apologized profusely for the added problems he had caused me through his negligence.

When he returned from the men's room, just before take-off, he said, "That was the only successful experience I've had since I reached this island."

•

In 1969, during the Reyes-Solar Ballet Español rehearsal, House Committee members found they needed costume hangers, several props, and refreshment for the dancers who wanted to rehearse until curtain time. I was the only Board member they could find home, so a half-hour later I was rattling along in my VW headed for the High School. A dozen coat hangers, two card tables, six wine glasses, a bottle of wine, and an ashtray for the Ballet's cafe number rested on the VW's back seat. A floor lamp for a piano behind the scenes peered over my shoulder. Beside me rode a large brown paper bag loaded with sandwiches and coffee. I felt like a one-man circus.

Again, once the dancers were on stage, the fiery and spirited flamenco performance brought thundering applause.

•

Props were often hard to find. In the late 60s, the High School music department did not own any music stands. We spent many trying hours collecting five for the New York Brass Quintet. With time, the department wangled a sufficient number of stands for their orchestra and generously loaned them to the Music Association when needed for a concert.

In return, we sometimes released our Steinway from its cage for the use of one of their budding pianists beyond the chop-stick stage.

The Romero Quartet, Spanish guitarists, needed four footstools. We did not have four footstools in 1967 but found four cement blocks we covered with black or red terry cloth towels. They looked quite dashing. The casualty was slight when Celin Romero gave his footstool a kick to change its position during their exciting Spanish music and flamenco concert.

Adventure with the Princeton Chamber Orchestra

A first-rate 1969 concert, but problem-maker, was the Princeton Chamber Orchestra with a whopping twenty-three members. Again accommodations were requested late during the peak tourist season. A week with our erratic telephones finally netted us enough rooms in three different guest houses. We engaged a tour bus to transport the group, then discovered the evening before the orchestra arrived that the bus was too large for the narrow, steep street to one guest house.

After several frantic phone calls, the Virgin Islands Sightseeing Company provided last minute taxis and mini-buses. The two basses and three cellos further complicated orchestra movements. They were like having five extra inert bodies, and bass players are more attached to their instruments than to their blood relatives. Still, by giving the basses TLC, all went well.

That is, all went well until the night before the orchestra's departure,

Photo by Susan Houston

In the Frenchtown section of St.Thomas, fishermen pull up their boats
and sell their catch directly to customers

when the worst tropical storm in a decade totalled the island. With the airport closed, the group could not leave St. Thomas at 8 a.m. the next morning as originally planned and had to cancel their Macon, Georgia concert.

The entire orchestra, some with portable instruments, milled around the crowded, bedlamic airport and mingled with disgruntled stranded tourists. Even after the runways opened, only a few orchestra members at a time were permitted to board departing planes. The last ones left at 9 p.m. They were the bass players. Getting them and their instruments on the same plane was not easy. What the orchestra needed were a few flying nuns.

P.S. I would advise aspiring young musicians to take up the piccolo. A nice handy little instrument and no transportation problems. Playing the bass viol means spending the rest of your life with a Siamese twin.

•

The brilliant Israeli pianist, David Bar-Illan and his lovely wife, Beverly, also had an unforgettable 1969 departure. Their boarding gate kept changing and I escorted them to the wrong one. Beverly wrote later: "Our last vision of you racing down that long, long breezeway at the airport in your effort to get us to the right gate has made us smile many times. I'll bet St. Thomas doesn't often witness such a display of activity!" Well, let us say it kept me from getting middle-age spread.

•

The Metropolitan Opera baritone, Frank Guarrera, in 1968 never did rehearse. The Steinway was being tuned, so Guarrera and his accompanist, Lowell Farr, settled for an upright piano in the High School's basement. When Frank Guarrera heard the first few bars, he shook his head and went back up to the auditorium. After emitting several well-rounded baritone sounds, he called it a day. "Testing the auditorium," he explained good-naturedly.

Lowell Farr followed in about ten minutes. His fingers did not take long to limber up on **that** upright piano. The lighting was not right either, but being the trouper he was, Mr. Guarrera arranged his own lights and gave a concert that had the audience standing and shouting, "Bravo!"

•

Although we encountered no unforgettable problems with the Lee Evans Trio in 1967, Lee Evans told me he would never forget the expression on my face during the after-concert dinner at our house. A Danish visitor—here for the semi-centennial celebration of Denmark's sale of the Virgin Islands to the United States in 1917—knocked over our six-foot, carved Indian screen.

As I served the salad, I looked up to see the screen about to crash into the buffet table loaded with crystal, china, and food. How I intercepted it a moment before it would have demolished everything remains a mystery.

Mr. Evans said, "I have never seen a face so horror-stricken!"
Had I seen it, I am sure I would have agreed. That is how I felt.

●

A worried couple of days came in 1968 when we lost the well-known French pianist, Michel Block. His New York agent notified us he would arrive two days before the concert. When Block did not pick up his hotel reservations, we called the agent. He insisted Michel Block was in St. Thomas. Well, he was not! One Board member said, "Do you think he's an island drop-out?"

We met planes and kept a "hotline" alive day and night to the Scott Hotel. It appeared we would not have a concert. We imagined all kinds of horrible scenarios where our pianist played the leading role: kidnapping, amnesia, dying in a hospital from an accident. Yet, like a cliff-hanging movie, Block turned up the afternoon of the concert. His agent neglected to tell us he was flying in from England. Block's delayed flight in London caused connecting flight delays all the way to St. Thomas. He could have gotten here sooner by swimming!

●

Although Al accused **me** of being lost for three days at concert-time, he quit complaining after Michael Maule's Dance Variations performance in 1968. Members of this talented ballet quartet wanted to relax a few days in St. Thomas before returning home. They found hotel rates in season, however, too high for "supporting dancers'" pocketbooks.

We offered our guest room to the two ballerinas, Jean-Marie Aubert from France and Dulce Anaya from Cuba. This compensated Al for my Music Association "lost weekends," but our male neighbors accused him of not sharing the wealth. He alone chauffeured the girls on sightseeing tours.

Dr. Virgil Tsuluca and Fred Morrison, owners then of the Riviera Boutiques and long time St. Thomas residents, offered the guest room of their Villa Riviera (featured in House & Garden) to danseur Larry Gradus and premier danseur Michael Maule. The ballet group loved St. Thomas, and Michael Maule and his wife, Joan, returned often for vacations.

●

Several times when we could not find accommodations for our artists, Board members housed and spoiled them. Once, Joe Marona, owner then of popular Thatch Farm guest house and restaurant gave free lodging to an entire dance troupe. Joe was not a Board member, but having been a dancer, identified with their money problems.

●

In a pinch, Board members ironed costumes, paced nervously during power outages that lasted until fifteen minutes before the concert, tight-rope walked across ceiling beams to adjust lights, and tolerated high school students operating the bank of lights. The latter sometimes left the artist in the dark and the audience in the spotlight.

Before the auditorium was air-conditioned, artists competed with the wind laughing through the window jalousies; noisy basketball games in the High School gym; drag races in an adjacent vacant lot; and curious faces peering through toothless places in the jalousied windows. They never complained even about the use of classrooms as dressing rooms, leaking plumbing, or the one small mirror for dressing and making-up. They all wanted to come back, except one soprano who did not think our high school auditorium had the right ambience for her usual elegant concert dress.

●

Because Betty DeLagarde was assistant principal of Charlotte Amalie High School, and I was always there for concert rehearsals, we were sitting ducks for last minute emergencies: sweeping the stage floor and setting up extra chairs.

The ratio of board members was half and half, black and white. None of them ever shirked responsibility, and I loved them for it. Unlike most such cultural groups where there are more Chiefs than Indians, we were **all** Indians.

Leta Cromwell's Musicals

Leta Cromwell, a small, vivacious woman with a good sense of humor was the Board member most generous with her home for after-concert dinners. She also kept her baby grand piano ready for concert artists wanting to practice.

Besides playing Fairy Godmother to the Music Association and other civic organizations, Leta sang with our celebrated Caribbean Chorale and sponsored summer musical festivals at her château in France.

Leta's yearly musicale for Board members featured her talented house guests or island protégés—violinist Pattmore Lewis and pianist Tony Harmer.

An unpredictable "happening" invariably enlivened this winter musical event. Electric outages offered the most diversion.

As comments and wagers on the electricity's reappearance flew back and forth like bats in the night, a variety of music lovers scurried around in the dark, lighting lamps and candles and bumping into each other. Accustomed to coping with outages, everyone stocks oil and battery lamps and has a drawer full of candles. Leta brought out beautiful silver candelabra.

Along with Liberace references, the soft light brought glamour to the piano and the dressed-to-the-teeth audience (made us women look as if we had face-lifts) while we peered and giggled at each other like high school spelunkers in a candle-lit cave.

The outages might last ten minutes or all evening.

Usually, after a few minutes of organized chaos, and whether or not the lights came on, the audience settled back to enjoy the music.

One night, along with our outage, we had the added attraction of a special telephone call.

Ordinarily, Leta's housekeeper discreetly answered calls on the first ring and dispatched them at once. This one turned out to be a long distance call for the guest pianist now in the middle of a concerto.

No matter.

Leta handed him the telephone. He chatted aimably for a good five minutes. The audience sat in the flickering candlelight, like children in Sunday school, and tried to pretend they were not listening.

After the pianist hung up, he smiled and nodded at his privileged listeners, and with his long, beautiful hands, adjusted the piano bench. He returned then to his fiery concerto. His savoir-faire made the holiday season for all of us. Such aplomb we had never seen.

Madame Lili Kraus

This brings me to the 1971 concert of the late world-renowned Hungarian pianist, Lili Kraus.

Roy Francis and I met Madame Kraus at the airport and took her to a hotel she found unsatisfactory. The room was too small and without a view. Her regretful, self-effacing manner sent us immediately to the telephone.

After numerous calls, we found a room at Bluebeard's Castle Hotel. Happily installed there, she "ohhhed" and "ahhhed" at the city view and harbor lights. My wristwatch read 9:30 p.m.

"Mr. Francis and I will say goodnight and let you get a good night's sleep, Madame Kraus—if there isn't anything else we can do for you," I

Streetside refreshment stand, Emancipation Park

said. "Oh, there is!" she replied in her heavy Hungarian accent. "I haven't practiced today, and I practice every day. Could you please take me to a piano?" she asked, half-pleading, half-apologetic.

After a moment of panic, Roy and I exchanged a quick glance. We both said at once, "Leta—"

I called Leta's house, but she was not home. I explained our problem to the housekeeper. Long accustomed to Music Associations predicaments, she told us to bring Madame Kraus at once and everything would be ready for her.

We left Madame Kraus alone at Leta's, energetically pounding away at the piano. When finished, she would call me, and I would return her to Bluebeard's Hotel.

Leta phoned an hour later. She said she would drive Madame Kraus to the hotel since she lived so much closer than I did. I was delighted.

The next day Leta telephoned early.

"I did the most awful thing," she said. "I was so tired and half asleep when she finished, I really didn't know what I was saying. But I wanted to make conversation as I drove her to the hotel and I said, 'When is your accompanist coming?' She drew herself up and said, 'I am zee pianist!' "

We both burst out laughing.

"I'm certain she thinks I don't know a thing about music," Leta said. "She was very quiet the rest of the way to the hotel."

After commiserating, I promised to clear up the matter. The next day when I picked up Madame Kraus for a rehearsal at the high school, she asked about Leta. Her tone implied Leta was not very knowledgeable about music.

I told her about Leta's interest in young musicians and her music festivals in France. She never mentioned Leta's faux pas and ended up in Leta's guest cottage for a couple of friendly days before she left the island.

The Lili Kraus concert was sensational.

Afterward I said, "Madame Kraus, that concert was simply magnificent!"

"On zat piano, it waz a miracle!" she shot back.

We both chuckled. All who came in contact with this delightful artist fell in love with her.

When I made arrangements to take Madame Kraus to the airport, she asked to see our gardens before departure time. Leta had told her about Hidden hill. We asked her for lunch.

Al went to pick her up at Leta's guest house. When he called out to tell her he was there and asked about her luggage, she said he could get it in the bedroom.

After he walked in, he saw that she was in panties and bra, brushing her hair into a great mound on top of her head.

"I just washed my hair," she explained, unperturbed, "and I will dry it at your house."

Al grabbed the luggage and hastened outside.

Upon arriving at our house, she pulled out combs and hairpins and let her dark hair swirl around her shoulders. As we strolled through the grounds, she swung it from side to side to dry. Lili (she told us to call her that) asked about numerous plants, flowers, and trees. What a joy to be her guide!

At lunch she told us about her harrowing years in a Japanese concentration camp during the early 40s. Shortly after she began a world concert tour in the Dutch East Indies, the Japanese arrested her on trumped-up charges. Subsisting on meager rations and sleeping in a crowded, filthy cell, she was forced to carry heavy buckets of water and scrub latrines with strong soaps and chemicals. Still, to keep her fingers nimble and her mental repertoire alive, she practiced daily on a table or any flat surface.

Finally a Japanese conductor she once played for in Tokyo, reunited her with her family in a "privileged" camp, where she stayed until the war ended in 1945. It was a long and difficult road back to the international concert circuit in 1948.

Lili Kraus spoke of many memorable concerts: in the world's celebrated music halls and performances for royalty. Yet her most cherished ones took place in 1965. She visited Dr. Albert Schweitzer and his African jungle hospital in Lambaréné for several weeks, shortly before his death. She played for him almost daily on a battered upright in the crude little mess hall. His favorite Lili Kraus recording was Beethoven's Fourth Piano concerto, and according to his nurse, he was listening to it when he died.

That luncheon with Lili Kraus, over 18 years ago, was a Paradise day. We heard from her occasionally and dropped her notes or Daily News clippings we thought would interest her.

Albert Daniels, our talented self-taught St. Thomas artist and sculptor, gave her a piece of sculpture, so we always sent news about him. After her St. Thomas concert, they chatted together. Since he rarely left the island, his vast knowledge of current music and art impressed her. It saddened us to send her his obituary.

We saw Lili Kraus in a PBS profile not long before she died in November 1986. No longer on the concert circuit, she was sharing her piano wizardry with talented young people on their way to becoming concert artists. They could not have had a more dedicated teacher.

●

The celebrated Italian violinist Pina Carmirelli asked me to carry her violin in 1970. I sprinted along jauntily until I asked its make.

She said it was a Stradivarius that belonged to the Italian government and was valued at $250,000. Gulping, I slowed down.

●

We loved the Vienna Choir Boys—all twenty-eight of them—with their three chaperones. We entertained the group for lunch at Hidden Hill in 1970: stacks of sandwiches, gallons of fruit punch, and enough cookies to last a kindergarten class two weeks.

They ate everything.

Unleashing them was like opening up an ants' nest. They scampered all over the grounds in jig time. Colorful tropical flowers: long, slim red Cat's Tail and cup-shaped yellow Allamanda; strangely shaped fruit: breadfruit and soursop; exotic trees: Bauhania drooping lavender orchids and African tulips with orange tulip-like blooms, excited the boys.

The blooming "Cutlass" trees with their flower petals shaped like cutlasses especially fascinated them. The small scabbards are bright red and when you pull out the hilt, the lower part looks like a tiny cutlass. The choir boys gathered them up by the dozens and stuffed them into pockets. I suspect that somewhere in Vienna today, a book preserves a dried "cutlass" from a Hidden Hill tree. I hope so.

•

The Alvin Ailey Dancers' performance, also in 1970, made a tremendous hit. St. Thomians love to dance. When they do, they move in a way that makes you know they were "born to dance." Even tiny children move rhythmically to music. The Alvin Ailey Dancers moved the same way, but more disciplined and sophisticated. A delightful group of dedicated young people that included the stellar Judith Jamison, they earned prolonged applause after each number. That night we set up all the extra chairs the auditorium would hold, but still people who wanted a glimpse of the acclaimed dancers had to wait outside.

When the after-concert dinner ended, most Board members stayed to talk with the group about dancing and their careers. The black dancers probably felt about St. Thomas as celebrated bass-baritone opera singer Simon Estes did.

At the time Al and I picked up Simon Estes at the airport in 1971, he was well-known, but now he is considered one of the world's great opera singers. A big six-foot, two-inch man, he did not fit comfortably in the back seat of the VW. As we made small talk, he seemed unusually reserved.

This was his first trip to the Caribbean, so we pointed out places of interest on the way to the hotel. He appeared receptive to his surroundings, but spoke very little.

After a long silence, he finally said, "I certainly don't feel like a minority here."

I turned around and grinned at him. "I do!" I said.

His deep laugh was a joy. From then on he warmed up, and our chit-chat was considerably easier and more pleasant.

Shortly after his concert here, Estes went to Europe, where he spent over a decade enjoying plaudits in famous European opera houses. He made his debut at the Met in 1982. He maintained he should have been singing there in 1966.

"And I would have, had I been white," he said.

I am sure that was true, but things are changing. Still Simon Estes will always belong to a minority—the élite one of the world's great opera stars.

•

St. Thomian Homer Bryant, our very own premier danseur, appeared

46

with the Harlem Dance Theater in 1973 and was the hit of the show for us residents.

•

Like many things, the Community Music Association is no more. The Reichhold Center for the Arts, in a beautiful tree and flower setting, replaced it. Given to St. Thomas by the late Henry Reichhold of Reichhold Chemical Company, the Center presents a yearly concert series along with other concerts, art shows, plays, and stage circuses.

I sometimes wonder about the Center's concert problems, but assume they are much the same as ours. I like going there, knowing the concert worries are not mine. I am also happy the Center will carry on—and we shall have music.

Yet sometimes I get nostalgic for our caged piano and the High School's squeaky auditorium seats.

Narrow Main Street in downtown Charlotte Amalie has many excellent stores that attract tourists. Many cruise ship passengers shop at Havensight Mall near the West Indian cruise ship docks, never coming downtown

CHAPTER 4

FORGIVE US OUR DAILY NEWS

Despite poking fun at it, I love the Daily News.

When someone kicks my pet rock, or I suffer from tropical rot, I always find an item in its pages to revive my funny bone.

The newspaper's humorous approach to news items delights me. For example, St. Thomas residents driving to work St. Patrick's Day morning in 1971, saw that during the night's witching hours, brand new wobbly stripes of green had been painted down the center of Main Street and waterfront drive.

Public Works, as well as Jack Kelly, well-known owner of an Irish linen shop, and equally well-known Rusty Hagan, Irish hostess-owner of popular "Rusty Roost's" restaurant, denied any knowledge of the prank. Bleary-eyed habitués of Trader Dan's, a slightly shabby open-air waterfront bar (long gone), shook their aching heads and also pleaded innocent. All efforts to solve the mystery came to a dead end.

Our Daily News finally reported: "Baffled, investigators concluded 'twas the work of the wee people—the Leprechauns." The case rested there.

On Thanksgiving Day 1972, a prankster blocked off Main Street.

Everyone strolled happily in the narrow thoroughfare's center. No dodging of taxis and cars. No bumping into people on crowded sidewalks.

The Daily News never found the person responsible for this act, either. Since almost everyone—except taxi drivers—favors Main Street being a shopping mall, I honestly believe no one, including the police, tried very hard.

•

Sometimes I find my laughter "fix" in The Daily News Classified ads. After an unusual amount of electric outages one week, this 1971 ad appeared in the "Personal" column:

"Congratulations to the V.I. Water & Power Authority on another fantastic week. We're behind you all the way. Amalgamated Brotherhood of Lamp Lighters and Candle Makers, Local 002."

A few days later came this reply:

"Will person placing advertisement in Monday's Daily News about candles, please come to Water and Power Authority Office, Bldg. No. 1 Sub-base and pick up the reward of 5 kilowatts, no delivery, bring shopping bag to take them home."

•

Speaking of outages, The Daily News in 1973 called them "outrages" and type-goofed "sour-cylinder" engines. Both on purpose maybe?

•

And who proofread this ad for Channel 12?

"**Garvel** to **Garvel** TV Coverage of the 16th Legislature Swearing-in Ceremony," or the one for Sapphire Beach Restaurant that promised a "**Karaft** of wine" with dinner.

•

Police reports are also grist for my laughter mill. This 1970 one is about an accident:

"Gifft told police that he was driving east on the Virgin Islands College road Sunday night when a donkey came out from the south side of the road and ran into the car's left front fender causing damage to the fender. There was no report on the condition of the donkey."

•

To prove things do not change, here is part of a 1985 article about island crime:

"Asked about the police shooting at a fleeing suspect, Hodge said officers have been told never to fire warning shots or shoot at someone who is running because it only makes them run faster."

No doubt!

•

The Daily News also reported that Consumers Services closed a brothel. How's that again? In an article covering the need for specific repair work on our roads, the newspaper reported that "pubic works" had taken care of it.

•

"Corrections" of any kind give me a chuckle. I never pass up The Daily News "Corrections" column. A 1984 favorite is:

"A sentence concerning Senate President Hugo Dennis should have read that he told business leaders just what they wanted to 'hear.' Due to a typographical error, the word 'hear' read 'fear.' " You can come out of hiding now, men.

Another bears repeating:

"A story in Friday's Daily News reported incorrectly that the ordination of Liston Garfield to the Sacred Order of Deacons will take place at 7 a.m. Thursday at the All Saints Cathedral. The ceremony will actually be begin at 7 p.m." Rigor mortis could set in if you missed that one and waited . . and waited . . and waited . . . .

And another:

"In Saturday's Scope story on artist Eljay Torger, the Harbor Arts Gallery—the site of one of Torger's previous exhibits—was incorrectly called defunct. Gallery management advised The Daily News Monday that the gallery is, in fact, still in business." Being "funct" is better than being "defunct." N'est-ce pas?

I am sure this Correction recipient thought so:

"In a caption concerning Claude O. Markoe School, the namesake of the school was referred to as the late Claude O. Markoe. This is incorrect. Mr. Markoe is alive and well. The Daily News regrets the error.

Their "Man-On-The-Street" column in 1973 asked thought-provoking questions and get thought-provoking answers.

To the question, "What are your secrets for living a long life?" A 95-year old woman said, "I gave up the boyfriends 50 years ago, so I haven't had too many problems lately." Natch!

And an 86-year old man replied, "Live a clean life! Extra girlfriends can cause unexpected situations to arise." You bet.

The Man-On-The-Street in those days occasionally interviewed dogs, as well as cows, horses, goats, and pigs to add zest to his column.

Asked, "Should America be given back to the Indians," a cow answered: "Yes, America has already gone to the dogs . . . ."

Today The Daily News has replaced the Man-On-The-Street with "Views On The News," which I do not find very funny. Maybe it is the news.

•

A tantalizing Daily News Classified Ad for men in search of a haircut in 1973 came from The Sip-N-Clip Barber Shop:

"Grab a tall glass of your favorite and gaze across the harbor while getting a fine professional haircut."

•

In the early 70s we enjoyed attending "Ship Plaque Presentations." This ceremony takes place when our Tourism Department presents a captain with a plaque commemorating his ship's first call to the port of St. Thomas.

One year The Daily News reported that the ship's captain was presented with a "plague." Bourbon-ic, no doubt.

•

This 1972 report in a Daily News column from St. John brought many chuckles:

"Ethel McCully was heard a few days ago on her radio telephone requesting a new copy of an old 1971 VITELCO (telephone company) directory due to the fact that her donkey had come into the kitchen and eaten out the entire St. Thomas section of the director. The donkey has no comment."

•

The late Ethel McCully, small and fragile-looking, was a Virgin Islands character. Fragile, she was not. She built her St. John house with the help of a donkey—same one probably—and published a book about the experience called, "Grandma Raises the Roof." She wanted to call it, "I Did It With My Ass," but such anatomical words were taboo then and the publisher balked.

An Hibiscus lover, Ethel McCully grew exotic blossoms in rare colors and always wore one tucked in her hair. She visited St. Thomas often and lunched at the Grand Gallery "Round Table," popular meeting place for Continentals, where she contributed her share of witticisms to sprightly conversations.

A particularly waggish Daily News ad appeared in 1973 under "Jobs—Men and Women:"

"LIEUTENANT GOVERNOR. No requirements as to race, creed, sex or political affiliations. Must be 30 years old, U.S. citizen and V.I. resident for at least five years. Write "Desperate" c/o Daily News, Box 644, St. Thomas."

Comments about the ad brought gales of laughter. Our Republican Governor, Melvin Evans, was trying desperately to replace Lieutenant Governor David Maas who resigned. Turned down by both Republicans and Democrats, the Governor finally persuaded a prominent and capable Democratic Senator, Addie Ottley, to change his allegiance and accept the job.

Evans lost the next election and his new Lieutenant Governor decided a politician's life was not his cup of bush tea. Addie is now a popular radio and TV personality and having the time of his life. There is a moral here somewhere.

•

In 1979, hurricanes David and Frederic took a bear paw's swipe at St. Thomas, dumped tons of water, and pounded us with furious winds. Phones did not function, electric lines coiled like snakes on highways, and rubble and boulders rendered many roads impassable.

After the storm, Woolworth's ran this ad:

"Aclaratory Note: Due to the hurricane, some of the items in today's shopper may not be available. But **rain** checks will be given." "Aclaratory" is not in my dictionary, and I never learned if the pun was intentional.

•

The bane of Al's existence is The Daily News TV schedule. He complains every night. He complains to Penny Feuerzeig, Executive Editor of The Daily News, and to Ariel Melchior, Jr., Publisher and Editor. Al believes in going straight to the top.

Well, the top is as frustrated as Al. The paper prints what the stations send. Often the paper is not sent anything. Even with the Gannett crystal ball, they are stymied. They tried a special service and now have a weekly TV insert. Al still is not happy. You simply cannot please **some** men.

•

Gannett has owned The Daily News since 1978, but J. Antonio Jarvis and Ariel Melchior, Sr. began printing the paper August 1, 1930. We have read it regularly for 25 years and found it an exceptionally good newspaper for a tiny little island in the middle of the ocean.

Not only did its owners successfully buck the depression years in the 30s, they coped with electric outages and Stateside communication breakdowns. Still they kept their presses clickety-clacking and their paper never missed an edition. No small feat. Besides I would not enjoy The Daily News nearly so much if it were perfect.

I admire the paper's willingness to "stand up and be counted." Several series of articles exposed government graft and hanky-panky. Through the Gannett Foundation, the paper has also given over a half-million dollars to worthy community organizations. Recent recipients are Boy Scouts, Multi-Service Center, Council on Alcoholism, and Island Center of St. Croix. The Daily News also prints letters that censure the newspaper. Bravo!

•

Back to the TV schedule. In 1981, the newspaper gave us David **Bunk**ley and Bob **Newhard**. When we received a flurry of government propaganda to brainwash us into accepting the metric system as the greatest thing since the yardstick, instead of the "liter," the paper discussed the "litter."

•

Daily News reporters that same year wrote about what our local "artisians" are doing in the schools—probably **well**! An ad waxed poetic about the beautiful "tracks" of land for sale on nearby Inner Brass Island. We wondered if the "tracks" were made by the "abominable sun-man."

•

A story about a mongoose in a school cistern received front page attention. The school had to close until someone removed the little animal. I will wager no other Gannett paper carried that item, but no one here found it strange.

•

The Daily News "Lost and Found" column is often interesting. Consider this 1982 ad:
"Left in taxi to Red Hood Ferry: Handbag containing eyeglasses, radio, cosmetic bag, medication and lawnmower parts. Call . . . " Only someone who lives in the islands can appreciate the need for this conglomeration of articles in a handbag.

•

After the 1983 Bastille Day celebration at Sib's Mountain Bar and Restaurant in Mafolie, The Daily News reported: "Entertainment was the Imagination Brass; the dancing was on the grass." St. Thomas has a large French population, covered in Chapter 11, "Cha-Cha Town."
Under "Help Wanted" in 1985, Zora the Sandalmaker needed:
"Man or woman. Slightly reverent. Pretty clean. Rather punctual. Very honest. Intelligent and eager to work as Zora's."
Zora tends to phone in her ads. One phoned-in ad for her Oriental Rug Room a couple of years ago came out like this:
"See Zora's electric collection of Oriental rugs."
I called her and said, "I see in today's ads that your Oriental Rug Room is all charged up," and read her the ad.
I will not quote her reply.
"I should know better than to use a word like 'eclectic' when I phone in an ad," she said.

The Daily News needles its readers from time to time, and I love it. In 1984 before Christmas, "Ho—ho—ho—your 1040 will be in the mail next week," headlined an article on taxes.

•

In a Daily News letter-to-the-editor that praised two postmen who extingushed a trash fire at Woolworth's, the manager said:
"In the event of the excitement one of the men got slightly scotched; that too was handled promptly." Watered down, no doubt.

•

Another intriguing letter-to-the-editor came from our St. Thomas jail and carried the headline "Grateful Inmates:"
"Dear Editor:
On behalf of the inmates of the St. Thomas jail we would like to thank the following organizations and/or individuals for their kind support during the year, and their special emphasis during the holiday seasons. The following ministered every week: the Apostolic Faith Ministry; New Testament Church of God; Full Gospel Businessmen Fellowship; Seventh Day Adventist Church; Bethel Baptist Church; Salvation Army; Women Aglow."
Women Aglow—ministering in jail?

•

Occasionally paid annoucements with black borders appear in The Daily News. Worthy of mention is a 1971 notice headlined TO THE FRIENDS OF MIKE QUIER:
"I wish I could personally thank each of you that helped make the burial of Mike possible. Without your help I could not have done what I think he would have wanted. He wore his loudest shirt and was buried at sea. When the boat left the dock, I announced 'Mr. Quier has opened the bar' and it stayed open until we returned. My particular thanks to Capt. Gillory, who donated the use of *The Reef Queen,* to Bob Conway, Harbor Master, who was present on his day off, and to Richard Hyall, the undertaker who did such a beautiful job on Mike and was also present on his day off.
I don't want to be facetious, but I think you, his friends, will understand the following: May I suggest that the next time you raise a glass, you mentally toast the Devil. After all, he now has Mike to contend with and we know Mike is arguing the price of coal and trying to get a piece of the action. My bets are on Mike.
Thank you very much.
Phyllis Fairchild Quier"

•

In September 1988, The Daily News bundled up its presses, swept out its cramped, rat-infested, 200-year-old building on Back Street, and trundled across town to a modern chapelesque dream of glare-proof glass and white masonry.

Equipped to cope with island quirks, the 16,000-square-foot building can withstand 150 m.p.h. hurricane winds. Well and rain water cisterns supply water needs, even for fires—along with fire alarms, extinguishers, hoses, and smoke detectors. Public fireplugs belch up only gargle-size spurts of water. Ultra-violet purifiers sanitize drinking water. During outages a generator creates emergency electricity; and battery power backs up the computer system. This is Paradise!

Though happy to leave Back Street, longtime employees nostalgically recall special anniversary celebrations; burying an obsolete printing press in the basement; typing by flashlight during electric outages; covering desks with plastic tarps when rain poured through ceiling cracks, rolling up pants and gathering buckets and brooms to bail out flood water; manning fire hoses to douse a fire next door; leaving behind the "ghost telephone" that rang mysteriously above the editorial offices, yet could never be found from the roof or ceiling space. It rang moving day.

"The old building has a lot of sentimental value for everybody," Mildred McFarlane said.

Ron Dillman, General Manager and CEO, showing off the new home, observed the smiling employees and lauded the paper's policy of hiring locals and helping them move up in the paper's ranks. Good luck, Daily News, don't stop keeping us informed—and entertained!

Portion of Daily News building. Man in front is Geraldo Guitry,
popular newspaper columnist and historian

CHAPTER 5

DOG DAZE

Beauregarde

Although a Basset Hound, Beauregarde did not know he was dog. He thought he was "people"—only built differently and with long ears. He was, however, our island's top celebrity dog in the late 60s and early 70s.

Sometimes his doleful face looked like people—hungover people—and so did the rest of him. Too fat and drooping all over like a melting wax sculpture, Beau would sit patiently beside the road observing passing cars—there were not too many in those days—until someone stopped to give him a lift.

When he wanted to alight—or "aheavy," in his case, a quick bark alerted his chauffeur. That could be in front of Trader Dan's, or the Carousel, popular waterfront bars, or someplace else where he would be plied with food and his favorite beer. It depended upon the time of day.

Beauregarde followed a loose routine: Yacht Haven, Morning Star Beach, and Rusty's Roost in the mornings. If he chose Rusty's Roost, and it was still closed, he rumbled the door until Rusty opened up, but she loved Beau and like everyone else, tolerated his idiosyncracies.

If Beau felt up to a formal dinner—and sometimes if he did not—he would go to Café Brittany, a prestigious downtown restaurant in Creque's Alley, now Royal Dane Mall. Owner Jerry Meyer tolerated Beau with good humor, but well-known Café Brittany organist, Paul Tomkins, another of Beau's devoted pals, saw to it that the dog ate gourmet fare. Prime rib, for example.

To my knowledge, no one ever fed Beau just plain dog food. He demanded better—and got it.

Beauregarde's favorite Café Brittany resting place was smack in the middle of traffic. Waiters, local senators, businessmen, snooty ladies, their escorts, and tourists had to step over or around him while he snoozed. Everyone laughed and went his way. St. Thomians adored Beau and tourists delighted in him as "local color." He could not lose.

Although Beau might appear a dog without a home, he had a comfortable pad near Smith's Fancy. Mrs. Tino McKay cherished him as a roué pet. Usually he came home at night and slept with one of her seven children. She would have been happier had he been more of a homebody, but she recognized him as an incorrigible wanderer at heart and a "people dog" who simply would not be confined.

When Beau stayed away overnight, his mistress was always glad to hear his sheepish bark at the gate in the morning and immediately forgave him for his dissolute ways. Like restaurant and bar proprietors, she could not resist his long-faced charm and fed him only the best. Sometimes an entire chicken.

Beauregarde did other things beside eat. By the time he was five he had cloned seven other Bassets, but it was not easy in the beginning.

Mrs. McKay bought Beauregarde from veterinarian Andy Williamson in 1967, and the dog had blueblood credentials. His official papers stated he was one year old and his name was "Brandy de Menthe." With a moniker like that he simply had to be a booze hound.

At first, hopes to mate Beau with a female Basset of equal lineage were fruitless, as were two other attempts. Beau returned from one "studding" experience five pounds lighter.

"He was nervous because he was watched," Mrs. McKay said. That figures.

When the Basset was taken to St. Croix for a coupling date, his low-slung, balloon sausage body had a hard time getting aboard the seaplane. He had even more trouble getting aboard the chosen Basset broad. Again Beau struck out.

Beau's only successful romance was with Sloopy, a young Basset and mother of Andrew, named after Andy Williamson. The important word is "young." Even canine roués like 'em young.

Andrew, Beau's favorite son and identical in appearance and habits, became a companion on his father's watering hole circuit. Stories about the two bar hounds abound.

My favorite concerns Rusty Hagan, owner of Rusty's Roost, who told how they came to an opening night party and plopped down in the middle of the terrace. She lettered a large sign: "Recommended by Beauregarde" and topped it with four stars. A large paw print authenticated the Basset's approval. Thereafter he came back with his son almost every night.

Unfortunately, Andrew disappeared one night, and even though friends offered a reward, no one ever found him. Beau took the loss very hard.

To drown his grief, the old Basset became more of a bar hound and carouser than ever. Patronizing his favorite waterfront haunts, he drank beer and socialized until 3 or 4 a.m., then staggered home. Many nights he had trouble climbing the stairs, but he finally managed and crawled into one of the McKay children's beds to sleep off "his night on the town."

The Basset also began visiting the piers when Greek cruise ships docked. He fancied Greek food and could polish off a spanakotiropita before I could pronounce it.

If Beau felt like going abroad, he hitched rides from Antilles Air Boat pilots to St. Croix. After a few days, he returned to Antilles, and a pilot brought him back to St. Thomas. It is even claimed that he once hitchhiked on the Carib-Star Ferry to Puerto Rico, but I cannot verify that.

After "Skitch" Henderson opened the Wooden Horse Restaurant in downtown Charlotte Amalie, Beau joined the other *bons vivants* who flocked there.

Radio interview shows sometimes originated from the restaurant, and once Lee Carle of WVWI interviewed Beauregarde along with other island celebrities. Beau gave a "doggone" good interview.

Beauregarde, a real canine swinger, never waddled into a café he did not like.

Marie Tallman, at one time co-owner of Carousel, said she always knew when Beau was really hungry. He went straight to the kitchen, oblivious to the dining areas's noisy activity. If not hungry, he plopped down to get acquainted with the diners. A "dog to people" welcoming committee.

Sometimes a kindhearted driver would find himself with an uninvited guest until Beau decided to move on. Bob Rosenberg picked up the Basset one evening before going to meet friends at Hotel 1829 and could not shake him. Beau liked the food there, too, and insisted on staying with the party.

When they were ready to leave, Beau got into the car and waited. Bob did not have the heart to kick him out, but he did not want the Basset as an overnight guest either. He stopped at The Mill, another favorite Beauregarde haunt, and helped the dog to alight (or aheavy), then got back in his car.

Bob said he would never forget the look in Beau's eyes when he realized Bob was not going to join him.

"He looked at me as if I was deserting my best friend," he said.

The demise of Beauregarde in 1976 was well-covered by newspapers, radio, and T.V. Everyone mourned the irreplaceable canine roué. Without Beau, Paradise would never be as much fun.

•

Another well-loved Basset, Napoleon, spent his first eight years aboard Yacht *Blue Shamrock* with his owners, Bill and Warren McKay. Then he took a land cruise of 9,000 miles with his people and toured the United States. They returned in 1980 to the *Blue Shamrock* to cruise the U.S. and British Virgins and Puerto Rico.

St. John's ferry dock at Red Hook Bay, St. Thomas

A delightful poem by a friend named Liz, dedicated to the Basset and Warren McKay, appeared in The Daily News in January 1982. Quite long and amusing, it expressed Napoleon's thoughts and ended with:

> I've got the longest, smartest ears
> Of any dog around
> And when I drop my head a bit
> They trail along the ground.
> I've got the biggest saddest eyes
> That you will ever see
> And even when I try to smile
> I look a misery
> It really isn't fair at all
> For I'm a happy lad
> I wonder why God made me seem
> To be so very sad?

•

The devotion of our island people to dogs is never-ending. Mohamed, "the dock dog," died at the age of fourteen and was mourned with a black-boarded obituary and picture.

Bullfoot

Bullfoot, a shaggy terrier, and another denizen of booze parlors in the 60s and 70s, was addicted to Kahlua and milk. He perched nightly on barstools at Katie's, Driftwood, Fat City, The Gate, Eddie's Backstreet, Sparky's, and Sebastian's.

David Felstein of Brooklyn, New York, reported his death in February, 1985 in The Daily News and reminisced on the dog's habits and escapades.

Bullfoot, who nursed his hangovers in various island spots, eventually found employment under the guise of a guard dog for the original "Cuckoo's Nest," a womenswear shop, not a bird-in-a-tree creation. Lying under a rack of long dresses, he bit the ankles of anyone who ventured near his tail.

Bullfoot definitely had unorthodox habits: eating mattresses, biting anyone who wore a workman's uniform, such as carpenters and painters wear, and eating his way out of any confinement—fiberglass airplane carrying cases and doors to locked rooms.

Felstein maintains Bullfoot would have spent his last years in our Fort jail if he had been human.

Bullfoot eventually migrated to New York, where he discovered his shenanigans were not tolerated as they had been in St. Thomas. His sins were pretty devastating. He killed a Yorkshire Terrier, crippled a kitten, an maimed numerous people. He also attacked a full-length suede coat. About to meet his Maker after eating a door frame, he was whisked away in the dead of night to permanent retirement in Brooklyn.

Here he had his own backyard and the run of a two-story townhouse. Semi-adopted by an independent black pre-school occupying the first floor of the house, the "lawless one" discovered a love for children. He allowed them to maul him and relished every minute of his play with the small fry. He never bit one nor even took a nip.

Two weeks after Bullfoot celebrated his 14th birthday, he was found to have an inoperable, malignant, and fast-growing tumor inside his body. He was put to sleep at the King's County Animal Hospital in Brooklyn and later cremated.

Felstein ends his account of Bullfoot with a sentimental salute.

"We're sure Bullfoot is running round Doggie Heaven at this very moment tearing up clouds, biting angels and looking for a bar that will serve him a drink. For anyone who remembers this feisty old renegade, lift your glasses high and let's all say, 'He was quite a guy.' "

Even a dog hater could not help but be touched by such a tribute from a man who loved a delinquent canine.

•

In 1981, Caribbean AMC Jeep and Budweiser sponsored a jeep road rally for the benefit of the St. Thomas Canine Corps. Each of the 109 entries, paying $10, received a T-shirt.

One was worn by Tracy Dodd's dog Tammy. The terrier looked better in the T-shirt than most of the jeep drivers. Evidently Daily News photographers Steven Rockstein and Richard Gibson thought so, too. Tammy, along with the jeeps, was the only one featured with a photo in the newspaper article covering the rally.

Waterfront produce stand

Radar

Certainly there is no place under the American flag where people love dogs more than in St. Thomas. I do know, however, of a dog-lover, veteran journalist, William Steif, who travels all over the world, but lives on St. Croix and has a Dalmatian named Radar.

When Steif is home, he writes a weekly column for The Daily News. Sometimes Radar Steif, a novice journalist, takes over his boss' space. I like William Steif's columns, but the truth is I **love** Radar's columns.

In one column, Radar maintained he learned to read "by sniffing the newsprint on the papers." He often writes about Guinevere, a shy German Shepherd, who also lives in the Steif household.

To avoid Radar's amorous passes, Guinevere hides in caves around the house.

"One of her favorite caves," Radar informs us, "is under the boss' typewriter table."

Even though Guinevere keeps clear of Radar, she is protective of him. Once when two Crucian dogs attacked him, shy Guinevere "came roaring up, growling and howling and chased them away." She also chased away a large Huskie.

Sometimes Radar enlarges on Guinevere's attributes.

"Guinevere has developed a lot of **chutzpah**—that's not exactly a Crucian word: It means guts or gall in Yiddish, and I plucked it out of Bill Safire's column in The New York Times one day before eating the editorials." Clever dog! I have wanted to eat a few of Safire's editorials myself.

Radar is worth watching. Someday he is going to replace Art Buchwald.

Our Island Dogs

Al and I are addicted to "island dogs." Descended from Rhodesian Ridgebacks brought from Africa for plantation managers, they have become almost indestructible through survival of the fittest. We have had four such dogs and feel they can compete with any breed. We are not alone.

This ad in The Daily News supports our point of view:

"FREE AND FOR IMMEDIATE ADOPTION: 100% thoroughbred St. Thomian puppies (¼ Labrador, ¾ dubious ancestry). Get a low maintenance mutt to cure your every need (love, security, devotion). Short on hair, big on bark. W—W—774-000 evenings."

Isla, meaning "island" in Spanish, was our first island dog. We brought her home from a cocktail party one spring night in 1966. Probably about eight or nine months old, she was one of the wild dogs—which I am glad to say we not longer have—that once roamed the east end of the island.

The dog had moved in on friends who already had two dogs and did not want another. They planned to take her to the pound the next day, where she would be put to sleep. Tan and brown, with medium length hair, and a little larger than a fox terrier, she was such a cute, lovable little thing, we could not stand the thought. This was before St. Thomas had an animal shelter and active humane society.

Shortly after we adopted Isla, a stray female adopted us. People had warned us not to feed strays, because they would never leave. Each night before Al closed the black wrought iron gates, he put her outside. But when he opened them the next morning, there she sat, ready to sneak back inside.

We closed the gates at night, because the Boschulte cows that lived up the road found Hidden Hill a good place for nightly meandering. Since we are not cow people, moving them was unnerving. Close up, cows are bigger than you think. Gentle persuasion failed. Waving a stick toward the gate, ditto. Only a two-legged Boschulte could budge them.

A week after their last visit, Al said, "I forgot to close the gate last night and the Boschulte cows called again."

"How do you know?" I asked.

"I just saw four tails going out the gate," he said.

Anyway, after the stray female came slinking in, I could not bear to see her go hungry. When Al was not looking, I slipped her food. Finally I told him so.

"I know. I've seen you do it," he said.

Sheepishly, I asked if he would give her to me for my birthday—the next week. He agreed. Like Isla, we took her to Andy Williamson for a good physical, all shots, a bath, defleaing, and a doggie hysterectomy. It made a bit of a dent in the budget, but she was worth every cent. We

Charlotte Amalie and harbor. Cruise ship docks upper left center, portion of Hassel I. upper right

called her "Mango," because she adopted us during mango season, when our twenty-five trees were loaded with the delicious fruit.

What a pair they made. Mango, a good solid tan and dark brown island dog of medium size, chased mongooses. Isla was flighty. She scampered after moths and stopped occasionally to smell a flower.

It was Isla's wild side that finally caused us to keep the gates closed all the time.

Although mostly sweet as fudge, cuddly and obedient, Isla had spells of wildness that confounded us. Without provocation she would race out to the road and run up and down, barking and howling furiously at nothing.

No amount of persuasion or treat could entice her inside the gates. When we finally caught her and carried her back into the grounds, she hid in the bushes until the gates were opened to let someone in. Then she dashed through like a mongoose running with a tail wind to resume her noisy chase up and down the road. This is how she was finally killed by an automobile.

The loss of this strange but wonderful little dog broke our hearts. I did not think about it at the time, but I wonder if a full moon had anything to do with her wild actions.

From then on, we kept our dogs inside the grounds and the gates closed.

After Isla came Joshua, who belonged to Gretchen and Ben Yates and their swarm of children and dogs and cats. When they found out we had lost Isla and were looking for a dog, they said they had one for us.

Joshua, a small tan island dog, the runt of a litter, came out on the short end of everything and Gretchen wanted a calmer household for him. She brought him over to meet Mango. Being a mother type, Mango accepted the pup immediately. Soon they were a team.

Two acres, however, were not enough for Mango and Joshua to roam in. They wanted to go adventuring, and they were sneaky about it.

Everytime they dug their way out, Al searched out the escape spot and filled it in with rocks and boulders.

I still laugh over the day Al was putting a last rock in a getaway hole and Mango and Joshua appeared outside the fence on the roadside. Having found their favorite male person, they wagged their tails happily and sat down to watch him.

Head down and absorbed in his work, Al did not see them until Joshua came over and, through the fence, licked his forehead.

"Oh, no!" he groaned. "Where did they get out this time?"

The battle never ended as long as we lived in Hidden Hill. The dogs thought all those rocks Al lugged around and put in gaps in the fence were a game he played just with them.

Sometimes, when they got out and we did not know it, they sat at the wrought iron gates and barked for us to let them in. Always deliriously happy to see them well and alive, we welcomed them like rich uncles. Neither one of us has ever been good at punishing or disciplining dogs.

When Mango had a stroke and had to be put away, we went to the new Animal Shelter and found Maggie. We had to do it right away, because poor little Joshua, trying to find her, howled and whimpered endlessly with grief. They had been inseparable pals for over six years. Before long, though, he loved Maggie as much.

With her soft silky tan and black fur, Maggie was our most beautiful island dog. She possessed an inbred dignity and often looked at less noble dogs with the disdain of an aristocratic dowager.

Like all island dogs, Maggie was a joy to have around. Her only failing was her violent trembling when it thundered, rained heavily, or the U.S. Navy target practiced off the coast of the nearby island of Vieques.

Al belongs to a men's luncheon club of great age that is devoted to foolishness. There are reports on such things as the Reverse Sunset Committee. Al was made chairman of the Earthquake Committee because he had Maggie, the "seismopup," whose tembling he recorded for earth tremor information.

Ellie Ellison still teases me about the night I quietly told Maggie, eyeing leftover goodies after cocktail guests left, "Please don't eat the caviar, Maggie."

Jacques, her observer husband said, "June should go to dog obedience school."

"Forget it!" Ellie said.

Our house guests and visitors found our dogs attractive, too, and wanted pictures of us and the dogs, but I always had to ask, "Do you want

Relaxing near bandstand in Emancipation Park

the front of us and the back of the dogs, or the back of us and the front of the dogs?"

No matter where we stood the dogs would face us.

•

One prominent St. Thomas family runs their own private animal shelter. Nancy Basford, a very active member of the Humane Society and Animal Shelter, works "like a dog" for the dogs, cats, horses, goats, or any other homeless island creature. She tops her activities with the Chairmanship of the annual Valentine's Day "Doggie Ball"—top social and charity event of the year that attracts around five hundred people. I remember the first one in the late 60s with about seventy-five people.

Nancy and her husband, Jack, practice what Nancy preaches. A recent roster of strays in their house included Woodstock, a brown miniature dachshund; Sally, a Basset Hound; Shannon, a Doberman; Sam, a mixture of collie and island; Sadie, a French poodle; and Sabrina, a cat of mixed breed. Never less than five or six animals roam the premises, getting love and attention.

If everyone on the island was like the Basfords, we would not need a Humane Society or Animal Shelter.

•

My final word on St. Thomas dogs:

If a sign on a gate in St. Thomas reads "Dog Within," or "Beware Bad Dog" and a Booth cartoon dog snarls at you from the sign, go no farther. Only the most intrepid native or adopted islander would dare enter without calling "Inside!"

Island dogs are protective unto death.

Charlotte Amalie Harbor. Cruising sailors from all over the world drop anchor in one or another of St. Thomas's harbors. They know a good thing when they see it!

CHAPTER 6

STRICTLY FOR THE BIRDS

Hidden Hill with its forest of trees, shrubbery, and flowers, was a perfect sanctuary for birds, indigenous and migrating, and a bird watcher's earthly heaven.

Al an inveterate bird watcher who can still whistle more of the bird calls he learned as a Boy Scout than I care to hear, recorded the comings and goings of our migrating birds. He did not record our local birds: the yellow-breasted Bananaquit—the official Virgin Islands bird, Grassquits, Flycatchers, Ground Doves, Cuckoos, Mockingbirds, Pelicans, Gulls, Frigate Birds, Black Anis, Pearly-eyed Thrashers (the gangsters of our bird world, called "Trashy Birds"), and Hummingbirds.

Parakeets

He did not keep track of the wild Parakeets, either. Yet our hearts leapt when we heard their raucous screech of freedom and saw flashes of green and yellow soaring through the crowns of the trees. Consequently, we wanted them nearer the house for a closer look.

"Hang a wooden tray high in a tree and stock it with sunflower seeds," a friend advised.

Al hammered together the wooden tray and used up a tank of gas finding the sunflower seeds. We waited with the expectant joy of four-year-olds for Easter Bunnies. No Parakeets. Only field rats banqueted on our goodies. While the Parakeets continued to skirt the treetops, the rats not only gobbled up the seeds, they gnawed the tray.

Remembering duck decoys, we bought a plastic Parakeet and put it in the tray as a lure. Still no Parakeets. Only undeterred field rats thumbing their noses at us. Since we had no desire to operate a soup kitchen for rats, we scratched the project. You can't win 'em all.

At Hidden Hill we never did see a Parakeet closer than our treetops. Here at Harbor Ridge East, since we look down on trees from our gallery, we often see a flock of five or six winging by. It always makes my day. Unfortunately, with the island's population growth, they are not as prevalent as they used to be.

We know of one captured Parakeet, caged and put on a gallery. Before long his past Parakeet pals came to visit him. They chattered like noisy children as the caged bird pressed against the bars and, with his beak, held out bird seed from his feeder, quickly snatched up by his buddies. A touching scene that stirred my heart. I was not unhappy when someone let the bird out to rejoin his feathered friends.

Migrating Birds

Al's record-keeping of our migrating birds was a boon to Dea Murray when she compiled her book, "Birds of the Virgin Islands" in the late 60s.

Dea created colored drawings of the male of each migrating species she could find and only mentioned the female in the text. Women's Lib groups might howl "discrimination," but mostly female birds are dull and uninteresting.

Our migrating birds loved us and returned every year. We gave them plenty of sugar and water for drinking and bathing. Most were Warblers: Black-and-White, Parula, Black-throated Green, Black-throated Blue, Pine, Palm, Prothonotory, Yellow, and Cape Mays. I would not know the names of all these birds if Al had not been an Eager Beaver Boy Scout.

One Cape May family came back each year in April and stayed until October. This upset our Bananaquits, Grassquits, and even the lizards. They considered the sugar tray attached to the wrought iron railing around the gallery their territory.

Even though the Cape Mays were not year-round residents, the male belligerently defended his squatter's rights. To stop the bickering, we finally put up another sugar feeder.

Papa Cape May almost had a nervous breakdown as he flitted back and forth and tried to dominate both trays for his family's exclusive use. Eventually, he wisely opted for one, and quiet reigned.

Bananaquits

After we moved from Hidden Hill to a Harbor Ridge East townhouse condominium in 1974, we missed the songs and ever-present activity of the birds. To attract Bananaquits, Al built another wooden tray for the gallery railing and religiously put sugar in it. I should add "building wooden sugar trays for birds" to Al's list of what he does all day.

Several months passed before we finally saw a Bananaquit nervously looking around while he nibbled at the sugar. He must have been a scout for our area Bananaquits. Within three days an army moved in. Most mornings a dozen birds ecstatically pecked away on the sugar tray. Even after 15 years, that Bananaquit count remains stable.

Now we have Grassquits along with the Bananaquits and a persistent Green-throated Hummingbird, locally called Dr. Bird, for whom Al provides a special Hummingbird feeder. The Bananaquits steal sugar water from it every day, but the Hummingbird is a pacifist. Unperturbed, he hums over to sip nectar from our Crown of Thorns, Hibiscus, or Slipper Plant.

Bananaquits are aggressive little birds. If we do not "chop chop!" in the morning to put sugar in their tray, they fuss and carry on like cookies-and-milk-time at nursery school. One comes right up to our breakfast table on the gallery and fishwife-chatters at us until we refill the empty tray with sugar.

Sometimes, if we leave the gallery door open, that same bird flies in and around the house and out again. It is his way of telling us he owns the place.

For convenience, we keep a sugar jar for birds on our gallery. When the tray is empty and we are not nearby, our yellow-breasted friend sits on the

The Virgin Islands Legislature building, known locally as "the green barn"

sugar jar and pecks at the lid. It is his way of banging a spoon on an empty plate to get service. Never use the term "bird brain" lightly!

We first became attached to Bananaquits when we stayed at the Anchorage Hotel in Antigua in the early 60s. We ate breakfast on a terrace beside the sea every morning, and the Bananaquits came right up to the table to get sugar from the sugar bowl.

Owners Andy and Marilyn Holm tried using sugar bowls with flip-up tops, but the birds soon learned the lid-flipping trick. They emerged with their bills looking as if they had been into whipped cream. The guests got such a kick out of this that Andy and Marilyn finally gave up. It probably cost them a fortune, because Bananaquits are instiable sugar eaters.

•

Since we now live high on top of the mountain, we rarely see migrating birds. We do not have the cover of trees that attracted them to Hidden Hill. Sometimes, though, an indigenous Red-tailed Hawk soars down to drink from the swimming pool.

The hawk came face to face with Al one day. As they stared at each other, transfixed, it was difficult to know which one was more startled. Al took off first.

The hawk is magnificent as he gracefully glides and scours the tangled vegetation below for prey. One day, in pursuit of something we never identified, he swooped in almost to our gallery.

The huge bird's rapid approach with landing gear lowered—talons tensely curved at the ends of massive thighs and legs, ready to grab an unaware victim—raced our hearts. Not more than 10 feet away, he sighted us and veered. That is as close to a Red-tailed Hawk as I ever want to be.

•

When we used to go to the beach or to the Inn at Mandahl, we loved to watch the Frigate birds diving and swooping, along with Gulls and Pelicans. Sea birds in their freedom seem to give us humans more freedom, because when you watch them, you tend to soar a bit yourself.

A Mockingbird at our post office sings up a storm from his light pole perch. When I do not hear his song for a week, I am fearful some boy with a slingshot has done him in. So far he has survived.

•

We hear Cuckoos and Ground Doves, but like the Mockingbirds, they are wary of humans, and for good cause. We take pleasure in the gentle doves and always know when they are around by the whistling sound of their wings as they fly.

Trashy Birds

The only island bird I cannot abide is the cackling "Trashy Bird." The big bully attacks other birds, robs their nests, and after wolfing down the eggs, destroys what is left. Officially the Pearly-eyed Thrasher, the bird watches everything with an evil eye. Instinct warns you he is mean, and Al kept telling me about their viciousness.

Bird lover that I am, I could not believe any bird could be so wantonly destructive. I would not let Al shoot Trashies until I actually saw one attack Bananaquits, ravage their nest, and eat the eggs. I could not get there fast enough to stop it.

For weeks I had carefully protected that nest, hidden in a large potted Agelica on our gallery. I had even blocked the sliding glass door from the living room to prevent human disturbance.

As the Trashy Bird swooped off, I stood there yelling at him and shaking my fist. I acknowledged then that birds have their underworld just as we do. I hated that Trashy Bird.

Charging back to Al, I cried, "Shoot every one you see!"

Seeing his puzzled look, I added, "Trashy Birds."

He breathed easier.

Sometimes after a rainless couple of days, when our birds enjoy a dip in the bird bath and exchange gossip during their morning "sugar klatch," a Trashy Bird sweeps down to our gallery to scare them off and steal their water.

As I rush the intruder, a righteous wrath that would do justice to Carrie Nation overcomes me. Complaining noisily in frustrated defeat, Trashy gives me the evil eye and flies away. I feel I have just saved the "good bird" world.

Peacocks

When we first came to St. Thomas, peacocks wandered the grounds of several establishments. I wanted one for Hidden Hill. Knowing more about peacock behavior than I did, Al discouraged the idea.

I still envisioned myself wandering around our beautiful grounds in a long, flowing gown with my magnificent peacock—in full bloom—trailing behind. I liked that picture. It would give Hidden Hill a "touch of class." The peacock, I mean.

Whenever I heard over the radio that someone had lost a peacock, I hoped he would somehow materialize at Hidden Hill. It never happened. Since then, I have learned that although elegant looking and beautiful, their characteristic call sounds like an alley cat's mating howl amplified a hundred times. Not the touch of class I had in mind.

In the 30s, Brooks and Jane Pratt had a peacock when they lived at Estate Havensight. Since the Pratts had lived in India for 12 years, they had an affinity for peacocks and did not object to their boisterousness.

The Pratts' grounds and gardens were not fenced in and the peacock had a habit of wandering off. He usually ended up at the West Indian Company offices where the ships docked.

This did not exactly spread joy among the company officials. If the peacock did not want to leave and pressure was applied, he might very well attack someone. Brooks would be called and dutifully march down the hill and retrieve his peacock.

This scenario became a much too frequent occurrence, and one day a company official had enough. He called the Pratt's residence and when Brooks answered the phone, shouted into the receiver.

"Brooks, your Goddam peacock is here again!"

"Did he deliver my message?" Brooks asked sweetly.

By now I have lost all desire for a peacock. Even if I had not, I do not believe one would manage very well in our 300-square-foot patio.

●

Several households and business establishments have pet Macaws. A popular one for years has been "Chico" atop his gnarly tree in the patio of El papagayo's Restaurant at Tillett Gardens. He says "hello" and whistles at the women, which seems standard practice for the island's pet macaws and parrots.

●

The Green Parrot Restaurant has a Green Parrot named Jerry. If he gets rambunctious and squawks too harshly when not getting enough attention, his owners put a cover over his cage. I think that would be a handy gadget for some people I know.

●

Recently, I was taken aback by this announcement:

"SHOOTING MEET: St. Thomas Shooting Association will meet at 7:30 p.m. today at For The Birds Restaurant. All interested parties are welcome."

Do you think they have an ulterior motive "strictly for the birds"?

Editor's Note: St. Thomas is fortunate in the abundance of its bird life. On some of the poorer Leeward and Windward Islands birds are scarce. This is because people eat them. The young men are deadly with slingshots.

CHAPTER 7

ON THE AIR

In early December of 1966, I adjusted my headphones, tapped the mike, and looked up to see the light on my side of the control room turn red.

No one else but this chicken was in the studio, and I was "on the air."

I took a deep breath and plunged in.

Judi Witty told me afterwards, "You came on like gangbusters." It was not a compliment.

If anyone had told me then I would sit in for 15 years, I would have said, "You're out of your mind."

That first day, I momentarily wondered "How did I get myself into this?" Not easily.

Mary Brooks Jackson, who initiated the women's radio show called "Mary-Go-Round," on WBNB (now WVWI), was on vacation and I was sitting in for three weeks. It had not started out that way. Judi Witty, Esther Loud, and I had each agreed to sit in one week. When D Day came, Judi and Esther had more pressing things to do, and I was left alone in the hen house.

Judi had been chosen because she was "show biz." In "That's Entertainment," after Judy Garland sang "The Trolley Song" and left the set, Judi sat down in her place. When the movie played in St. Thomas, "our Judi" got more applause than the "other Judy."

Esther was chosen for her pleasant voice, and I, because I was writing a syndicated radio show for Beverly Stark, U.S. Electric Utilities spokeswoman.

Just because you are **writing** a radio show does not mean you know what to do behind a microphone. Though interviewed numerous times in mainland USA, I found being "behind the mike" and being "in front of it" the difference between being on stage or in the audience. A few people I interviewed froze before the mike. At least I did not do that.

I learned fast with the help of disk jockey John Knight and news commentators Rick Ricardo and Lee Carle. They all wisecracked me out of "foot in mouth" attacks, and made me aware of little tricks.

For example, when I mispronounced a word, I confessed to forgetting my "pronunciation pill" that morning—and went on. It worked. Listeners laughed.

Starting with a funny story or punchy one-liner made the program flow smoother. So I invented the "Morning Brightener."

Disk Jockeys

When Stan Soltowsky became the morning D.J., and I said, "Now, for my Morning Brightener," Stan took off like a pelican fish-diving. I gratefully called the M.B.s my "Stan Vanishing Act." He hated them, but they spared me the torture of his creative, deadly ribbing.

In the 60s, B.S. (Before Stan), WBNB offices and broadcasting studio were in the Virgin Isle Hilton Hotel. The studio where Mary-Go-Round was broadcast resembled a Grand Central Station cubbyhole.

We sat at a table beside the control room window, where we could see the D.J. and everything that went on around him. On the wall to the left of our mike table, and a full four feet away, was the door to the john, a table with coffee makings, and another door leading into the newsroom.

Every time someone opened the door, people talking and the clickety-clack of the news machines wafted in like noise from a schoolhouse playground. Since there was no place else to go, that "someone" passed through to the control room, the john, or made himself a cup of coffee. Whatever—it was unsettling, but I did not look up.

"The Guys" soon thought I had served my apprenticeship and began treating me like one of the gang. That means they tried to distract me as they passed through so I would laugh "on the air."

They did not succeed, but they came close. I concluded all male D.J.s and news commentators were crazy as coots and never changed my

Blackbeard's Castle Restaurant, tower, and pool

mind. Stan Soltowsky was undoubtedly the most outrageous of the dozen D.J.s I worked with during my 15-year period of sitting in. Stan left no quip unturned. His comments on the news items in "Today in History" did wonders in making history come alive. Not always in the way the script intended.

Still, the truth is, I have yet to meet a D.J. I do not like. If "laughter is the best medicine," D.J.s are loaded with restoratives. I wish I had scribbled down some of Stan's prize witticisms over the years, but since they poured out like Niagara Falls, writing them down was impossible.

Newscasters

A few attention-getting remarks, however, from Rick Ricardo and Lee Carle during the morning or evening News Hour come to mind. In speaking about a man on the island of Jamaica who just died, Rick said, "He left 48 children and died of cardiac arrest." Pausing, he added, "What else?"

Stan, at the control board, said, "I wonder if they buried him face up or face down."

After reporting on a burglar who had been shot in the buttocks, Rick commented, "The burglar is in the hospital, but he's not sitting up."

When Yugoslavia's Tito died, Lee Carle talked about the funeral and all the ostentation, ending with, "Tito liked pomp and ceremony, especially when he was on **dead** center." Whether the pun was intentional or not is still a mystery.

After Lee reported the island of St. John had purchased a new hearse, he mentioned the death of a Mr. Moorehead. "Mr. Moorehead was the first one to get to use the hearse," he said, making it sound like a stroke of luck.

Lee left WVWI, but while he was there, I was a devoted fan. He could dramatize a broken water main so it sounded like the Hoover Dam had sprung a geyser.

One of our bottled gas companies had a devastating explosion in 1971. Against a background of screaming sirens, Lee, mike in hand, ran down the street toward the havoc. His breathless blow-by-blow account of the mini-explosions—that sent pieces of hardware flying hither and yon like Fourth of July fireworks—was a reporting masterpiece. I felt I ran beside him. Miraculously, only one person died. The destruction indicated dozens.

Lee's heroic involvement sometimes got him into trouble.

When the *Angelina Laura* cruise ship caught fire and burned at our harbor's West Indian Company dock in 1979, Lee was johnny-on-the-spot. The police tried to control the curious. They also tried to move Lee from his vantage point. That was like telling General Patton, in combat, to go from the front to the rear lines.

Lee stood his ground. He shouted that bringing people "live" news events was a public service and police rules did not apply to him. To the police **that** was tantamount to sedition. From our gallery, we had a box seat for watching the fire's huge leaping flames and billowing smoke, but our group became more engrossed in the wrangle between the LAW and

Arches make Grand Hotel distinctive

Lee than in the burning ship. The Police Chief cited Lee, and the hearing went against Lee. Lee remained undeterred.

Some people found Lee's reporting too dramatic, but I admired him for always being in the thick of things: fires, floods, hurricanes, bad accidents. During such crises, Lee and Rick stayed up all night, even sometimes for a couple of days when power and telephone lines were down, broadcasting news and first aid information. Both have been honored for Community Service. I will take drama to ennui any day.

Lee only had problems when he described what women wore. His biggest faux pas occurred the day he talked about the sparkling "rhinestones" worn by Her Royal Majesty Queen Margethe II of Denmark on her visit to St. Thomas in 1978. He probably could not have told they were diamonds even with a jeweler's loupe.

For several years, Mary Brooks Jackson and Lee Carle broadcast the New Year's Eve celebration from the Virgin Isle Hilton Hotel. One New Year's Eve, Lee lost Mary. After a round of sprightly snippets describing women's attire and a few interviews, she disappeared.

Lee kept calling plaintively over the air, "Mary, Mary, where are you?" as if he had lost his little lamb. "Come in, please, Mary. I need you."

The boisterous festivity in the ballroom was impenetrable. No one heard him, but giggling and dying of curiosity, those of us listening at home did.

After an inordinately long time, we heard Mary say, "Here I am, Lee."

"Where have you been?" Lee demanded, annoyed.

"To the ladies room!" she snapped.

"It certainly couldn't have taken all **that** time!"

"Well, it did! You try going to the bathroom in a jumpsuit!"

We listeners guffawed. No one but "our Mary" would broadcast the problems of going to the Virgin Isle Hilton's ladies' room in a jumpsuit on New Year's Eve. Such funny, spontaneous happenings do not occur anymore. We are too "big-time" now.

All the D.J.s and news commentators who worked with me had dirigible-sized senses of humor and endlessly needled each other, both off and on the air.

•

Occasional bantering and funny goofs still take place, but not often. Not long ago, a commentator no longer with the station, said, "And now for the weather report. . . ."

After pausing, he said, "The weather today is a mystery. I don't **have** a weather report!"

When this happens, I love it. It makes me laugh and sets up **my** day. I did not love it when I was on the air. As a great Chinese philosopher must have once said, "It makes a difference where you sit."

•

The most distracting D.J. I worked with shall remain nameless. He fell in love with one of the office secretaries. During my hour behind the mike, she would sashay into the control room and contribute her part to a torrid wrestling match. Even though I had written the commercials, I had difficulty keeping my mind on them. The show in the control room, even surreptitiously observed out of the corner of my eye, was far more interesting.

No one ever walked in on the D.J. and the "movable" secretary. I pretended not to notice. I am sure they did not care one way or the other. Hots is hots!

•

In the beginning, the studio did not have a clock, so I carried one of mine. It was like taking your own fire hose to a fire, but a wristwatch is not adequate. Even when a LARGE studio clock stares you in the face, timing your commercials correctly and getting off the air promptly is similar to having a Nazi interrogator standing over you with a whip.

Being clockless is even worse than leaving your commercials at home. All the years I sat in, nightmares about forgetting my commercials and not remembering a single word plagued me.

•

The studio was not exactly soundproof, either. Since the Virgin Isle Hotel was near the airport, planes landing or taking off sounded as if their air space included the studio! The installation of a ceiling light while I was on the air, though, begot my most trying and noisy broadcast. We took more music breaks than usual.

•

That first Christmas, the radio show's preparation almost did me in. At the end of the three weeks, I was a large "market-basket" case. To prepare for the hour on the air, it was necessary to call on all 15 accounts each week, gather material for eight daily commercials and write them.

In addition, we found stimulating (we hoped) interviews, and if we did not have an interview, looked for reading material that would keep listeners from twirling the dial. I also clipped items for Morning Brighteners and Sign-off Chuckles, selected my own records for music breaks, and planned time so I did not run over or run short. Life resembled a six-day bicycle race. Every day!

"I'll REALLY be glad to see Mary tomorrow when she gets back to St. Thomas," I said to Al the night before she returned.

"What are you going to do if she doesn't come back?"

I did not hesitate. "Cut my throat!" I said, determined never to do the show again.

It did not work out that way. Time exorcised the drudgery. I decided part of it had been fun, and shortcuts would lighten the tedious work. So—several months later when Mary needed a vacation, I agreed to sit in.

•

After a couple more three-week stints, I concluded the third week must go. Two weeks were enough. By accident, I found Carol Griffin for Mary, and the three of us worked together like a well-oiled machine. If Mary wanted to be gone six weeks, I took the first two weeks, Carol the second two, then we each did a week. It worked for 10 years, until Mary retired to live in a 400-year-old house on the Spanish island of Majorca.

Louise Noble followed Mary as hostess. We kept somewhat the same routine for five more years before I retired. Louise left the island soon after, and a series of hostesses took over. No one lasted very long. Finally the show went off the air. Like many other things, a St. Thomas era ended.

Mary Brooks Jackson

Of all the hostesses who did the women's radio show for what eventually became radio station WVWI, Mary Brooks Jackson was the only one "just right." A dancer, she toured Europe with a popular U.S. chorus line before becoming part of one that high-stepped for the Nelson Eddy-Jeannette McDonald movie musicals, and she could relate many hilarious stories about the making of those movies.

A born trouper with a great sense of humor and the stamina and health of a thoroughbred mare, Mary easily took the radio show in stride. Except for vacations, she never missed a day for 10 years and was always on time. Mary had a devoted following. Everyone wanted to hear what she might say. Unlike me, Mary did not know any "radio no-nos" and was unpredictable. No one monitored her, and her comments were fresh and funny. Also she could ad lib her commercials and everything else. Certain of going blank right in the middle and forgetting everything, I was afraid to ad lib, so wrote them out. Carol was somewhere in the middle. She ad libbed some commercials and wrote others.

Everyone listened intently to Mary for fear of missing something humorous she might say—mostly not intentional. One day she interviewed a doctor about vasectomy operations. When he told her about the snipping part, Mary uttered an effective, "Ouch!" Every man must have flinched. Another time when doing a commercial about a new bra, she said, "It will either be the peak of chic, or a flat bust."

Interviews

Although I mostly enjoyed interviews, sometimes I interviewed myself. These were trying programs—for me and the listening audience. I would ask a question, hoping to bring forth an anecdote or lively description.

"What did you like about Bora Bora?"

A pause. "It was beautiful." Silence.

"The Pacific island is filled with lovely beaches and tropical vegetation, isn't it?"

Pause. "Yes." Silence.

After a half-hour of this word pulling, you feel as if you have just scaled Mount Everest and cannot move another step. With a buffoon's smile and a jolly "this has been most interesting," I have upon occasion simply terminated the interview with a music break. Reading an article from my emergency file to fill in time saved me from committing mayhem in the studio.

Among my most rewarding interviews were local "bahn heh" (born here) celebrities such as Enid M. Baa, after whom our Enid M. Baa Library was named. A scholar and historian with a sense of humor and ready wit, she was always a first-rate interview.

Admirer and acquaintance of Leopold Sédar Sénghor, once president of Senegal, Miss Baa often talked about the gifted poet, nominated in 1962 for the Nobel Prize for Literature. Her readings of his poetry were like listening to a softly moving brook.

Laura Moorehead, one of our famous St. Thomas cooks and owner of "Mampoo Kitchen," divulged West Indian cooking secrets and recipes, and told interesting island stories.

Leona Bryant, involved in tourism and now our worldwide-honored Tourism Director, had a bottomless stock of stories that pointed up special facets of Virgin Island life. A dyed-in-the-wool Virgin Islander, she became fierce as a tigress if someone attacked the islands unfairly. Interviewing Leona alway meant a sizable listening audience. When we walked down the street together after the program, everyone, including taxi drivers, would lean out car windows or stop her and say, "I heard you this morning on radio, Leona. Really enjoyed it." I kept telling her she should run for office.

Noble Samuel, once a St. John senator, has had a long career with the National Park Service. He loves these islands as much as any local person I ever interviewed. He also has done as much as anyone to preserve the Arcadian quality of St. John.

When Ladybird Johnson came to St. John in the early 60s, Noble Samuel was asked to show her how to snorkle. Because of her curiosity about fish, she drew outlines of various ones on a sandy beach. If not right, Samuel rubbed out any inaccuracy and corrected it.

Samuel spent five days with Mrs. Johnson. They even hiked to Reed Bay. When she learned her guide had never been to mainland USA for

National Park training, she arranged for him to attend the Harper's Ferry Training Center. After training at the Center, he began to preach conservation.

In a delightful history of St. John, Called "St. John Backtime," compiled by Ruth Hull Low and Rafael Valls, Senator Samuel is quoted as saying, "The simpler we keep St. John, the better it will be."

We need more Virgin Islanders like Noble Samuel. I wish St. Thomas were simpler and had a National Park to preserve green space.

Old-timer Continentals were excellent interviews, too, because they had been here during the donkey-and-dirt-road days.

The late Erva Boulon and her husband Paul came in 1928 and, for a number of years, lived on St. John without electricity, telephone, and plumbing. Her experiences and island recipes never failed to make a hit with listeners.

Fred Dixon came in the 30s to help set up the St. Thomas school system. A born storyteller, he related wonderful tales about those days.

Continentals who came in the 50s included Maxine Carter, who danced with Don Loper under her maiden name, Maxine Barrett. They appeared in MGM movies and toured Europe and South America, where they danced in fashionable night clubs and hotels.

Maxine's Hollywood buddies, the same as those of Judi Witty included the likes of Carole Lombard, Clark Gable, Ginger Rogers, Gene Kelley. Her stories about such people poured out like good wine and transported us listeners back to less complicated, glamorous days.

For our first "Doggie Ball" held at the Mountaintop Hotel in 1968 for the Humane Society, Maxine, Judi Witty, and other local theatrical people were the smash-hit entertainment.

Actress Leslie Caron—whose father was French consul for the U.S. Virgin Islands and also owned C&M Caron, a Charlotte Amalie store with exquisite French imports—was a special delight. Like Maxine and Judi, she brought with her the charm and poise of top-notch show people.

Leslie's brother, Aimery Caron, an authority on atoms, teaches at the University of the Virgin Islands. When I interviewed him after he spent a year in France doing esoteric research on atoms, I suggested he supply me with the questions to ask. I did not want to sound as dumb as I am on that subject. For me, atom research ranks somewhere above Einstein's Theory of Relativity.

Karl Gullers, photograper by appointment to the King of Sweden and around-the-world tripper, was an easy interview. He has snapped thousands of photographs for his 50 published books. His one-man photographic shows have been hits in Rome, London, New York, and San Francisco as well as Buenos Aires and Mexico City. He had a lot to talk about—and did.

Karl's wife wrote a book, "The Crewel Needlepoint World" under her maiden name, Barbara H. Connelly. Karl's original photographs accompanied the text. Barbara, one of America's foremost experts in needlepoint and crewelwork, has a background in set designing and interior decoration. Her enthusiastic interview beguiled me into attempting needlepoint.

The chapter "Simple as Painting By Number" hooked me. I needle-pointed an eyeglass case, a few pillows, then designed and finished a small rug. After that I had nothing to do.

Regarding Al, I said, "I don't know what to needlepoint next."

"Well, don't look at me, " he said.

My rising arrow of creativity fell to the ground, ending my budding career in needlepointing.

●

Being "on the air" gave me an opportunity to be part of the community in a way I could otherwise never have been. People still recognize my voice and stop to say they miss me. It makes my day extra sunny. In retrospect, I treasure those 15 years as good ones in Paradise.

Now it is time for my chapter Sign-off Chuckle: "Good listeners are not only popular everywhere, but after a while they know something."

Charlotte Amalie High School. Note students in uniform

PART TWO: INSIDE HIGHLIGHTS

CHAPTER 8

SANTA UNDER A PALM TREE

On our first Christmas in St. Thomas, a huge evergreen Christmas wreath from Wisconsin decorated our gallery railing. With the purposeful dedication of the Three Wise Men, our friend Dr. Richard Anderson carried it and Wisconsin cheese in his lap all they way from Madison.

Dick knows I am allergic to cheese, but that did not lessen the gift's value. Anyone bearing gifts from Wisconsin includes cheese. It keeps their cows in business. For Al, the cheese bonanza was like winning a Fort Knox gold bar. He is a cheeseoholic and not allergic to anything.

I loved the wreath. Fresh and beautiful for weeks, it eased our transitional Christmas away from longtime friends.

Just because Santa has practically no chimneys to slide down in the islands is no reason to underestimate the importance of Christmas in St. Thomas. It is celebrated as enthusiastically here as in the States. Where else would you find a policeman directing traffic as he played "Jingle Bells" on his whistle?

•

Another just-before-Christmas vignette I will never forget was the truck driver stopped at a traffic light, eating an ice cream cone. A small boy looked up at him longingly. Suddenly the driver leaned down and gave him a couple of licks before the light changed and the truck moved on. That little boy's face lighted up as if he had just had a close encounter with Santa.

•

Of course, there is the commercial side. Stores bulge like a fat Santa's tummy with Christmas decorations, gifts, and toys. Christmas music rings out from open doorways of air-conditioned shops into the narrow canyon that is Main Street. Our Danish forefathers scorned wide streets.

•

In the countryside, elaborate creches and Santas with sleighs and reindeer decorate private yards, Stars of David top roofs, and colored lights bedeck house eaves. Lights flashing all night symbolize Christ as "The Light of the World."

A strong feeling of old-fashioned Yuletide spirit permeates the air as Christmas approaches. Puerto Rican, Danish, French, African, West Indian, and mainland USA residents cling to many of their Christmas customs.

Three King's Day

Instead of Santa Claus, "Father Christmas" gives West Indian children presents. On January 6th, the "Three Kings" bring gifts to Virgin Islanders of Puerto Rican descent.

Because our sister island, St. Croix, has a large Puerto Rican population, Three Kings' Day there is an important occasion for celebration. Even though of Spanish origin, the day has become an integral part of each Virgin Island and is a legal holiday. Remember our ten extra holidays? This is one.

Three King's Day also climaxes St. Croix's Christmas Festival. Before the Festival, masqueraders disguised as Zulus, Indians, cowboys, and troupes depicting exotic nations such as Japan and China, filled the streets and danced to scratch band music. They join the official Three King's Day parade—much like our St. Thomas Carnival parade—with steel bands, floats, troupes, floupes (a combination of floats and troupes), and Mocko Jumbis in brightly colored costumes cavorting on stilts.

Much going back and forth by seaplane links the islands for the Christmas Festival, our St. Thomas Carnival, and little St. John's Carnival in July.

Christmas Trees

For the most part, artificial trees and live evergreen ones from the States, bring cheer to homes inside and out. A long time ago, when cargo ships were not as dependable as today, the Christmas trees went to another island by mistake and did not arrive until after Christmas. Can you imagine a less saleable item? Like having the bride's dress arrive after the wedding!

Our first few Christmases, when the number of VW "Bugs" on St. Thomas seemed to indicate this was their breeding place, I got a tremendous kick out of the "little beetles" skittering up and down the mountains and through narrow downtown streets topped with huge Christmas trees. They looked like baby porcupines with their quills painted green!

Not many years after our arrival, the islanders' traditional Christmas tree, the native Inkberry, a green shrub with sharp thorns, began to be replaced with Stateside evergreens. Our population explosion depleted the large areas of virgin vegetation where they grew.

At one time groups of schoolboys foraged in the hills to find these trees for their school programs. After the boys decorated the branches with garlands and ornaments, they stuck wax candles on the tree's thorns and lighted the candles only briefly to herald Christmas. A bucket of water always stood nearby in case of fire. Unfortunately, this charming custom has vanished.

A few islanders now replace the Inkberry with the Century Plant, used also by Continentals. Native to Middle East dry areas like Israel as well as St. Thomas, the plant blooms after about sixty years. The stalk rises from the plant at this time, reaching a height of fifteen to twenty-five feet.

If the living stalk is cut, it is said that the plant will not die as it otherwise would. A member of the Agave (from the Greek word *agavos* meaning "admirable") family, this stately ornamental succulent's uncluttered symmetry lends itself "admirably" to decoration with bright bau-

People gathering in Emancipation Park for a program to celebrate Martin Luther King, Jr. Day. Statue is King Christian IX of Denmark who was King when St. Thomas' slaves were emancipated in 1848. Grand Hotel in background

bles, tinsel, and candy canes. The dried stalk is especially handsome when sprayed gold, silver, or white, but I also like its grayish natural color.

Many owners keep their Century Plant long after Christmas (no pine needles, no mess) and redecorate it for Easter, birthday parties, bridal and baby showers, the Fourth of July, Thanksgiving Day, and not infrequently the next Christmas. The Century Plant is often kept for years as a house decoration. Alive or dead, the plant's mileage can be matched only by the old Model T Ford. On top of that it is free.

Carolers

Church choirs start long before Christmas to practice their carols for midnight services on Christmas Eve and Old Year's Night. On both occasions many years ago, singing groups serenaded townspeople with carols from midnight until dawn. Then for several years, because of the growing population, the trend was away from homes and to public squares and hotels.

In 1977, however, a group of young islanders, lamenting the decline of the true and traditional meaning of our local Christmas, decided to keep the caroling tradition alive. Leaders Calypsonian Glenn "Kwabena" Davis and Vernon Finch mustered their forces and the first Christmas Challenge of Carols took place in 1977. Finch, leader of the Party Hardy

Carolers, proudly boasts that once revived, the singers have never missed the Christmas Challenge of Carols.

The "Guardian Angels" choir is made up of school crossing guards and Traffic Bureau personnel. Eleven members are female. Other participating groups include the Voices of Love, the Bethel Baptist Choir, Dorothy Elskoe's Merry Carolers, and the Bovoni Village Choir.

The Christmas Challenge choirs begin spreading their Christmas cheer at eleven p.m. Christmas Eve and visit different island neighborhoods, starting with Estate Tutu. The repertoire includes everything from "Silent Night" and "The Battle Hymn of the Republic" to "The Guavaberry Song" and choir-composed songs, such as Voices of Love's "Are We Welcome?"

In the beginning, the choirs, still strumming guitars and singing, reached Emancipation Park around daybreak, where the Challenge of Carols began. Each group performed several songs on the Emancipation Park bandstand. After individual group presentations, the six choirs assembled in the nearby parking lot and each one selected its favorite carol. Everyone sang at the same time and tried to sing louder than the others. In this Challenge, everyone was a winner, but the listening audience felt themselves the real winners as they enjoyed the Christmas songfest of these dedicated young Virgin Islanders.

Vernon Finch says the Carolers want to emphasize to friends and community the meaning of giving and sharing at Christmas instead of its commercial side. The Challenge of Carols has also been held in Lionel Roberts Stadium, but returned to Emancipation Park where trees and plants create a more Christmas-like atmosphere. Hats off to these young people! They are making our island a better place for all of us.

Bands

Scratch bands, made up of scored gourds for scratching, homemade whistles, and tin can drums, have their heyday at Christmas time. Volume overcomes technique as band members play everything—back-ups, marches, calypso, and holiday music—in the streets, in public parks, and for private and community affairs.

Near Christmas one year, I had a sandal fitting at Zora's sandal shop when a scratch band noisily passed by in the street. Suddenly a pained expression twisted her face.

"What's wrong, Zora?" I asked anxiously.

"It's that scratch band. It's so out of tune!"

"They're great!" I said, leaning out the window and tapping my foot. The cacophony and jaunty appearance of the slightly shabby men's group shuffle-dancing down the street as they played their primitive instruments, fascinated me. Momentarily, I forgot Zora's musical talents and finely tuned ear. Unlike Zora, I had not played the French Horn with the Hawaiian Symphony Orchestra and Canada's Montreal Women's

Zora fitting shoes on tourists. Zora's store also sells popular handmade canvas bags shaped like fish, and has an art gallery and Oriental rug room on her premises

Symphony. Always involved in chamber groups, Zora also spent six years as a member of the St. Thomas Community Band and was Bandmaster for five. It's incongruous, yes, but why shouldn't a sandalmaker play the French horn?

Among the Community Band's biggest events of the year is Carnival, when the group leads the parade. Zora is short, and in order for all Band members to see her directing, she held up a long, sturdy branch of bougainvillea, denuded except for the mass of red blossoms that crowned its top.

Umpah—umpah—it was quite a sight to see her as she marched along, wearing a carnival straw hat and conducting the Band in expert Drum Major style with a bougainvillea baton. She claimed scrambling around the bushes searching for the right bougainvillea branch was not one of her finer musical moments.

Zora also led the Band through many rousing Christmas performances, from those in the Queen Louise Home for the Aged to the ones in the Knud-Hansen Hospital's parking lot next to the emergency room. I wonder about that juxtaposition.

Other outstanding Christmas concerts are given by the Caribbean Chorale with around 100 voices. Performances now take place at the Reichhold Center, but in the old days it was the Charlotte Amalie High School. Chorale singers come from all walks of life and embrace all ages. Their Christmas concert, televised on our PBS station, is a highlight.

Severina Williams, at the Queen Louise Home, sang the same love letter to the world for over fifty Christmases:

Thank you God for the world so sweet
Thank you for the food we eat
Thank you for the birds that sing,
Thank you God for everything.

Recently added to our Christmas festivities is the appearance of our Virgin Islands Folkloric Company at Reichhold Center. Company Director, Arona Petersen, commented on their 1986 "Christmas of Yesteryear" performance of folk dancers and singers.

"It's going to be an evening of nostalgia and enjoyment to get everyone in the old-time Christmas spirit," she said.

Eat, Drink, and Be Merry!

Traditional island Christmas foods include Johnny Cakes, ham, sweet bread (also called Christmas Cake), sweet potatoes, tarts, and old-time sweets.

The most favored Virgin Island Christmas drink is guavaberry, a traditional fruit and rum-based liqueur. Recipes vary with the maker, and the drink is usually made in the fall when the guavaberries are ripe. Prunes, raisins, brown sugar, cinnamon, mace, cloves, nutmeg, and vanilla, in varying quantities, are brewed together with the guavaberries to make the rum base.

A customary Christmas greeting—in calypso—for well-wishers entering a home is:

Good morning, good morning,
And Ah wish you a Merry Christmas
Good morning, good morning
Ah come for meh guavaberry

When Christmas day is finished, so is the guavaberry—and many of its imbibers. One elderly lady once said, "Too much guavaberry will tip you down!"

The Governor officially opens the Christmas season by lighting the community tree in Market Square. Thereafter, the festivities—religious, community, and social—are underway.

On Christmas Day, West Indians open their homes to friends, family, and acquaintances. Even enemies are welcome, and all are treated to the best the family can afford.

The Virgin Islands spirit of goodwill and generosity also manifests itself with gifts and cards. Many cards show Santa Claus in his sleigh loaded with gifts. Others show snow scenes of cottages, small churches, and horse-drawn coaches. I prefer the locally created cards with Santa lolling under a palm tree, or of reindeer swimming joyfully from a palm-shaded beach and giving Santa a hard time about returning to the North Pole. For such a little island, there is an overwhelming abundance of Christmas cheer.

Now to the "be merry" part. During the holiday season, there is often dancing to regular bands, or steel bands, that lasts through the night. Since we moved from Hidden Hill in 1974 to one of six townhouse condominiums atop a mountain above Charlotte Amalie, we can attest to this.

The sound of the music rolls up on the wind currents, pounding, pounding, ebbing, and flowing, until it seems inside the room and you. Finally you fall asleep, exhausted. Music is an integral part of Christmas, and the revelers are undoubtedly dancing the Bamboula, one of the oldest island dances with origins in Africa. So who is going to complain? If I were younger, I would be there with them.

The year's holiday season ends with Old Year's Night welcoming in the New Year with a big pot of Kallaloo, made with a hambone left from Christmas and simmered with okra, hot pepper, onions, herbs, spices and a bale of fresh spinach. There are parties galore.

Our second New Year's, we were fortunate to be invited to the home of Virgin Islanders Dante and Limpie DeCastro for a traditional Old Year's Night. Told to come around midnight, we did. (For many previous New Year's Eves we were in bed shortly after that.) A steel band arrived soon, and not long after, enough food to feed a Russian regiment appeared: Kallaloo, fungi made with cornmeal, and a marvelous sweet potato dish were only a part of the many delectables. Some I could not identify.

Guests came and danced and drank and ate and had a high old time, including ourselves. We began to fade around two-thirty. We thought the party would break up soon, but more people kept coming. Finally at three-thirty, dead on our feet, we sneaked out quietly.

The day after New Year's when I called to explain and thank the DeCastros for including us, I asked how long the party had lasted. Limpie laughed. "Until five-thirty New Year's afternoon," and giggling, added, "You should have come back after you had a good sleep!"

We were invited to the DeCastro party every year for a long time and always put in an appearance. They lived near Hidden Hill, and it was too

View from Sapphire Beach Resort

good a party to miss. We would go to bed after dinner, get up around eleven, and take off. Still, our endurance never went beyond three o'clock.

We know now that this is the kind of party given by old Virgin Island families on Old Year's Night to welcome in the New Year. It must be a lifetime of good, fresh air that gives them so much energy. We arrived here too late.

•

In Arona Petersen's newspaper column just before New Year's one year, she had "lil hints to help you mek a lucky New Year in case you had bad luck last year."

This was my favorite: "Sweep out all ole year dirt befo New Year come in so it cud find a clean house."

Before Christmas in 1987, a heavy black-bordered box like a funeral announcement, ran in The Daily News "Lost and Found" ads for several days.

Topped with "Notice!" in angry black letters the ad read:

"To the person that 'took' Mainland Appliance cat's Christmas collar— May you find kitty litter in your stocking!"

As I have said before, Paradise has its asps. The Mainland Appliance cat, well-known and friendly, spent most of its time wrapped around the cash register. It would not have raised a paw to scratch a "tief." Unfortunately.

•

One holiday season this ad appeared in The Daily News:
Merry Christmas and Happy New Year
to
All the people of the Virgin Islands
from
The Thirteenth Legislature of the
Virgin Islands
1979
It could only happen in the Virgin Islands.

•

Never sell the Virgin Island-style Yuletide season short. "Deck The Halls With Boughs of Holly", coming from a steel band playing on a palm-fringed beach, makes for a many-splendored Christmas.

CHAPTER 9

CARNIVAL CAPERS

If it is April, it is Carnival. An island madness sets in, terminating in revelry that would do justice to a Roman festival.

Benjamin Disraeli once said: "I have a great confidence in the revelations which holidays bring forth." Well, I would be interested in Mr. Disraeli's palm reading of our St. Thomas Carnival.

The first ripples of its approach start when meeting notices of The Raunchy Bunch, a Carnival troupe, appear in The Daily News' "Calendar of Events." This is the harbinger of St. Thomas emerging from its cocoon to become a glamorous, iridescent butterfly for a fortnight.

With the vigor of a jolly giant, Carnival magically sweeps the daily grind under the seaweeds and transforms the island into a frolicking, make-believe world of steel bands, feasting, drinking, dancing, singing, contests, and parades—unrestrained West Indian pleasure. Every businessman knows he cannot expect work from employees during Carnival. Islanders say, "It's traditional."

Do not knock it. Carnival is the safety valve that keeps the island sane—sort of—the rest of the time. Regardless of any terrible things that happen during the year, everyone forgets them when it is time to "bambooshay."

Bambooshay, from the French bambocher meaning "to live it up," expresses the same desire as "kill t'ing pappy" and "roas-a-time." The latter was coined by Virgin Island Delegate to Congress, Ron De Lugo, founder of St. Thomas' modern carnival in 1952. All are island patois for "enjoy yourself."

Preliminary Events

The "windup," as used in baseball, starts the week before official Carnival Week. The Carnival Queen, as well as the Prince and Princess for the Childrens' Parade, are chosen—and the competitions have the fierce intensity of a Miss America Contest. Calypso singers from the entire Caribbean also compete for Carnival "Calypso King" in the Calypso Tent. Not held in a tent, as in "tent," I hasten to add, but in a ball park or hotel.

Hundreds of people come to hear the singers. Calypso, with its addictive rhythm, goes back hundreds of years. Its inspiration came from many nationalities, and the lyrics may be chants, doggerel, or limericks.

The audience boos those who do not measure up, and cheers their favorites with names such as Mighty Sparrow, Lord Chalkdust, Lord Kitchner, and Lord Blakie. Women also compete. Calypso Rose, Marjorie V, and Lady Tashika are prize winners; so is Mighty Whitey, one of few white contenders.

If you were not born in the West Indies, chances are you will not understand the subtle meanings of the witty calypso lyrics that comment on politics, social matters, love and life. Occasionally obscene songs are banned, but most are hilariously critical of politicians, other public figures, and unusual events.

•

Carnival Week activity centers around Children's Village, with its amusement park rides, and the Adult Village, with its colorful, cartoon-decorated booths. Erected especially for this spectacle of music and fantasy, the Adult Village forms a huge square in our largest downtown parking lot. This snarls traffic into a riled hornet's nest for a couple of weeks, but nobody in his right mind bucks Carnival.

In the middle of the Village is a sturdy bandstand, festooned with brightly-colored maypole streamers and an aurora borealis of hundreds of lights. Nightly it supports ear-splitting orchestras and steeldrum bands. Their throbbing rhythms sweep up the mountains behind Charlotte Amalie and across the bay to the harbor islands.

Mostly, onlookers listen. Some dance or "jump up" (a street dance, tramp, or other disorganized dancing. "Jamback" and "trash back" are also dances). Others mill back and forth between the bandstand and booths, munching fried chicken legs and sipping Maubie. Made from Maubie Tree bark, spices, orange peel and sugar, this popular local drink tastes like root beer.

More potent drinks are also served. "Fire one" in Carnival parlance means to have a straight alcoholic drink.

Market Fair

Carnival Week brings other diversions such as horse races, boat races, Carnival hat contests, and toddlers' races. The most popular event, except for the parades and J'ouvert, is Market Square Food Fair on Tuesday.

Held in Rothchild Francis Square, once used for slave auctions, the Fair began in 1953 under the auspices of Mrs. Mildred Anduze and Mrs. Maude Proudfoot (who always wears a hibiscus in her hair, whether it is Carnival or not).

The Market Fair started out small. Even when we first came to St. Thomas in 1965, it was possible to walk around leisurely and make studied selections from the tempting displays of food, drink, plants, handmade straw hats, and brooms made out of palm fronds. The brooms make a "clean sweep" of everything, and we keep a beribboned one in a corner of our gallery as a conversation piece and to add local color.

Today, the square's streets are packed curb to curb and from a balcony above look like a brightly colored mass of fractured cloisonné. It is all you can do to squeeze through.

Steel bands pound out foot-shuffling, body-swaying Caribbean music, and rapacious as hungry Frigate birds, the crowd pushes toward the native delicacies, many offered only at this Fair.

Women vendors wear Market Women costumes of the past: kerchiefs around heads, white peasant blouses, multicolored full skirts.

A mind-boggling array of baked and cooked West Indian specialties make display tables groan. There are stewed fruits: mangoes and tamarinds, plus gooseberry preserves; lobster, crabmeat, and meat pies; banana fritters; coconut bread, carrot cake, and jawbones, a hard peppermint candy.

One woman standing before an unbelievable quantity of enticing, fragrant dishes was asked how she got them all to the Fair.

"Dahlin', you know how: Strugglin' and bufflin' (hurried confusion)."

It is hot and noisy as you press through the chattering crowd. You are enticed by the redolence of fried fish, stewed whelks with peas and rice, roast pork with sweet potato stuffing, and goat stew. No one can resist the tempting aromas of pies, cakes, puddings, and candies that lure you like sweet magnets. It takes Arona Petersen to tell it as it is. Her description of Food Fair: "the usual confusin, monkey tricks and pascalam (full of fun)."

•

Kay Bailey, a long-time island resident, is famous for her unusual Carnival hats. They average two feet high and three feet wide, and feature three-dimensional Carnival-inspired scenes. Instead of having her Carnival float on wheels, Kay wears it on her head. In 1986 she received special recognition for her 25 years of prize-winning Carnival hats.

At one time, Kay had a popular radio show on WSTA and interviewed me once about a Music Association Concert. I never recovered from Kay knitting during the entire show. Her commercials came out smooth as

Street produce vendors outside the roofed market. The market's business is going downhill from competition on the waterfront, alongside Lionel Roberts Stadium, and from supermarkets like Pueblo and Grand Union

aged wine, and she never missed a cue—or stitch. Would that I had her knack for the ad lib when I was hostessing WVWI's radio show.

J'ouvert

J'ouvert ("daybreak dancing" and pronounced joo-vay) starts at 4 a.m. on Friday morning of Carnival Week and heralds the beginning of the parades. Thousands of revelers tramp from Carnival Village through the streets and join others along the waterfront drive, dancing, gyrating, singing, as they follow the bands. Only rarely are there "incidents."

Most participants have been up all night, but this uninhibited salute to the last two days of Carnival is good-natured and spirited even though it occasionally waxes a bit bawdy. Men sometimes wear outlandish costumes, from women's dresses and nightgowns to gorilla outfits. The thickly packed throngs have been known to force buses, cars, and even garbage trucks to be abandoned on the street. J'ouvert peters out around 7:30 a.m.

The Parades

The Children's Parade begins assembling an hour or so later at Western Cemetery. Both parades start at the cemetery, and some adult participants are ready to take up residence there when Carnival ends.

Angels, spangled insects with airy wings, papier-mâché animals with movable parts, smoke-belching monsters, lavishly dressed dolls, dream world creatures: all interpret the Carnival theme and originate from the children's lively imaginations. Their parade is a children's Alice in Wonderland "happening" accompanied by musical groups and steel bands.

Although scheduled to start at 10 a.m. on Saturday, the Adult Parade almost never does. Headed by the Carnival Queen, the parade, depicting a popular or historical theme, is made up of floats carrying everything from old-fashioned, side-wheel river boats to elaborate replicas of our old fort; of troupes in glamorous costumes of satin, sequins, ruffles, and plumed headpieces, representing subjects from Arabian Nights and Magic Birds of Fire to Greek warriors and royalty.

Interspersed are a wide range of bands: marching; on trucks; on flatbeds pushed and pulled by dozens of happy-go-lucky, sweaty, brawny men. Steel bands predominate, and their irresistible beat has long been the soul of Carnival.

Gertrude Melchior, a yearly regular and honored for her faithful support in 1989, has basked in glory on some of the most elaborate floats imaginable. Dorothy Elskoe, a mainstay from the first carnival, was honored in 1986 for her many years of hard work and solid backing.

Over the years, the Elskoe-Roebuck group has presented many spectacular, prize-winning entries. A favorite was "Julius Caesar," which portrayed a full assembly of Roman soldiers and maidens swaying to the beat of West Indian music. Their additional winning entries included

Helen of Troy, Joan of Arc, and Samson and Delilah. There are too many other headliners to mention. Come to Carnival and see for yourself!

The first time Al and I ever heard a steel band was in Old San Juan, Puerto Rico. I had never experienced anything so compelling as we joined the crowd trailing after them. For a while I thought I was not going to get Al back to the hotel. Steel bands have an overpowering toe-tapping appeal.

Speaking of bands: One year a U.S. Army Band played for Carnival. During their first appearance they performed with the solemn dignity of Military School cadets on inspection day. By the Adult Parade, however, they sported carnival hats and open-necked khaki shirts. Jammin' and jivin' along with our island bands, they grinned and waved like jackpot-winners to the rousing cheers of applauding spectators. It warmed your heart to see an Army band having such a once-in-a-lifetime spree.

Many prominent local people: bankers, lawyers, senators, and other VIP's, male and female, prance along the parade route in fancy costumes, ranging from Egyptian lancers and belly dancers to spanish Dons and Louis XIV courtesans.

Bands blare out the catchy tune they hope will win the Road March; drum majorettes step high and twirl batons; agile acrobats do handsprings; dancers execute intricate routines.

Over 70 parade entries, serious and comical, pause at Post Office Square before a temporary viewing stand, filled with government and Carnival officials, to perform clever skits or well-choreographed dances. These are repeated and judged at Lionel Roberts Stadium after the parade.   The Road March, a term originating in Trinidad, is the musical selection played most often at carnival parades by steel bands and other

Produce market outside Lionel Roberts Stadium

musical groups. Each Road March enjoys popularity until another one wins the title the next year. For your Carnival Glossary, remember a "steel pan" is a steel band's basic instrument, and to "beat pan" means to play in a steel band.

Always popular participants are Alli Paul's and Hugo Moolenaar's Mocko Jumbies on 12-foot stilts. In voluminous, vividly colored skirts or pants and ruffled shirts, they defy gravity as they frolic along the parade route. Loud cheers and clapping follow their progress as it does when they perform at the Super Bowl Parade, other spectacular nationwide events, and in Africa, Europe, and South America.

•

One morning long ago, before an Adult Parade, a nearby noisy clamor sounded to Harrison Murphy like a truckload of tin cans out of control, turning over and over—bump, bump, BUMP! Silence. Murph ran out of his house on Skyline Drive, now Valdemar A. Hill, Sr. Drive, and saw a badly battered VW at the roadside. A bumper dangled from a tree branch and VW parts lay strewn like pieces of a dismembered Tin Man as far as the next curve.

Anyone in the car would be badly injured, maybe dead. He raced back in the house, telephoned the hospital to send an ambulance, and hurriedly returned to the VW, just in time to see a man slowly extricate himself from the wreckage. Dazed, unsteady, but seemingly unscathed, the man stood up, shook his head, and looked around.

A moment later another man crawled out of what was left of the VW and staggered around getting his balance. Not a scratch marred the smooth dark skin of either one. Neither spoke. The first death defier reached into the car, pulled out a Carnival hat, and put it on. The other man leaned in, yanked out a similar one, coaxed it back into shape, and plopped it atop his head. Then, arm in arm, they started to weave their merry way toward town, headed for the Carnival parade.

Murph ran back to the house and telephoned the hospital.

"Is the ambulance on its way?"

"Not yet."

"Forget it!"

The VW carcass and car pieces, looking like a stripteaser's discards, stayed along the roadside until Carnival was over. Then the pieces and the VW hulk were gradually consumed by automobile vultures.

•

During Carnival our police give out daily warnings on their morning radio Traffic Report. "Go slow on the bottle, enjoy the road. Don't drink rum," and "Stay sober on the road. Don't make any skylarking! Traffic cops are getting rough." Of course everyone strictly obeys!

•

One year, a group of mischievous brawny athletes who worked out weight lifting chose to be a ballerina troupe. All big men, over six feet, they had shoulders like Hercules. Just seeing them, in their pale blue tutus and size 12 matching satin ballerina slippers, set off howls of laughter.

Someone, probably Kay Atcheson, founder of the St. Thomas School of Dance in 1965, and of the Ballet Theatre of the Virgin islands in 1967, had taught them the basic ballerina steps they performed along the parade route. Whistles, shouts, and guffaws followed them the entire way.

They were the hit of the parade, but the best was yet to come. Several of the men were volunteer firemen. When a fire alarm sounded before the end of the parade, the men raced to their cars and charged off in their tutus to fight the fire. I deeply regret I did not see that show.

•

During the parades, sidewalks, second floor windows, tops of walls and roofs, and balconies are lined with merrymakers dressed in crazy Carnival hats, wild shirts, and gaudy dresses. Youthful spectators even perch in trees. Backed by the colorful banners and streamers that decorate buildings, telephone poles, and streets, the observers' flashy attire often vies for attention with the flamboyant costumes of the paraders.

•

During the confusion of Carnival festivities one year, a St. Thomas prison inmate escaped from Fort Christian, slipping past prison guards an hour after being jailed. He chose to exit over a fort street-side wall and climb down through the thick cover of tree branches there. No way was he going to miss Carnival!

•

The Adult Parade always ends with troupes of clowns, American Indians, and African Zulus—600 to 800 strong. Shouting, laughing, jump-

School children marching down Main street en route to Martin Luther King Day celebration at Emancipation Park

93

ing up, singing, they surge down narrow, crowded Main Street to disgorge at Post Office Square. There they spread out to perform their lively antics, looking like a throng of brightly costumed circus fleas.

It gives our energetic young people a chance to be part of the Adult Parade, and there would not be as much good-natured boisterousness without them. Others must enjoy them as I do, because they always receive a big hand.

•

Months of planning and meticulous work go into the fabulous floats, clever skits, intricate dances, and elaborate costumes. It never ceases to amaze viewers how the many beautiful and original floats can be hidden until parade day, when they seem to materialize from a genie's lamp. It is the secretiveness and originality combined with the tinseled and sequined appeal of a fantasy world that keeps Carnival alive and well from one year to the next. No two are ever alike and never should be.

After the Adult Parade, a spectacular display of fireworks at 8 p.m. marks the end of Carnival. The gaiety continues until all hours of Sunday morning, ending only when the last weary parade marchers and spectators are completely exhausted. St. Thomas has survived another Carnival. Hardly anyone will work on Monday. It is traditional.

Still I am with Harry Belafonte when he sings, "PLEASE don't stop de Carnival!" John Thompson in his Daily News article, April 28, 1970, "Carnival First Impressions," agreed also. "Please don't stop the carnival," he wrote. "Just let it get started on time."

Wishful thinking. Since we have been here, Carnival has only started on time once, in 1988. Will the tradition be broken? I do not believe so. We would have nothing to complain about.

Editor's Note: St. Thomas' Carnival compares favorably with those of other Caribbean Islands that are more heavily promoted. Many groups practice the year round. The Calypso competition attracts the Caribbean's best. St. Thomas Mocko Jumbies are unique. Try to time your visit for Carnival time.

CHAPTER 10

ISLAND HAUNTS AND HISTORY

GHOST STORIES

All West Indian islands have their ghosts.

St. Thomas is no exception. Whereas most people would not opt for one ghost, Marti and Tony Giovan opted for two. Some people cannot get enough of a bad thing.

The Giovans inherited their first ghost in 1964 when they moved into a house within a dagger's throw of Blackbeard's Tower—the nefarious old pirate's stamping grounds.

Blackbeard's Castle

Blackbeard's Saracen-style tower looks like a sugar mill, but stories about its one-time owner have nothing to do with anything sweet. Supposedly he imprisoned his women in the tower and carried on wicked activities too terrible to mention.

The tower did not start out evil. After the colonial Danes began building Fort Christian on the waterfront, mosquitos forced them to higher ground to avoid the yellow fever plagues that killed many settlers. They chose the hill above Charlotte Amalie.

At first the Danes clustered in houses around the tower. Then the English made a deal with pirate looters throughout the Caribbean and pardoned those who agreed to stop plundering. This seems to me like bargaining with a mad dog to go lie down. Afterward, several ex-pirates, including Blackbeard, headed for Charlotte Amalie.

Blackbeard arrived first, kicked out the Danes, claimed the tower for his own, and ruled the island by terrorism. Six feet six inches tall with a long, bushy black beard, he sported dramatic wide-brimmed hats and flowing black capes, earning him the nickname "the black devil."

Legend has it that Blackbeard, when a practicing pirate, stuck sulphuric matches in his beard a moment before he went over a ship's side to plunder it. The sight of this huge, fierce-looking man with his beard seemingly ablaze so demoralized the men that they became easy victims.

Some people believe ghosts are disturbed spirits with unfinished business, or spirits of the mentally ill. Either theory could apply to Blackbeard.

The pirate's legacy of violence plagued the tower and its environs for years. A Victorian mansion erected at the tower's base burned to the ground in the mid-fifties, but the fire only scorched the tower. Afterward, a psychiatrist built a house, later occupied by four successive owners, all mercilessly badgered with problems. None stayed longer than two years.

Blackbeard's Castle and pool. See also photo page 71

Undaunted by ghost gossipers, the Giovans and their five sprightly off-spring moved in and loved the tower.

"Fie, on Blackbeard's curse!" they said.

The children, their mystery-loving little friends, and an array of animals, including everything from a great Dane—not left over from colonial days—to a lively monkey, must have created enough bedlam to put the fear of God even in an old reprobate like Blackbeard. Nary a ghost went bump in the night. I believe Blackbeard could not take the heat, so stayed out of the pandemonium. Children and animals charging about proved too much. He did not have a ghost of a chance.

Still, one of the Giovan children's friends named Seth claimed Blackbeard was there and kept searching for his ghost. One night, Seth talked Marti into a "Ghost Watch" in the tower.

A group of children, led by Marti holding a hurricane lamp with a lighted candle in it, trailed up the tower's circular staircase like kids behind a Pied Piper. Stopping at the tower's second story, Marti put the lamp in the middle of the circular floor. The group sat around it on cement bags. This was not your run-of-the-mill séance.

Seth requested quiet. All complied, except for an occasional giggle.

Seth began to speak. "I am going to ask questions. If the candle's flame goes higher, it means 'Yes'. If it goes lower, it means 'No.' "

"Blackbeard, are you here?" he asked.

The flame flared up. No giggles now. Everyone sat up straight as exclamation marks.

"Are you happy, Blackbeard?"

The flame definitely lowered.

The questions and answers continued in a conversational manner. Marti confessed she was so startled she could not speak. Suddenly the candle went out. She swore that a chill, a kind she had never felt before, came over everyone.

"Icy cold," she said, adding that she never would have believed the experience if she had not been there herself.

A subsequent attempt to recreate the event ended in failure as Seth had predicted. Is Seth the only one who knows for sure if it was a hoax?

Blackbeard, or whoever never called again, but Marti felt a great respect for her ghost as long as she lived in the family's quarters around the base of his tower. She always spoke about him in the present tense.

Bluebeard's Castle, not haunted

Frederick Lutheran Church. People are all inside!

"Blackbeard did it!" the children claimed when something was missing, broken, or things went wrong. Of course, we parents know that is worth as much as a bag full of leprechauns.

Still, an experience worth recounting happened to a reporter who wrote a story about Blackbeard's Tower. His camera jammed after he took only a few shots of the second story location of the "séance." He reloaded and took more interior shots, checking exposure. When he developed the roll, not a single shot came out.

"Perhaps the large, inscrutable cat that appeared on the stairway out of nowhere jinxed the pictures for Blackbeard," he said.

What do you think?

Blackbeard's is now a charming small restaurant-hotel and ghostless— I think.

•

When the Giovans had Blackbeard's, the indomitable family flew to Rhode Island every summer. Their flight was like moving Barnum and Bailey's Circus. They warned Pan Am they would have animal cages, but never mentioned the number. Panic broke out when they arrived with six or so cages housing their menagerie. Add five children and all their luggage and sports equipment. It was enough to make any crew sit down and cry.

Villa Olga

The Giovans acquired their second ghost when they signed a 99-year lease in 1967 for Frenchtown's Villa Olga and turned it into a popular guest house and restaurant. At one time, various fort sites were located around St. Thomas, and according to some old papers, Villa Olga is near one of them.

Before the mansion was called Villa Olga, it had several names: Albino's Place, Estate Altona, Careeninghole—which goes back to when ships dry-docked there for repairs—and Manecke Villa, just prior to Villa Olga.

When Russians first came to St. Thomas to open a consulate here, well over a hundred years ago, they settled in this area. They brought in coal for ship fuel and built large cisterns above ground. Each one held a half-million gallons of water from catchments behind them. For many years the cisterns supplied all of St. Thomas' water. The prison-look-alike structures can still be seen near the original Villa Olga, now a Chart House Restaurant.

Not long before Chart House opened in June, 1981, a fire of inexplicable origin almost completely destroyed the structure. Undeterred, the leaseholders rebuilt, and any ghosts **appear** assuaged. Not one has been reported since. The fire did 'em in.

One of Villa Olga's ghost stories centers around an aristocratic young lady of the Russian court, married to the Consul General, who came to St. Thomas during the Russians' sojourn here. She expected the glamourous life of the more sophisticated European consulates.

On her arrival, she discovered she was pregnant from a clandestine affair at court. Eventually she delivered twins, who were mysteriously murdered and buried in the Villa Olga grounds. The young woman grew rest-

Old Colonial Quarter viewed from Blackbeard's Castle restaurant.
The large white building upper right behind Denmark Hill is the
Danish Consulate. That land still belongs to Denmark

99

less with the unexciting life of St. Thomas and returned home to Russia after a year.

Following the young Russian lady's departure, Villa Olga changed hands frequently and gradually lost the elegance of her occupancy. Sometimes the mansion's reputation became questionable. When it was a gambling house and bordello, a murder was committed there.

In 1965, a fire destroyed several buildings, but the main house, over a hundred years old, and another building equally old, were not damaged.

Although Marti and Tony knew the history of Villa Olga, they did not take seriously having supernatural guests as well as live, paying ones. After extensive renovation, they opened their guest house and restaurant.

Weird "goings on" started when Marti complained the door to the newly converted ladies' room would not stay shut—no matter how carefully locked. One of her daughters had the same experience, yet it never happened to anyone else.

Soon a foreign-looking couple arrived for a stay at Villa Olga. The woman, described by Marti as "strange," claimed her mother, the daughter of European servants at the Villa, had been born there. She showed Marti a very old picture of four small children—two boys and two girls. She maintained one girl was her mother and left the picture with Marti. After putting it in her office, Marti forgot about it.

Later, one of Marti's close friends came to Villa Olga for a visit. The woman's mother was a practicing medium, so she had been raised in an atmosphere of psychic phenomena. After making a trip to the ladies' room, the friend told Marti she had a mischievous ghost on the premises. The door had behaved in the same way for her as for Marti and her daughter. Marti told her the full story of the door, including the picture incident. The friend advised Marti to put the picture in the powder room. She said it might be that the ghost was one of the children who simply wanted to be home again.

Investigation revealed the powder room **had** originally been servant's quarters. Marti put the children's picture in the ladies' room, and there was no more trouble. For a while.

After a couple of years, the picture mysteriously disappeared and was never found. The door went back to opening and banging. A new manager insisted he sometimes heard a child calling when he was in his room—which backed up to the servants' quarters. A friend substantiated his claims.

Now, too, lights began flickering on and off as if a prankish child were playing tricks. The manager also heard the banging door. He did not stay much longer at the Villa.

Stories of Villa Olga's ghosts spread. Several psychics who visited the Great House heard children scampering about and a woman sobbing. One visitor claimed to experience a "sensation of pain and sadness" that emanated from the mansion. Marti speculated the spirits were those of the consul's wife and her children.

Without ghosts, no ghost-hunters have prowled Chart House, which means no more good "ghost stories."

Harbor View Hotel

Another haunted house belongs to the late Arlene Lockwood and Lenore Wolfe who bought Harbor View in 1961 and turned it into a hotel and popular restaurant. The handsome old Danish mansion dates back to the late 1700s.

Supposedly built for the French Consulate, it was later owned by the Lockhart family, followed by Gertrude Gardner. From 1940 to 1961, Harbor View had various owners: Bebe Paul, who served pheasant under glass in its gourmet restaurant; Ricky and Francis Chalifoux, who ran it as a hotel and restaurant; and Gun and Bertil Agell, who hosted another gourmet restaurant there until Lockwood and Wolfe bought it.

The latter duo should have been awarded four stars for endurance. I cannot think of any other restaurant that has been under the same man-

"99 Steps" on Government Hill is the most famous of Charlotte Amalie's
historic street steps. Up these steps to the right is Cotton House,
one of the few remaining Danish mansions

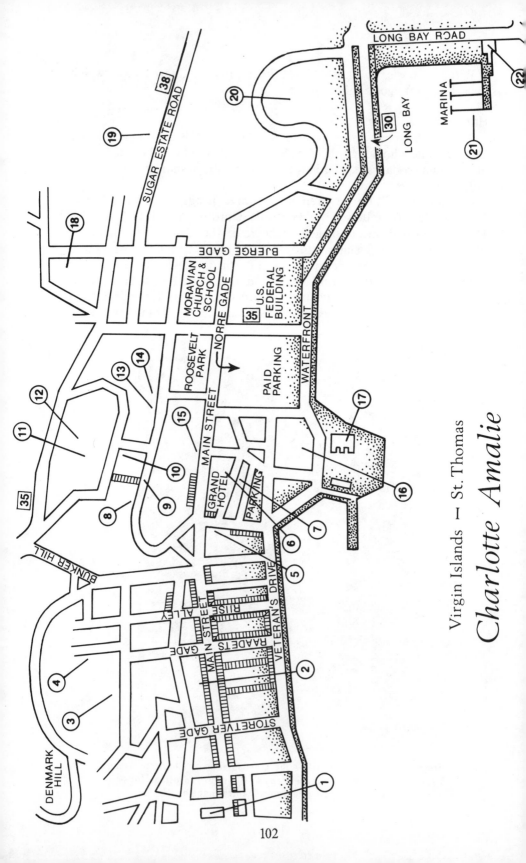

Virgin Islands — St. Thomas

Charlotte Amalie

1. Market Square
   (Sloane Market 18th Cent.)
2. Camille Pissarro Building (18th Cent.)
3. Synagogue (1833)
4. All Saints School and Church (1848)
5. U.S. Post Office with
   Stephen Dohanos mural
6. Hospitality Lounge (for tourists)
7. Emancipation Garden and
   Bandstand (1848)
8. Hotel "1829"
9. 99 Steps
10. Crown House (1750)
11. The Mark St. Thomas

12. Blackbeard's Castle Hotel
    and Restaurant
13. Government House (1867)
14. St. Governor's Office
15. Frederick Lutheran Church and School
16. Fort Christian and Museum (1671)
17. Legislature Building
    (Green Barn)(1874)
18. Lionel Roberts Stadium
19. Charlotte Amalie High School
20. Bluebeard's Castle Hotel
21. Kon Tiki
22. Hotel

Numbers in squares are road route numbers
☐☐☐☐ Duty Free Shops
Route 35 leads north to Magens Bay and Drake's Seat
Rental cars at airport

agement for as long and maintained such an enviable reputation. Their ghost, however, is a friendly one, who mostly walks through the halls and disturbs no one.

Once, as Arlene sat on the porch, she noticed someone walking through the lobby. She checked, but no one was there. Another time when she was in her apartment, she heard someone clear his throat in a room to the left. She thought it was the manager, the only other person in the house, until he came in from the right.

Former owner, Gertrude Gardner, claimed there definitely was a ghost. She identified him as a man who had died in the house long ago. No one, however, worries about the Harbor View ghost. The employees believe he is harmless and simply making sure all goes well at Harbor View Hotel and Restaurant. If you are going to have a ghost he seems the best kind to have around.

ISLAND HISTORY

Let us leave ghosts behind now and visit St. Thomas haunts bewitched only by fascinating histories. Within a radius of a few blocks in downtown Charlotte Amalie, these buildings can be viewed in a couple of hours. Great adventure is afoot in Paradise!

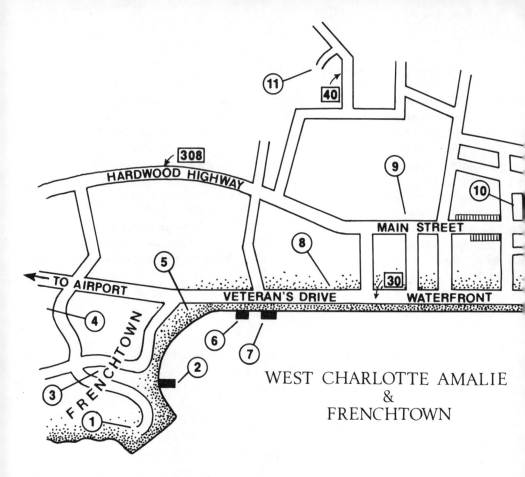

WEST CHARLOTTE AMALIE
&
FRENCHTOWN

West Charlotte Amalie and Frenchtown — Legends

1. Chart House (Villa Olga)
2. Avery's Boathouse
3. Normandie Bar
4. St. Anne's Church
5. U.S. Post Office
6. Seaplanes to St. Croix and St. John
7. Ferry to Tortola
8. Windward Passage Hotel
9. St. Peter and Paul Cathedral and School
10. Market Square
11. Harbor View

☐☐☐ Duty Free Shops

Fort Christian

The island's oldest structure is Fort Christian, built by the Danes. Although Columbus discovered St. Thomas in 1493, the small, mountainous island with its hostile Carib Indians did not interest the Spanish. The hardier Danes, nevertheless, occupied it in 1666 and began constructing the fort. They did not establish a permanent settlement until 1672, nor complete the fort until 1680.

In the meantime, Fort Christian, crammed with the court, government offices, Lutheran Church, military police, and barracks, served as seat of government and living quarters for the governor and other officials. Talk about mass confusion. A residence solely for the governor was not purchased until 1720.

In 1678, on the hill above the Fort, the Danes built Skystborg, a watchtower overlooking the harbor and later called Blackbeard's Tower—where our aforementioned wicked pirate Blackbeard lived.

Today, parapeted Fort Christian, red brick, with gold accents on its handsome crenelated clocktower, arched gothic windows, and entrance, looks more like a fairy tale castle than a fort.

For a long time, the fort was ignominiously demoted to being the St. Thomas jail. Inmates yelled and whistled at women passing by and made men targets for anything tossable. The casual comings and goings of prisoners also caused concern. Another jail was built nearby. Nothing changed. Knotted sheets dangled inmates to freedom. Some simply walked out. Island criminals are not easy to confine.

Happily, the Fort is now a creditable museum, exhibiting island and Fort Christian history; an array of pre-Colombian artifacts—pottery, idols, implements; and an authentic 17th century dungeon with chains and a torture rack. Cultural events also take place there, the most popular being the Virgin Islands Folkloric Company's dance performances in the courtyard.

The Green Barn

Across the street on the Fort's waterfront side (entrance to the Museum) and enclosed in a black wrought iron fence, stands an impressive two-story Italian Renaissance edifice painted a lovely spring green. It could be a setting for a military school musical.

Kindly, and unkindly, called "The Green Barn," it is the Legislature Building, home of the 15-member Unicameral Virgin Islands Senate. Built in 1874 as barracks for the Danish police, the structure was used as a U.S. Marine Corps Barracks from 1917 to 1930, and afterwards, a public school until 1957. The "goings on" here are something to behold, but we will get to that in Chapter 14.

Charlotte Amalie

Not until 1691 was the town named Charlotte Amalie in honor of the Danish Queen, King Christian V's wife. In the beginning, the Danish set-

105

Memorial to St. Thomas soldiers killed in war, Roosevelt Park

tlement was called "Tap Hus," or Beer Hall, because of its watering-hole popularity with traders, smugglers, and pirates. The clientele has changed, but the island's watering-hole popularity has not.

Rampant piracy diverted legitimate trade from the island until after 1700. During that time, the pirate Bluebeard occupied Bluebeard's Castle—not to be confused with Blackbeard and his Tower. The former is now our scrumptious and popular Bluebeard's Castle hotel. No ghosts.

A 1681 census, the first, listed 37 people living in the town. Declared a free port, which it still is, in 1764, the town grew rapidly. In 1799 Charlotte Amalie's population was 7,000—about ten times that today.

From 1804 to 1831, fires and other disasters demolished most structures. Consequently, surviving mansions such as Crown House have become cherished landmarks.

Crown House

Our famous "99 steps" lead to Crown House from Kongens Gade (Gade means "street" in Danish. It's pronounced gah-dah). This bougainvilla-flanked stairstep street, built around 1700 by the Danes with bricks used as ballast for sailing ships, solved the problem of getting around the town's hilly terrain—and still does. (See photo page 101.)

A magnificant harbor view from the top of the stairsteps awaits its climbers. To the left, facing the harbor, is Crown House. Built prior to 1750 on Government Hill above Government House, the mansion, known for lavish parties, was once the elegant residence of Vice-Governor Peter von Scholten. During his tenure, the Vice-Governor added many distinguishing touches to enhance its beauty. Among them is an exquisite chandelier from Versailles.

After von Scholten became Governor in 1827, he moved to St. Croix and under pressure, freed the island slaves July 3, 1848. Emancipation Park, also called Emancipation Garden, in St. Thomas, commemorates the event.

Grand Hotel (See photo page 73)

Across from Fort Christian on Main Street is Grand Hotel, built in 1839-40. Our oldest hotel, it has only offices and shops today. Its gallery overlooks Emancipation Garden and the harbor, and the building covers a city block. Originally three stories high, it shed its third story in a hurricane near the end of the 19th century. It has managed very well without it.

During the island's Elysian years, before 1970, Grand Gallery Restaurant occupied a large section of the Hotel's second floor. "Petsey" Powell operated the Restaurant with Alvin Nibbs ("Mr. Nibbs"), steward, prize-

Entrance to Mark St. Thomas Hotel. This 200-year-old building was once an Episcopalian parsonage and is on the Register of Historic Homes. Its 8 rooms are furnished with antiques. It has been praised as one of St. Thomas' outstanding restaurants

winning bartender, and creator of the Fuzzy Navel. Make your own wise-cracks about that one. I would not touch it with a ten-foot moray eel.

Mr. Nibbs used to made an Al Brown Rum Collins that only a few people knew about. The recipe's special ingredient was a well-guarded secret. I suspect a dollop of heavenly nectar. Assisted by a parrot named Nausea, who ate his favorite delicacies off your plate if you lunched at the bar, Mr. Nibbs managed the Grand Gallery Restaurant during the six months each year Petsey was off-island.

The Grand Gallery Round Table, named after the Algonquin Hotel's famous Round Table, was the island's most popular luncheon place for Continentals. Camaraderie and fun reigned. The table also served as grapevine center. The regulars knew "everything" happening on St. Thomas. It took a good Round Table joke or a choice bit of gossip about two hours to be diffused throughout St. Thomas.

When Mr. Nibbs chose a bride, Petsey threw a real bash at the Grand Gallery. Superb food and "jump-up" music rattled the ancient hotel's bones. The old, sagging ballroom floor, loaded with dancers, swinging and swaying, bounced up and down like a trampoline. Mr. and Mrs. Nibbs received guests' congratulations and wishes for happiness from two rattan fan chairs on a dais. I doubt if there has ever been a more festive island wedding celebration.

•

Across Main Street from the Grand Hotel is the stately Frederick Lutheran Church, official church of the Danish West Indies and established in 1666. (See photo page 98.)

When the Danes ran the island, any Dane who did not attend church was fined twenty-five pounds of tobacco, good way to smoke 'em out. The present Gothic Revival building replaced two other structures at this site which burned down in 1750 and 1789.

Government House

After the first Government House (1720) deteriorated to the point where a new residence was mandatory, Catherineberg, considered the first Danish West Indies country house of its day, seemed an inspired choice.

The imposing Greek Revival mansion on Denmark Hill had served well as a residence for the Vice-Governor. Unfortunately, many little wooden houses on small plots surrounded it. Numerous people thought that the highest government official on the island, the governor, should live in a "more upper-class neighborhood." Consequently, in August 1864, the construction of a new Government House began on Kongens Gade.

Loud grumblings about irregularities in awarding the bid and about cost overruns reverberated throughout the island. Same complaints today.

In April 1865, on the forty-seventh birthday of King Christian IX, councilors and elite gentlemen assembled for a levee at noon in Masonic

Hall. They generously toasted the King's health before proceeding to Government Hill, where they laid the Government House cornerstone in a "glow" of good fellowship. Seems Danish Old Boys are just like U.S. Old Boys.

The cornerstone inscription reads:

"God grant that justice, honest endeavors for the welfare of this community, and a Christian domestic life may ever dwell under the roof of this building."

In no time the "Christian domestic life" had a setback.

The trouble, believe it or not, was over a privy. Occupants of the previous Government House used the one next door belonging to the Frederick Lutheran Church Parsonage. The Danish Parson decided, however, that now, since there were "altered relations" between church and state, state could no longer use clergy property, especially anything as intimate as a privy.

Plans were presented for a Government House masonry privy at a cost of $450. The Council Chamber huffed and puffed over the "exhorbitant" cost, maintaining two small houses could be built for the amount. After "delicate negotiations," as day follows dawn, came compromise. Government House got its privy, a wooden one, at a cost of only $130. That took care of the seat of government. The Governor was now among the privy-ledged.

Dedication of the Guardhouse

Before we leave Government House—open to the public at certain

Government House, with Danish sentry box outside,
a gift from the Danish Government

hours—I must mention the bright red "Toy Soldier" guardhouse at the mansion's front steps. Danish sentries used these to guard many of Denmark's public buildings. The Danes presented this one as a gift to Government House in 1967. The sentry box commemorates the fiftieth anniversary of the transfer of Virgin Islands' ownership from Denmark to the United States.

Governor Ralph Paiewonsky conceived and successfully carried out the 50th Anniversary celebration, undoubtedly the Islands' most spectacular official event. Built around a Governors' Conference in the U.S. Virgin Islands and preceded by a cruise from the States, the three-day production was Hollywood stellar. I have never been so proud of our island. Would that we could always be like that.

For once, the island was spick and span. The weather perfect. Glamour reigned. A sleek limousine with fluttering U.S. and Danish flags stood ready to transport each governor and his entourage to all events.

Ronald Reagan, then Governor of California, and Nancy were among the most sought after of the Governors and their wives, along with Governor Warren Knowles and his wife, Dorothy, from Wisconsin.

Mary Brooks Jackson interviewed Dorothy Knowles most successfully during lunch beside Hidden Hill's pool. She also interviewed Nancy Reagan on the cruise ship that carried the Governors and their wives from St. Thomas to St. Croix. Although Mary found Nancy more aloof than Dorothy, she also enjoyed that interview, but never dreamed Nancy Reagan would someday be the First Lady.

A scene I shall never forget is Mary Brooks Jackson hanging over the ship railing, wildly waving a white hanky and shouting my name, just before the cruise ship took off for St. Croix. Al and I stood on the pier bidding Governor and Mrs. Knowles goodbye. Hundreds of people milled about on the crowded, noisy dock, or pressed forward to see the limousines disgorging their celebrity passengers. Bands blared, flags waved, men, women, and children shouted and laughed.

Finally I heard Mary Brooks Jackson and spotted her along the thickly packed crowded railing—reminiscent of an immigrant ship. I waved back. Certain she had something important to tell me, I wriggled through the throng to the ship's side. I looked up expectantly.

"I'll write when I get work!" she shouted, grinning down impishly.

All those nearby burst into laughter, especially the ones who knew her, and almost everyone did because of her Mary-Go-Round radio show. That was our irrepressible Mary and her ebullient sense of humor. Unfortunately, after a few years on Spain's island of Majorca, she moved to California.

Synagogue Hill

Two short blocks north from the center of Main Street, on Crystal Gade, in an area known as Synagogue Hill, is the Western Hemisphere's second oldest synagogue, a small architectural gem. Covered with sand, the floor commemorates the Jews' exodus from Egypt. Graceful stairs lead to a columned porch and the interior, highlighted with well-polished mahogany woodwork, welcomes visitors.

Like St. Thomas, the synagogue has, since 1796, offered a tranquil haven for the Jewish immigrants who became active in island business, political and civic affairs. Ralph Paiewonsky was our first native-born business-man appointed governor. He also worked tirelessly for the establishment of the College of the Virgin Islands on St. Thomas, now the University of the Virgin Islands.

Jews have lived on St. Thomas since 1665. They first came as ship chandlers and brokers, and later became shop owners. The synagogue was not built until after 1796, after several families formed a congregation. They called their place of worship "Blessing and Peace."

In 1801 nine families comprised the congregation. The number grew to twenty-two in 1803. After a fire destroyed the original synagogue in 1804, several others replaced it, but were also destroyed by fire. The present one, completed in 1833, was named "Blessing, Peace, and Act of Piety." The Service of Consecration took place September 14, 1833, and Governor Peter von Scholten and his entourage, in brilliant gold-braided uniforms, cock-hats, and swords, graced the premises for the auspicious oc-

Synagogue entrance

casion. Every tourist should see the synagogue and its priceless historic treasures.

•

Our island's mixture: Carib Indians, Spaniards, Africans, Danes, Germans, French refugees, Russians, and Jews, along with other immigrants from the world's nooks and crannies has given our island a past as lusty as a Dumas novel.

The entangled history of little St. Thomas rivals that of London or Paris, but is unknown to the world in general. We are now considered simply a sun, sand, and surf Caribbean vacation island. Nevertheless, our heritage is as unique as an El Greco painting: a potpourri of plantation owners and sea captains, pirates and adventurers, aristocrats and rogues. On second thought, things have not changed much in this respect, either.

•

We shall visit two more buildings of interest before ending our historic tour.

Going West on Main Street from the Grand Hotel, to the left and across the street, is a Stephen Dohanos mural in the Post Office. Painted in the 30s during the WPA program for artists, before Dohanos became famous, it is worth seeing.

Camille Pissarro Building

On down Main Street a couple of blocks on the right is a sign swinging over the sidewalk that says: "The Camille Pissarro Building." The famous Impressionist painter Camille Pissarro was born here, July 10, 1830.

Market Square

112

Sometimes protected by heavy streetside doors, a black wrought iron gate that is folded back during the day, marks the entrance to a dark brick-paved passage leading to a small courtyard. There, a masonry stairway goes up to the original Pissarro living quarters, filled now with offices and shops. It is not difficult to transport oneself back a hundred and fifty years and imagine young Pissarro climbing the stairs. The boy lived in Charlotte Amalie until 1841, when his parents sent him to France to be educated. His father, a prosperous Jewish merchant of Spanish origin, had also lived in Portugal. His mother was Creole.

Although Pissarro had an exceptional ability for drawing, his parents did not encourage his artistic talent. His father wanted him to be a merchant. He called his son back from France when he was seventeen to start his apprenticeship. The young man tried hard to juggle his business and art for the next five years.

Around 1850, a Danish painter, Fritz Melbye, sent to St. Thomas to study art in the colony, was impressed by Pissarro's natural gift. He persuaded the artist to go with him to his next post in Venezuela.

Pissarro wrote later, ". . . thus breaking the chains which bound me to a bourgeois existence."

A new world of cultivated people, music, and art lovers opened up for him. Pissarro returned to St. Thomas in 1854, but left for France in 1855, where he settled permanently. The rest, of course, is history.

In its collection of fine paintings, Government House has a couple of Pissarros in rooms used for entertaining. The paintings are only on display at formal functions, but plans are underway to have visiting hours for the general public.

Tuck this bit of Pissarro data away for upmanship. Few people know he was born on St. Thomas. Pissarro's works have enjoyed renewed favor since 1981, so when someone mentions his name, casually comment:

"I've seen his St. Thomas birthplace."

Thus ends my art history lesson. It also ends my coverage of St. Thomas haunts with ghosts and those with unusual histories.

**Bakery Square on Back Street is filled with attractive shops.
At one time the building housed a bakery**

CHAPTER 11

CHA-CHA TOWN (See chart page 104)

French settlers in "Frenchtown," on the West end of Charlotte Amalie's Waterfront, once considered the nickname "Cha-Cha Town" derogatory. Many islanders insist the term was neighborly. They maintain the origin of Cha-Cha Town started with the French fishermen in Carenage—the area's first name when it serviced boats. The men sold their daily catch on the streets, or in the market place, and prospective customers often haggled to lower the price.

In disgust, the anglers replied, "Cha-cha," the sobriquet for an insignificant fish in the waters around the island of St. Barthélémy, their former Caribbean home. "Cha-Cha" implied the price offered beneath consideration.

Amused by the fisherman's retort, St. Thomians, never intending to be pejorative, began calling the area "Cha-Cha Town."

To the Frenchmen, however, a person called "Cha-Cha" inferred he was worthless, so applying the name to where they lived insulted them. Fortunately, with time, the Frenchmen realized the term was friendly and the people of their adopted island considered them an integral part of the community. "Frenchtown" is used almost entirely now, but I like the sound of "Cha-Cha Town." It suits the hard-working, high-spirited fishermen there.

History of Frenchtown

The exact date the French arrived in St. Thomas is in question. It appears that well over a hundred years ago they began to emigrate to St. Thomas from St. Barthélémy in the Leeward Islands, frequently called "St. Barths."

A fire in 1852 demolished the town of Gustavia, St. Barths. Later in the year, a hurricane devastated crops and homes. Soon after, the shorter route to the United States from Europe became more profitable, and steamers serving the tiny island gradually withdrew. This forced many French citizens, originally from Normandy and Brittany, to find another island for survival.

St. Barths' original arrivals in St. Thomas—LaPlace, Quetel, Bryan, and Querard families—came from its productive farming region. They settled in Estate Tutu as tillers and gardeners on the estate of Mr. Magens for whom Magens Bay is named and on other landowners' estates in the region. Later they moved to Mafolie, Barette, and Hull areas.

Fishermen—Danet, Magras, Ledee, Olive, Bernier families—from St. Barths' Gustavia district migrated to Carenage on Charlotte Amalie's little, circular Gallows Bay.

Above the Bay, Gallows Hill overlooked the entire settlement. At one time, island criminals and pirates sentenced to die were hanged on the hill's summit. As late as 1916, pieces of the gallows' scaffolding still remained there—grim reminders of swift island justice in the past. The Great Hurricane of 1916 scattered and destroyed the last vestiges of scaffolding.

In 1921, the Redemptorist Fathers chose Gallows Hill as the site for St. Anne's Church, and Mr. J.H. Boschulte donated the land. His Lordship, Right Reverend James Morris, Bishop of Roseau, Dominica, dedicated St. Anne's Church on Christmas Day, 1922. Except for the renovation of its chapel in 1934, St. Anne's remains unchanged. The attractive small church, painted a warm yellow and trimmed in white, crowns the hilltop with the dignity of a 14th century bishop's miter and is a landmark for sailors and residents.

In early days, the bells of St. Anne's Church rang out from its steeple at 6:00 a.m., summoning faithful members to Mass at 6:30. Sundays it rang 15 minutes earlier. No rest for the holy. At dawn, Philip Baptiste, tall, ageless, revered, trudged up the hill's rocky path from his home below to peal the awakening bells. Old-timers say that to the children, he seemed an awesome figure, representing "church, God, and eternity."

Since no funeral home existed then, Baptiste, a carpenter, fabricated all

Frenchtown, where fishermen pull up their boats. See also photo on page 39

the community's coffins. Older Frenchtown people remember him as a humble, religious man.

"As a child, I always thought of him as St. Joseph," one said. When awakened by the bells, Frenchtown came alive quickly.

Ever-present roosters crowed; fishermen, vigorously as Swiss yodelers, called to each other from house to house while preparing to leave for their day's fishing; storefront shutters clattered open as proprietors readied for customers. The aroma of fresh coffee permeated the air; small children wandered out of neat clapboard cottages to play beside small shrines in immaculate fenced-in yards; and donkeys bobbed along the winding roads.

The Normandie Bar

The Normandie Bar, closed from 2:00 a.m. until 6:00 a.m., opened. Who were customers? Perhaps a couple of hotel night clerks, a night watchman or two, a sprinkling of returned fishermen, and bartenders just off duty from other watering holes—like postmen taking holiday hikes.

Frenchies boast every tale about Normandie Bar, which celebrated its 50th anniversary in 1988, is true.

"Plots are hatched there; lots are cast there," they said. Politicians filled and vacated jobs; drafted, amended, repealed laws until the Bar became known as the "downtown Senate."

Although politics remains a hot subject, Normandie Bar patrons these days are vastly interested in sports, with Big League baseball the favorite. Wagering is mostly confined to drinks, but during the World Series a "sou" or two may change hands.

Every night Frenchtown bustles with activity, making it a Caribbean version of New Orleans' French Quarter. "Downstairs" Normandie Bar—

Café Normandie, elegant French cuisine upstairs,
Caribbean downstairs, and a lively bar

windows and doors wide open—along with drinks, serves Puerto Rican fare. Noisy, relaxed, filled with gesticulating Frenchtown habitués, it is the "local color" that tourists love.

"Upstairs" Café Normandie's air-conditioned environment is refined, urbane as a small three-star Paris restaurant, with classic French cuisine and impeccable service. The juxtaposition of the two restaurants is an anomaly, but each is an adventure, one in people; the other in food.

Other Restaurants

In 1976, 14 bars and restaurants watered and fed Frenchies and other St. Thomians. Today the number remains about the same, but turnover is constant. Restaurants range from elegant Café Normandie on Rue de St. Barthélémy, "upstairs" from "downstairs" Normandie Bar, to Percy's Bus Stop, a retired double-decker bus with odd appendages and West Indian Food.

•

Quarter Deck, next to Avery's Boat House—a St. Thomas landmark for sailors in dinghies or sleek yachts, who need charter boats or boats repaired, docked, or stored—has been popular with boat people ever since we came to St. Thomas. In 1987 the Quarter Deck closed, and, under new management, became "Hook, Line, and Sinker."

Editor's Note: *Avery's is still going strong. Dick Avery had the first bare boat charter fleet in the Virgin Islands, now featuring a variety of Pearson sailboats.*

Quarter Deck will be missed by us old-timers, but we wish Hook, Line, and Sinker success. We also hope it continues to preserve that "Ahoy there, mate!" quality that made even us landlubbers want "to go down to the sea in ships and smell the briny deep."

Parochial school children at Mafolie Catholic Church, Our Lady of Perpetual Help. The little shrine is lovely

Today St. Thomians and tourists go to Frenchtown's Alexander's for Wiener Schnitzel, Chez Jacques for classic French cuisine, Chart House for American steaks, Barbary Coast for Italian specialties, Johnny Cakes for Italian and Caribbean fare, and the new and attractive seaside Sugar Reef Café (formerly Gregerie East) for Continental Cuisine.

•

Affectionately called "Frenchies," Frenchtown inhabitants love music. The boys' choir at St. Anne's, accompanied by organist "Bing" Magras, was once renowned throughout the Caribbean. Favored instruments included the tambourine, accordian, maracas, and steel band pans.

In the past, Carnival marchers assembled in Frenchtown and many steel bands got their start there. Things have been changing, though, in Cha-Cha Town. The rapid growth of island population has altered priorities. Education is highly regarded and Frenchtown children capture a large portion of honors and awards at Sts. Peter and Paul High School. Current generation Frenchies have their sights on Stateside Colleges or the University of the Virgin Islands. The traditional life of Frenchtown fisherman that satisfied their forefathers no longer tempts them.

Gustave Quetel

Still our Conservation and Cultural Affairs Department in 1987 honored Frenchtown's oldest fisherman by naming Frenchtown's fishing center for eighty-two-year-old Gustave Quetel. Popularly called "fish house," the facility became officially "Gustave Quetel Fishing Center."

Quetel started fishing at age nine. Although he held other jobs on boats, they were "just work." He says, "Fishing is not just work. It's a way of life."

In the early days, Quetel started out in his row boat around 3 a.m. to reach a good fishing spot at daybreak, which is considered the best fish-

Gustave Quetel Fishing Center

ing time. Once a large wave hit the boat, and he lost his oars, but the tidal current drifted the boat close to shore. In the 40s, French fishermen traded their oars for outboard motors, and life at sea became easier.

Quetel remembers the days, fifty or so years ago, when fish sold for 10 cents a pound. Today's price is two dollars a pound. Although Quetel only fishes occasionally now, he still makes fishpots and fishnets. He also laments the younger generation's lack of interest in fishing. Though a good number of older fishermen remain, the future does not look bright for Frenchtown's fishing industry.

French Farmers

A number of young Frenchmen are still interested in farming, but not small-time. On the rainy Northside, they produce fresh vegetables and limited fruit for supermarkets. Some operate profitable plant nurseries. Others have opened bars and restaurants there, using their own crops. The Berry family's "Place In The Sun," with fresh produce and inviting garden atmosphere, enjoyed great popularity for several years in the early 80s.

When the first French farmers came to St. Thomas from St. Barths, the steep, rocky mountains of our Northside discouraged them. Overgrown by dense vegetation once cultivated and planted by slaves for sugar cane and bananas, it bore little resemblance to St. Barths' rich, level land.

Need to survive and rapid migration of families from other Caribbean islands, however, made food their top priority. Soil preparation and hard, backbreaking cultivation of the precipitous hillsides began.

From the onset, the Frenchmen knew they must control erosion by terracing, and they moved large rocks by manpower to construct rock barriers. Despite the rugged, steep slopes, the land proved productive. Those original terraces hold today and the rocks laid at their outer edges still preserve precious topsoil and retain rain water needed to grow vegetables—a tribute to a job well-done.

Bastille Day

For years, the most popular drinking-eating spot in a garden setting between town and the Northside has been Sib's Mountain Bar and Restaurant, owned by the prominent Sibilly family.

In the Estate Elizabeth-Mafolie area, Sib's became the focal point for many local French festivities. The July 14th observance of France's revolution—Bastille Day—is a big French event. One year other Northside residents joined local Frenchies on a grassy plot across the road from the restaurant. A temporary miniature village erected there and stocked with native dishes and refreshments served the revelers food and drink while they sang and danced until early morning.

In contrast, Frenchtown gourmets have hosted wine-tasting and hors d'oeuvres parties at Café Normandie and ended their celebration enjoying leisurely sumptous dinners. Alexander's also has contributed to Bastille Day merrymaking with people shuttling between the café and

**Sib's Mountaintop Bar & Restaurant is prominent in St. Thomas'
celebration of Bastille Day**

Normandie Bar throughout the night, sipping champagne and nibbling canapes.

Before Sib's, Bastille Day in Frenchtown meant music, parades, tramps, drinking, and eating. French flags fluttered atop roofs and people sported traditional red and white French berets. I remember a spic-and-span French naval vessel in the harbor long ago with rows of sailors, in spotless white uniforms and red and white berets, standing at attention on deck during a welcoming ceremony. The impressive spectacle still tingles my spine.

For a while Frenchtown's Bastille Day changed.

In 1977, a woman complained, "Now everything happens at Mafolie." She blamed the younger generation for not keeping up the Day's tradition in Frenchtown.

"Today's French people are becoming Americanized," she said, recalling special past events on Bastille Day: sports, boat races, music. But the past is returning, and both Sib's and Frenchtown now proudly celebrate French holidays.

Father's Day

Frenchtown's Father's Day celebration has always been an important occasion. A Mini-carnival. A colorful, noisy parade circles through the streets. Mocko jumbies, clowns, Sebastian Majorettes, Oswald Harris Court Majorettes, marching bands—the Frenchtown Troubadours and the Mountain Kings—participate. A Queen and escort lead the parade and festivities.

One year, a parade float carrying Frenchtown fishermen and their catch in an authentic fishing boat took top prize. The Moby Dick Troupe wearing kangaroo suits and doing a kangaroo dance came in second. Dancing with a kangaroo would really be "jumping up."

The Frenchtown Civic Organization, Frenchtown Community Center, Apaches Softball Club—Frenchtown has its own Joseph Aubain Ballpark—the Cain Magras Troupe, and Moby Dick Committee sponsor the popular Father's Day events.

A tournament for Frenchtown fishermen takes place on Saturday, and during the Sunday night award ceremony, the Committee announces prize winners. Among awards are "smallest fish" and "hard luck," the Hard Luck award one year went to Felix Greaux, whose steering gear broke while he trolled. He rigged up a broom for steering the boat that got him safely back to shore—and that is no fish-tale.

La Belle Department Store

For many years, a popular shopping place in Frenchtown for both French people and other St. Thomians has been La Belle Creole Department Store, now La Belle Department Store. It carries everyday items not easy to find in St. Thomas.

Downtown we have Gucci, Cartier, Courrèges, Guy LaRoche, Louis Vuitton, all the luxury items from Europe, but when you need a yard of gingham or a roll of elastic, it is La Belle.

In 1986, La Belle Department Store, tucked away at the west entrance to Frenchtown, celebrated its 40th birthday. The family-oriented business started because of Leopold Magras' one-story home built in 1942.

When finished, the house seemed to the family a perfect place for a café. The Modernaire Bar was born and became a popular Frenchtown gathering place. Then in 1956, the Margras clan had another brainstorm and converted the bar to LaBelle Creole Department Store. Quaint and smartly run, the store catered to the needs and fancies of local residents.

Eventually, the two-story complex became what it is today, a family corporation operating a laundromat, two guest houses, and the leased-out United Nations Bar to prove Frenchies are not chauvinists. One never knows where a simple home can lead.

•

It is evident that Cha-Cha Town, although an integral part of the whole community, remains distinctly French. I hope it stays that way. The French presence gives St. Thomas a special flavor, like adding a dollop of white wine to midi ragout.

Photo by Susan Houston

Dock at Frenchtown where fishermen clean and sell their fish

Happily, many "old country" French customs prevail.

This one appeals to my sentimental side: A charming Normandy tradition continues with fathers reading certain letters before sitting down at the wedding dinner. Letters from parents of the Bride are addressed to the Groom's parents, and letters from the parents of the Groom are addressed to the Bride's parents. Each father graciously receives the offspring of the other as his own, and both families express their good wishes and happiness to the newlyweds. An effective way of cementing family ties.

•

Over the years, Frenchtown residents honored their streets with French names such as Rue de St. Barthélémy; constructed their own Community and Recreational Center; celebrated Bastille Day and Father's Day; and organized a Fishermen's Cooperative.

They built their picturesque Frenchtown St. Anne's Church, and, in a lush setting of trees and flowers, Northside Frenchmen lovingly created their charming little Mafolie Church and Shrine, Our Lady of Perpetual Help.

Even while preserving their roots, the French slowly reached out to assume important roles in St. Thomas: commercial and mercantile business, building trades, political affairs, and successfully ran for the Legislature. In the 80s, the Senate had two members of French descent: Lorraine Berry and Cain Magras.

•

Thirty years ago, older French ladies wore high-crowned straw hats and black dresses, like those worn in their native part of France. Mothers kept their small houses immaculate as a French boulangerie, tended tiny gems of gardens with miniature shrines, and taught basket weaving to the younger generation.

In the 50s and 60s, Frenchtown women also helped build the island's tourist industry with their woven baskets and hats, embroidery and other souvenirs.

With changing times and values, however, the younger generation is moving away from weaving, embroidery, fishing and farming. Such endeavors are hard work and not lucrative enough, so they educate themselves for banking, legal work, politics, and merchandising.

A few small private enterprises remain: French gardeners sell plants in Frenchtown, and until recently, a building the size of two telephone booths, opposite Normandie Bar, carried a sign "Harry's Cuts." Bright red and blue, accented with white, it was a barber shop. Cute as a button, it looked as if it belonged in Disneyland. I miss its gay, light-hearted touch.

Pauley and Gilligan's

Frenchtown has had its share of "characters." We found one a few years ago on a Sunday morning as we maneuvered around Frenchtown potholes on our way to Gilligan's Seaside Bar and Garden Café for our first breakfast there. Passing Normandie Bar, we noticed a round-faced, cherubic man standing near its open door wearing a hat decorated with a sailboat under full sail. The boat rested in a sea of purple bougainvillea and red hibiscus blossoms that supported an American flag.

A beer can in one hand, he chatted nonchalantly with a group of men. He could have been a Carnival spectator or a "hat party" participant. Yet there was no party and Carnival was months away. His fanciful headgear seemed a one-time joke.

The following Sunday we saw him again at the Normandie Bar. A towering creation, topped by a seaplane and nestled in bougainvillea and hibiscus teetered on his head. Afterward we saw him every Sunday, and he always wore a festive hat. Sometimes he wandered as far as Gilligan's. Once we saw him strolling blithely along Charlotte Amalie's waterfront. He looked as if he were promenading on the Champs Elysées.

Finally our curiosity needed satisfying. After several inquiries, we found out our hat-man's name was John Paul Greaux, well-liked and nicknamed "Pauley." We also learned he had been wearing his imaginative hats nearly 10 years and his sizable collection had started with Carnival. As the millinery creations grew more elaborate and not confined to Carnival, they became his trademark.

Once for Bastille Day, however, he wore a snappy neck scarf and an elegant cowboy hat encircled with a white ribbon hatband. No floral arrangement. Employed by Avery's Boat House, Pauley sometimes raced with Dick Avery on sailboats.

Chart House Restaurant, formerly Villa Olga

Greaux always smiled pleasantly at passersby and looked as if he was having the time of his life. From what we were told, he did indeed enjoy life and was part of what makes Cha-Cha Town colorful and unique.

We stopped seeing Pauley because Gilligan's closed, and we had to seek another restaurant for Sunday morning breakfast. The demise of island eating places ranks with the night moth death rate.

Our Sunday morning breakfast ritual takes explaining. When the Inn at Mandahl closed in 1986, we had to find—after 15 years—a new place for eating our Sunday morning banana pancakes. Not as easy as it sounds, since we prefer to eat between nine-thirty and ten and on Sundays most island restaurants open around noon for Sunday Brunch.

After two months, we found Gilligan's in Frenchtown on the gallery of Villa Olga Hotel, popular with Stateside holidaying scuba divers. Now it's all spruced up and called the West Indies Inn. It also caters to divers, and Joe Vogel, owner of our oldest diving company, takes people out on dive trips.

Gilligan's offered the Somerset Maugham-tropical-island atmosphere of St. Thomas 25 years ago when two traffic lights directed traffic and people rode donkeys to town. The restaurant might run out of bottled gas, limiting the menu, or champagne, limiting our Mimosas. Sometimes service was slow, but everyone remained relaxed. Besides, Al could ogle the mermaids with beautiful legs as they carried skin diving gear to the sea.

An itinerant organ player, Vance, who hauled a loudspeaker system and mini-organ around in his car, played for the hungry. Yet, to us, Gilligan's star attraction was Crosby, a Golden Retriever belonging to owner Cathy.

Crosby wandered around, wagging his tail and holding a teddy bear in his mouth, hoping for a tug-of-war. If he liked you, he collected coconuts to lay at your feet. His mistress often bought him snuggly stuffed animals. He promptly plucked off tail, ears and bows. Crosby loved everybody, and everybody loved him, so his streak for "stuffed animal" mayhem remained an enigma.

With Gilligan's and Crosby gone, we also lost Pauley and his hats. We settled for a green parrot named "Jerry" at Magens Point Resort Hotel's Green Parrot Restaurant, within a mango's toss of where we live. This meant (horrors!) moving Sunday breakfast to ten-thirty. Still it is a good compromise, and their banana pancakes are delicious.

•

St. Thomas needs Cha-Cha Town. It brings a special *joie de vivre* to the island that would not be here if those French immigrants from St. Barths had not set sail for Paradise long ago. With great sadness we read of Pauley's death in January 1990. Though we never met him, he represented to us the spirited individuality of our picturesque Frenchtown community.

Vive la France!

CHAPTER 12

CASTLES AND OTHER PLACES

EDITOR'S NOTE: In this chapter, June gives us vivid descriptions of selected St. Thomas' unique and/or magnificent homes. These are all private homes. **None of them are open to the public,** *and therefore we have not located them on our maps. However, we are including this chapter because a description of St. Thomas and her history would not be complete without knowledge about these unusual homes. You'll understand better how this island got to be the way it is after June takes you to each of these private homes.*

Paradise should have a castle. So, of course, St. Thomas has one. A magnificent one.

Louisenhoj Castle

Called "Louisenhoj Castle," or sometimes "Fairchild's Castle" after the man who built it, the structure is made of island rocks combined with red or yellow bricks. It resembles south France's small medieval châteaux rather than the royal palaces of creamy quarried stone in the Loire Valley.

Nestled among tall trees on the spine of a mountain adjoining the Mafolie area, Louisenhoj's towers overlook the Caribbean Sea and Charlotte Amalie to the south and the Atlantic Ocean and Magens Bay to the north.

In 1918, financier Arthur S. Fairchild, after culling ideas from castles he had seen in Italy, began building his own Italian *castello* on the remains of a 17th century plantation Great House, called "Louisenhoj." More than three dozen Italian craftsmen crossed the ocean to work with and teach native St. Thomians and local Frenchmen the art of building such an intricate edifice. Fairchild lived in the castle during its construction, and throughout his life travelled the world in search of rare treasures to enrich Louisenhoj's interior and exterior. He kept adding rooms until he died in 1951.

Certain walls contain prehistoric, medieval, and historic stones, collected on Fairchild's travels or presented to him by friends. He carefully catalogued each one. The catalogue remains at Louisenhoj, and Sir Charles Carpenter Batchelder, present owner of the castle, has added several notable pieces to Louisenhoj's unique "wall collection" of venerable fragments of history.

Louisenhoj means "Louise's hilltop" in Danish and was named for Danish Queen Louise, wife of King Christian V, and Louise Magens, wife of Harbormaster Magens, appointed by the King. When the King and Queen visited St. Thomas in the late 1600s, the Queen fell in love with the plantation Great House. Magens—for whom Magens Bay is named—decided to call it Louisenhoj to honor both women.

At the time we moved to St. Thomas, the Joseph Green family occupied Louisenhoj. Filled with Green family heirlooms, the castle offered an enchanting leap back in time. On one wall of the Greens' vaulted ceiling dining room, a Tibetan *thanka* (religious scroll) hung beside a 1732 grandfather clock.

Other cherished items included a wall display of 15th, 16th, and 17th century duelling pistols that a Turkish Sultan presented to Green's English ancestors, who served as British Ambassadors to Constantinople. A prized sword of the Sultan of Mysore, killed in 1799 by Lord Cornwallis—who surrendered to General Washington at Yorktown—also had a place of honor. In addition, because of his service in the British, Canadian, and American Navies, Green had an impressive array of plaques conferred on him by visiting naval captains.

A tournament suit of armor from the 1400s that belonged to a Green ancestor, stood near the castle entrance. Complete with a lady's favor around its neck, it looked as if it belonged to a member of King Arthur's Round Table. Affectionately called "Mortimer" by the Greens, it encouraged many witty remarks.

Joe and Vivien Green enjoyed sharing their fairy tale castle with friends and visitors. They entertained often during cocktail hour, using a roofed terrace and pavilion at the side of the castle. Paved with a geometric design of yellow bricks, once used to ballast ships, and pebbles washed smooth by the Caribbean, the terrace looks down on Charlotte Amalie and the harbor. Old spreading trees and well-tended gardens embrace the area and provide the perfect setting for relaxed conviviality.

Joe Green had a stroke in 1968. The difficulties of negotiating steps on various levels as well as numerous stairways caused the family to give up Louisenhoj and move into a home on one floor. If all the castle's steps and stairways were collected in one place, they would rival Rome's Spanish Steps.

Sir Charles Carpenter Batchelder, known to his St. Thomas friends as "Batch," acquired the castle February 1969. He immediately refurbished it with **his** family heirlooms: fine antique armoires and tables, regal chairs, and rare oil paintings.

In the dining room, he kept the Italian Victorian chairs, dining table and sideboard belonging to Fairchild. The room lacked proper lighting, so envoys shopped for and found, in a Philadelphia antique shop, a magnificent gold-leafed chandelier with a rococo foliage design. The size and shape of a small pine tree, it would look at home in Versailles. The elegance of the dining room, with its imposing elk antlers and oil paintings, warrants a silk rope across the doorway to preserve it old world aura.

On the west side of the dining room is a restored "cloister" with a lush garden patio. Containing Arabic and 7th-century Roman gravestones brought from Europe by Fairchild, this secluded spot offers the ambience of an Arabian Nights' hideaway. A small open room on its far side is called "The Morning Room," because the morning sun bathes it with golden light and makes it a cheerful place for breakfast.

Down the corridor, past huge Chinese Foo dogs, and in the base of the "great tower" is a small sitting room, the centuries old original room that became the nucleus of the castle. Its walls are stone, put together with beach sand, molasses, and donkey hair. In the olden days, everything for this room was created by hand. Now called "The Card Room," it is furnished with a bridge table, large T.V., comfortable dark brown velvet sofas, Oriental rugs, and pictures of Batch's family, highlighted by a Waterford chandelier.

Near this room is the castle's large, thick entrance door, painted shiny black, with knocker and studs painted gold. Striking. When you enter the spacious foyer, you are tempted to whisper. Similar to small, private Paris museums, exquisite collections of glass and porcelain are artistically arrange on étagères and glistening tables along foyer walls. A photographic portrait of Queen Elizabeth II, once a huge Christmas card sent to Batch direct from London, is a stellar attraction among the portraits. She seems at home there. Next to the Queen is a handsome photograph of Dame Margot Fontayne.

Louisenhoj Castle entrance, "Act of God Chapel" at top of stairs

An imaginative stained glass window deftly blends island and castle motifs with a family escutcheon. Created by Batchelder's niece, Cynthia du Pont Tobias, its glass casts colored sunbeams past a small hand-painted stone cat curled up on a velvet cushion that graces a miniature marble window seat. The cat looks so real you want to stroke it. The sunbeams continue across the gleaming tiled floor to the Great Hall entrance, lightly touching a suit of plate armor along the way. (Not the Greens' Mortimer.) This suit of armor, called "Arthur," is not a Batchelder heirloom.

Still I love its story.

The present master of the castle decided he should have a Mortimer for Louisenhoj. After much searching, he espied such a plate armor suit in the men's clothing department of a discount store. No, it was not looking for a cloth suit. It was being used to display the neckties that hung all over it.

Questioning revealed the suit of armor was an antique made in Toledo, Spain. The store's owner confessed he did not have the foggiest notion of what to do with it. Suits of armor were not a hot item. Since he did not want it and had a live prospect in hand, he soon set a reasonable price. Mission accomplished.

After some shipping problems, the knightly attire arrived at the castle in a box that resembled a coffin. When the delivery men unloaded it at the service entrance, the head man said: "Sir Charles, your suit of armor is finally here, but I don't think you'll want to wear it downtown."

Batch's chef-d'oeuvre is the Family Chapel, dedicated to all faiths and completed February 1978. A devastating storm in 1976 washed out a large hole near the castle entrance. The insurance company maintained the building was on a mountaintop, so could not be flooded, and since it was an "Act of God," no insurance money would be forthcoming. Consequently, Sir Charles used the hole to build a concrete foundation for what he calls his "Act of God Chapel." This lovely little chapel of stones and red brick looks as if it has always been part of the castle and a 16th century princess should be praying there. Waiting for her are kneeling cushions needlepointed by a close friend, Nat Norris (whose unusual Oriental house "Kaleidoscope" we will visit later).

Cynthia du Pont Tobias also created the chapel's spiritually pleasing stained glass windows, and friends contributed various religious artifacts. The peaceful atmosphere and seclusion offer a perfect environment for reflection and gentle thoughts.

Steps lead from the chapel to Italian gardens with fountains, Italian statuary (maidens in Grecian dress), and a Doric-columned pergola. Overlooking Magens Bay is "The Lookout," said to be the original "Drake's Seat," where the famous English buccaneer, Sir Francis Drake, spied on the sea lanes for vessels he could attack with his ship, *Golden Hind.*

The castle's large French doors on the north side open into Louisenhoj's 30- by 40-foot Great Hall. With its stately musician's gallery, the hall offers a dramatic setting, especially for concerts and festive occasions.

Drake's Seat has a tremendous overlook of Magens Bay

A memorable musical experience for me was listening to the Westminster Singers there for an Antilles School benefit concert. The dulcet voices in that palatial room—with dimly lighted wall sconces reflecting on crystal chandeliers, old portraits, and a pair of crossed swords—resounded like a celestial choir. The singers, graduates of Westminster College Choir in Princeton, New Jersey, have sung at Tanglewood and Spoleto Festivals. Each one is a professional musician and music teacher. All friends, they formed the group through mutual love of music and singing. Their repertoire included selections from long ago such as "O, Yes Has Any Found A Lad" to the more modern "Embraceable You."

In the castle's East Tower, beyond Great Hall and the dining room, near the kitchen, is a completely round room. Once divided in two and used for kitchen servants, the room has now chameleoned into a luxurious master bedroom suite, made comfortable with more antiques and easy chairs. Just outside is a gazebo in an attractive vegetable garden setting used for luncheons and small dinners.

As expected of a castle, Louisenhoj has two ghosts. They are inclined to float around on Sundays—undoubtedly their day off from other spirited adventures. Seen by Batch as well as house guests (one took a credible photograph to prove it), the ghosts are thought to be Arthur Fairchild and an Italian man, who, when alive, was Fairchild's "guiding spirit" in creating his Italian castle. Like all bona fide castles, Louisenhoj has a dungeon with slave chains—hear them clanking? It is used now for a liquor locker.

Another outbuilding, long ago a Danish kitchen, is a Treasure Room Museum. It contains two ancient iron-bound chests that cannot be opened without mangling them. One is alleged to have belonged to Bluebeard and the other one to Blackbeard. My money is on

Blackbeard's holding a bejewelled, female skeleton, one of his 14 wives whom he diabolically introduced to **his** Treasure Room. The game of speculation about the contents of the chests will continue until more ancient keys are found, an earthquake—or other natural disaster—solves the mystery.

Sir Charles has carried on the castle's tradition by keeping its character intact and sharing it with friends, island visitors, and civic organizations. An effective storyteller, he enjoys relating both historical facts and amusing stories about his castle.

I like one he tells about a lady house guest who was imparting her castle knowledge to a visitor. As they stood on The Belvedere (a north terrace), she fluttered her hand at the great expanse of water to the horizon and said, "From here you see the Atlantic Ocean and from the other side the Pacific." The dear lady was obviously "all at sea." A heated black swimming pool reposes here.

Charles Borton, who assists Batch with the monumental task of keeping Louisenhoj a show place, loves the old castle as much as its owner does. An authority on its history, he also enjoys relating amusing anecdotes as he guides visitors through its maze of rooms. Unfortunately, Louisenhoj Castle is not open to the public.

Lambert "Castle"

Because of Louisenhoj Castle, we have another castle. It came about because the late Stanford ("Casey") Lambert, owner of Lambert Laboratories (makers of "breathtaking" Listerine), was a friend of Arthur Fairchild. Seeing Fairchild's Castle aroused in him a desire for his own castle, and he went about building one near Cowpet Bay.

Our second castle compares in no way to Louisenhoj. Constructed more as a whimsy, it looms beside the sea on a rocky promontory and looks like what it finally became—a crenelated mammoth white elephant.

When in residence, Lambert adhered to an afternoon ritual that attracted a good bit of attention. At five o'clock, as the castle's American flag was lowered, he shot off an antique cannon, aiming at a rock in the middle of his private bay. He had read this was an old castle custom, and he was for keeping such formalities alive.

Lambert had various idiosyncrasies. Another causing wide comment was his insistence that women house guests wear high-heeled, black patent leather shoes, not too comfortable on sandy and cobblestoned beaches, or tripping up and down the castle's steps. It was also rumored he told his house guests what presents to bring when they came for house parties.

After using the castle a few years for elaborate entertainment, Lambert lost interest. He died shortly after. Only there once, we did not find it a "cozy" place. The castle was sold and became a guest house, then later a private home.

Several private homes, not in the castle category, but of historical or highly original architectural interest have, over the years, become our "one-of-a-kind" favorites. None of these homes are open to the public. Following are our top winners.

Canaan

"Canaan," which belonged to the Herbert McConnells, is especially rich in history. Once a sugar estate called "Canaan and Sherpen Jewel," and hidden in thick vegetation, it overlooks Magens Bay. According to records, it is well over 200 years old and, in 1733, had a working sugar mill.

In 1805, 35 acres of sugar crop and 115 acres of bush composed the property. Male Negro plantation workers and female slaves not doing cultivation totaled about 60. Its owner then, named Westerman, lived abroad and had a white manager.

The plantation had several owners before Arthur Fairchild acquired the present 36 acres in the 20s. In 1940, Mr. and Mrs. Havercamp bought Canaan and converted the manager's house into today's attractive residence. They also replaced the privy with two bathrooms. Electricity was installed in 1953, shortly before the Herbert McConnells purchased the property.

Noteworthy architectural features include a tray ceiling in the living room and typical Danish squares that decorate corners of doors and windows. A concealed trap door in one bedroom leads to a hurricane shelter, and small glass peepholes in the heavy outside shutters are still usable when the shutters are closed against tropical storms. Tiles on a spacious, flower-laden terrace on the north side of the house came from the old St.

Goats are a constant hazard on St. Thomas' narrow roads

Thomas Hotel Italia, torn down many years ago.

A complete set of prints of town and harbor scenes of the three Virgin Islands by lithographer C. E. Baerentzen of Copenhagen, Denmark, decorate living room walls. Inspired by oil paintings of daguerreotypes, each print is by a different artist: two each of St. Thomas, St John, and St. Croix. The series, popular in the mid-1800s, became known as "the Baerentzen prints." Copies may be purchased now at A. H. Riise's Art Gallery or the Fort Christian Museum Gift Shop. The prints at Canaan are augmented by contemporary island artists and a brass alms dish depicting "Return from Canaan." Joe Green found the alms dish at an auction in England.

As was the custom of the day, the kitchen with 19-inch thick walls is not attached to the house. This kept any kitchen fires from spreading to the main residence. The kitchen is separated from the living room by a wide passageway. In past times, owners sprayed the "cooler" with water to preserve foods such as eggs and butter. A masonry oven for baking bread is in the back part of the kitchen, and two little chimneys remain for the stove and oven. Generations of soot darken their inner walls.

On the left of Canaan's driveway is the old horse mill, once driven by oxen or mules. Syrup flowed into a trough and onto large containers, called "coppers" in the boiler house. Its ruins still stand. Two of the coppers are now used for garden planters.

Remnants of a road below the boiler house descend to Magens Bay, and a narrow path leads to a spring. Cattle were driven this way for water, and even during Arthur Fairchild's time, water was brought from the spring to make cement floors in the dwelling house. Now the spring is dry.

Canaan's slave quarters are believed to have been located on the property where small foundations and bits of pottery were found. A McConnell miniature outdoor museum preserved a whale harpoon, branding iron, old working tools, pieces of pottery, and other plantation relics.

Some evidence indicates that Henri Christophe spent a brief time at Canaan as a slave. He later became King of Haiti and built one of the world's wonders, La Citadelle near Cap Haitien. Louisenhoj Castle has an original cannon ball from Haiti's Citadelle installed on the South Terrace parapet.

I cannot leave Canaan without emphasizing its unusual and attractive grounds. Huge lichen-covered boulders form an effective background for giant-size rock gardens. Tall mahogany and gnarled old turpentine trees, supporting "Dancing Lady" and other orchids, shade the boulders, driveway and low, one-story house. A Japanese garden with ponds of water lillies, a stone Japanese lantern and temple dogs blend agreeably with the veritable botanical garden. Colorful tropical flowers and plants, clinging to boulders, create the illusion of a "Midsummer's Night Dream" setting.

The Venus Pillar

Another house, built by Arthur and Judi Witty in Mafolie, is of unusual historic interest. Not because of age, but because this gracious and beautiful home has a lovely large tree-shaded terrace built around the Venus Pillar. The Pillar marks the site of the 1882 Brazilian astronomical expedition in St. Thomas to observe that year's transit of Venus.

Since transits of Venus are rare, no living astronomer had viewed the remarkable spectacle of the small black disk (with a diameter of about 1–30 of the sun) move slowly westward across the sun's brilliant face. During the present century, there will be no Venus transit. The phenomenon only occurs every 243 years, at intervals of 105 ½, 8, 121½ and 8 years. In **exactly** 243 years, Venus completes 395 revolutions, or approximately 13 revolutions in eight years. Consequently, for many centuries, there have only been four transits of Venus.

I do not understand a whit of this, but here goes the explanation, courtesy of the St. Thomas Historical Trust:

The reason for this rarity is the 3.4 degree inclination of the Venus orbit to the earth's orbit. Venus at inferior conjunction usually passes well north or south of the sun's disk. A transit can occur, however, only when both planets arrive almost simultaneously at the intersection line of their orbit planes. Since the invention of the telescope, transits of Venus have occurred in 1631, 1761, 1769, 1874, and 1882. The next will occur in 2004 and 2012.

The 1882 Brazilian expedition to St. Thomas was one of a coordinated international effort, begun during the 1874 transit. The Brazilians established their station on the heights above Charlotte Amalie because this site has an exceptional field of view. Observations and calculations were made by the team, and a report on the expedition and its results was published by the Imperial Observatory of Rio de Janeiro in 1887.

The Venus Pillar marking the site of observation is a 13.5-foot high obelisk with a pyramid cap, constructed of rubble masonry with a find sand stucco. The original instrument station, a 31″ by 29.5″ marble tablet with four stabilizing holes, has been placed on the north face of the obelisk and contains an inscription of the event.

An expedition from Denmark also participated, but they packed up and went home after the transit. The Brazilians stayed on, relaxing and enjoying the social life of St. Thomas while they built their obelisk. What else can you expect from a country that produced Carmen Miranda? Bravo Brazil!

Star Gazing

St. Thomas is a box seat for viewing such sky extravaganzas. Al and I saw Halley's Comet from the swimming pool's corner. It juts out from the mountain like a ship's prow. Having seen the comet as a small boy, Al wanted to be one of few people alive who could say he had seen it twice.

One night when the comet was supposedly visible from St. Thomas, we went out about 4:30 a.m. and searched the sky. I finally found it with binoculars, but once we knew its location, we could see it without them. It was an exciting moment, reminiscent of our first glimpse of Sputnik one cold, wintery night from the middle of iced-over Lake Mendota in Madison, Wisconsin. Makes you feel pretty insignificant, but still elated to witness such a "heavenly event."

Kaleidoscope

"Kaleidoscope means 'beautiful views with ever-changing colors,' " claims Nat Norris, owner and creator of "Kaleidoscope," the St. Thomas house he and Ed Schoenhardt call home six months of the year. No name could be more appropriate. People who do not know Nat and Ed, however, call the residence "the Oriental House with the Torii Gate."

Located in our Crown Mountain rain forest, the house is embowered with a jungle of tall Royal Palms, giant Norfolk Island Pines, African Tulip trees, and a cornucopia of flowers from red and yellow Heliconia and pink Anthurium to fragrant white-flowered Stephanotis. They paint an

Photo by Susan Houston

Nat Norris' home 'Kaleidoscope" on Crown Mountain Road. Shows Torii Gate entrance, Japanese lily pond and bridge, and part of house.

effective foreground before your gaze sweeps across lush green woodlands and valleys to the Atlantic ocean's Scotch Cap, Cricket, and Cockroach islands.

Nat, who has spent his life painstakingly restoring authentic Newport gambrel-roofed houses, decided he wanted something different for his winter home in St. Thomas. How different? Oriental. You cannot get farther away from 18th century gambrel roofs than that. Not one to let mushrooms grow under his feet, Nat engaged architect David Ping Chung Chang, graduate of the prestigious Princeton Architectural School, as architect. Started in 1962 and finished in 1966, the house could be transplanted to Japan, and anyone would think it had grown there.

During the four-year gestation period, Nat made two trips around the world to buy Japanese garden seats and cranes, stone lanterns, exotic door handles, bronze finials for the Japanese bridge and gallery railing, and roof tiles copied from Japanese temples.

For three years, he also spent his yearly six months in St. Thomas living in a tent on the property and working with construction people and his contractor, St. Thomian Albert Joseph, to ascertain roof pitch, overhang, gutters needed for rain run-off, etcetera. With supplies constantly arriving, Nat needed a post office box. Because he lived in a tent, the Postmaster refused to give him one. Tactful persuasion finally convinced the man Nat was as reliable in his tent as he would be in his house.

The finished Kaleidoscope is a masterpiece. With well over 2000 square feet on **one level**, the structure is a miracle for mountainous St. Thomas. Terrazzo floors throughout are part of the architect's will to make the house earthquake and hurricane proof. Though everything can be closed up against nature's rampages, walls and doors also open completely to the usual St. Thomas sun and soft breezes.

The Torii Gate and Moon Gate, along with the zigzag approach—to keep evil spirits away—of the Monet Japanese bridge, authentically carry out a Japanese motif. "Happy life" and "long life" symbols abound, and well-placed little ponds add beauty and visual interest. Some ponds have water as well as carp, others have only pebbles, used by Japanese gardeners to simulate water.

Just inside Kaleidoscope's main entrance are two large pieces of highly polished Bamboo inscribed with Japanese characters in a soft green. Purchased in Macau, one reads "Birds and flowers are lovers in this garden," and the other "Lakes and mountains make fabulous views."

Tinkling wind chimes, hanging baskets of begonias and ferns, Imari bowls, coolie hats, paper lanterns, temple dogs, and Japanese screens make one feel transported to Kyoto.

The interior *pièce de résistance* though, is the "conversation pit," a large rectangular sunken section of the living room that must be stepped into via couches lining the complete rectangle. No stairsteps. No way out. Except to scale a couch. You have to stay there and TALK. I think that makes it a good conversation *pièce*.

A low rectangular table in the pit's center is—once you manage to get yourself and tray inside—just the right height to make the area a great spot for buffet suppers. You are completely isolated from conversation "crashers," so uninterrupted talk ripples as merrily as a bubbling spring. Unless no one else is agile enough to join you.

Nat and Ed use the pit for naps. Handsome Oriental pillows in needlepoint, 20 in all made by Nat, are strewn about and a blanket or two are within reach. A perfect place for stretching out. You cannot fall off the mountain.

Nat once brought a bag full of "coqui" frogs from Puerto Rico. They croak, "Ko-Kee—Ko-kee—." A lovely sound. Nat gave us one for Hidden Hill, and it is still there "ko-keeing" with all its heart. The tiny frogs are everywhere in that area now. Torrential rains from a sizable storm carried them down from Nat's rain forest and distributed them afar. God's way of sharing the wealth. Once you hear or see one of the big-eyed dainty frogs, you will be hooked.

Smiths'-On-The-Rocks

One of St. Thomas' most dramatically situated homes belongs to artist Ira Smith. Rambling over a rocky point of land high above the Caribbean, the house is sheltered on the land side by a grove of trees. On the other side, gardens and terraces cascade down cliffs to the breaking sea.

Ira designed the house and supervised its construction during 1963. The modest, but attractive entryway is deceiving. Basically a carport, it has a 6-foot stone wall on one side that is a continuation of the driveway wall and extends into the house. A simple planter of greenery is along the opposite wall.

The two walls are separated by a masonry one with an artistic arrangement of small rectangular pieces of chartreuse or blue pebbled glass. The main entrance is in this wall—a plain, heavy door studded with brass ornaments from Morocco and Spain. A Moroccan brass "Hand of Fatima" knocker and a spray of metal bells hanging beside the door announce guests.

Although not your run-of-the-mill entrance, it still does not prepare you for the interior. When the door in what Ira calls "the unimposing façade" is opened, you step into an indoor-outdoor world that mixes nature and aesthetic wizardry with surprising dexterity.

A strategically placed room divider—with a potpourri of Ira's paintings on the entry side and on the other a group of his botanical paintings of orchids—separates the entrance from an expansive covered area open to breezes on two sides. To the left is a luxuriant Japanese garden inside a low stone wall and backed by the driveway's six-foot stone wall. Between wall and ceiling, open space creates a lush tropical painting.

Beyond, suspended concrete slab steps lead to a stone-like shelf that extends over an ornamental pond where silvery carp idle. The shelf serves as entrance to two bedrooms and baths. Earthen planters filled with trailing Peperomia swing above it, and underneath is an Indian frieze of exotic Hindu figures. You have the sensation of being in another world.

Though the two bedrooms are enclosed, the space beside them is not. There, the roofed center of the house is open to the rocky cliffs and sea horizon. Next, an enclosed living room looks out to the Caribbean through floor to ceiling walls of glass. This inviting room is a showcase of whimsy and objets d'art, many pieces collected during world travels.

A sampling starts with a full-sized carousel horse and Ira's late wife's collection of glass and ceramic frogs. It ends with two Japanese Tonsu chests and a spectacular antique church mirror from Lima, Peru. Ira carried the mirror in his lap on the flight home. A sunburst of gold and mirrors with sharp pointed ends, the work of art is about two feet square. It must have been as comforable as carrying an aroused porcupine. Yet what a treasure. Although a large square mirror fills this one's center, the dazzling frames are mostly used in Peruvian churches for religious paintings.

Behind the living room is a large combination kitchen and office, a dressing room and bath, and an orchidarium. The orchids come from parts of the world with climates similar to St. Thomas: Vandas from South East Asia and Dendrobiums from there and Hawaii. Since temperature variation near the shore is minimal (unlike ours in the mountains), Ira also selects orchids that do not require temperature change.

Caged Budgerigars—a kind of Australian parakeet—serve as alarms for anything threatening the orchidarium. Looking out beyond the orchids, one may see large iguanas high in the trees, eating blossoms from

Photo by Susan Houston

Ira Smith's home, showing pool and entrance to bedrooms.
This is a huge central room that opens out to a view of the sea.

Pink Cedars. A nice prehistoric touch. The trees are not really "cedars," and neither is our official island tree, the Yellow Cedar.

Next to the orchidarium is Ira's studio. Once a small concrete building that housed a U.S. Corps of Engineers' searchlight (they wheeled it out nightly to search for German ships during World War II), it was the only solid structure on the property when the Smiths bought the land. Naturally Ira incorporated it into the house.

The door to the studio is a work of art that arranges colorfully painted half-turnings in an eye-catching design. A nearby antique commode with a shell decorated mirror (another Ira Smith creation) picks up the door colors.

Now we have come full circle and are back at the entrance door. All previously mentioned rooms cluster around the large indoor-outdoor center like perimeter jewels in a brooch. Any walls there are filled with paintings and accented with living plants. A collection of Baerentzen prints includes one by Danish artist Fritz Melbye, Pissarro's mentor. Memorabilia abounds, but with no feeling of clutter.

Free form pieces of green carpeting, scattered on the concrete and stone floor, give the impression of grass under the tables with chairs and the comfortable couches. This informal, live-in expanse reaches out hospitably to welcome you and make you feel at home. It succeeds. Only an unerring artist's eye could blend everything so artistically.

A ship's weathered figurehead—created by Ira—curves out from the wall next to the bedrooms. He thought one would look "right" there. It does. Against another wall a Victorian hat rack holds an assortment of hats, including plain and Carnival straw creations and a black sombrero from a Mexican Mariachi band. A jaunty touch. "Eclectic" describes Ira's house.

Now to the swimming pool. Above the house on a rise of rocks, the pool accommodates swimmers who do not want to climb stairs to swim in the ocean. When the Smiths built the house, they preferred the sea, but with time, the convenience of a nearby pool became apparent, so they built one. On the pool's far side hangs another Ira Smith art work, a single rectangular mosaic of a colorful fish. Two lavish dressing rooms with baths, and a covered pavilion that looks out to the sea, contribute to the pampering of guests. From this vantage point you can see the path Ira created amid the weather-sculptured boulders that stand like sentinels along the stony seashore. He planned it so guests and family could enjoy walking beside the water or swimming among the rocks. Guests who want "to be alone" use the path to reach a foliage-concealed Robinson Crusoe lean-to on the beach.

We leave this extraordinary home, featured in House and Garden, with the Smiths' crowning touch. They named it "Smiths'-On-The-Rocks."

Flag Hill House

Flag Hill House, the eyrie home of Nick and Maxine Carter for 30 years, has always been an island showplace. Not because it is a stately, luxurious mansion, but because it is a "real" island house, traditional West Indian style, and perfect for island living.

Maxine explains it best. "Everything is open. We simply lived under a roof," she says, adding, "Beauty was all around us, and we wanted to capture it, so the house was secondary—a frame for all of Flag Hill's tropical beauty." That is it in a cashew shell.

Jolting along on donkeys, Maxine and Nick found their property in the 50s by following a native guide as he machete-hacked a trail through heavy underbrush to Flag Hill's summit. Nick had simply pointed to its crown and told the man, "I want to see the view from up there."

Since Nick's death, Maxine treasures the memories of those days when St. Thomas was an untouched, relaxed island, and everybody knew everyone else. We treasure those days, too, when you could park on Main Street, leave your car open and filled with packages, and no one would touch a thing. That time is gone forever, however, and there is no sense in crying over spilled Paradise.

Nick was not a man to dilly-dally. Once they saw the view, the property was soon theirs, and they designed and built the house in 1957.

We have known Flag Hill House since 1963. The first time we climbed its straight-up road in a pink and white striped jeep, I refused to ride the final 200 yards. Terrified and certain the jeep would back-flip, I got out and walked. The driveway at the top appeared to end with a suicide cliff. Al drove on. When I reached the top, they were all laughing at me. Still my heart was back where it belonged, and I was overjoyed to see the house was on flat ground and not hanging from a rock.

As I walked into the delightful top-of-the-world living room, past the sunken bar and family room with handsome stone support walls, tiled floors, and inviting couches, I had an exhilarating sensation of space. Everything **was** open. Reaching the huge covered gallery with a colorful fabric ceiling and matching curtains that could be closed against rain, I stood spellbound. I knew then the true meaning of the word "breathtaking."

The vista swept across the harbor's Hassel Island and Water Island to Charlotte Amalie's waterfront. There, white houses with red roofs rose in cake layers up the sides of the mountain chain that ripples from Louisenhoj Castle to the western tip of St. Thomas. Harbor waters glistened azure blue.

Looking down from a height of well over 800 feet made me feel like Zeus. As many times as I have been in that house, I always go first to the gallery to see if the view is still there. To me, it is the most spectacular one from that side of the island. Before Hong Kong decided to have a skyscraper competition, the view from Kowloon to Hong Kong Island looked very much like this spectacular view from Flag Hill House. I hope St. Thomas does not go the skyscraper route to accommodate our fast growing population.

Most walls of Flag Hill House are folding doors, only closed during tropical storms. Since we have known it, a new dining room and garden terrace have been added, and the tea house glass-enclosed.

The tea house, with a panoramic view of the island's south and east side, St. Croix, and St. John, was a favorite breakfast spot for the Carters. Removed from the main house, this cozy place of seclusion was also enjoyed by house guests. Its view any other place would be a show-stopper, but it has to take back seat to the harbor view.

To get to the tea house one must walk through the garden terrace. Fringed umbrellas shade white wrought iron tables and chairs in a setting of magnificent old trees and low stone walls that hold back a profusion of flowers—red, yellow, pink and white. Flowing out from the dining room and living room, the garden terrace seems to be the catalyst that makes Flag Hill House a lavish floral tiara crowning Flag Hill. A toast to Flora, the Roman goddess of flowers!

•

The selection of these last five houses will cause comment, and I will be told about all the prized ones I missed. I do not question that. This chapter is not about St. Thomas houses. It is about St. Thomas' "one-of-a-kind" houses we have known for more than 20 years.

Photo by Susan Houston

Ira Smith with carrousel horse in his glass-enclosed living room

CHAPTER 13

HASSEL ISLAND

Our Charlotte Amalie harbor islands are Water island and Hassel Island. Water Island, although used sometimes in the past for military purposes, is now residential, but the greater part of mile-long Hassel Island belongs to the National Park Service and all of the island is on the National Register of Historic Places.

No public transportation to Hassel Island is available at present, but *The Reefer*, a 26-passenger boat at Frenchman's Reef's Sea Adventures Dock, will transport passengers between Frenchman's Reef and Hassel Island for $5 round trip. *The Reefer* shuttles from the Hotel to Charlotte Amalie's waterfront on a regular schedule and passes Hassel Island each way, making spontaneous or planned trips easy. The boat will even take you to Hassel Island's Careening Cove. Like a kind of water activities smorgasbord, Sea Adventures offers a varied menu: sunset cocktail cruises, scuba diving and sailing, harbor tours, day trips to St. John and the British Virgin Islands. Their approach is personal and flexible.

Big plans are underway by the Park Service to develop Hassel Island's commercial and maritime history as a tourist attraction. Cotton and tobacco were cultivated on the island in the 1600s, but the growth of steamship traffic between Europe and the Caribbean turned it into a coaling and ship-repair-yards station during the 1800s until the mid-1900s. First, the ruins of Creque's Marine Railway Complex across the water from Frenchtown will be freshened up. Built in the 1860s, Creque's was used until the 1960s to haul up boats for repair. Remains of a steam engine, two 200-foot railways, a 30-foot cradle and winch, repair shop, and a 200-foot pier are still there.

Shortly after Hurricane Hugo, trails to Hassel Island's Fort Willoughby at the St. Thomas Harbor entrance and to Cowell Battery above were cleared of debris and readied for tourists. The Battery, built by the British

View from Skyline Drive. Three cruise ships at West Indian Dock, one waiting outside. Hassel Island in foreground, Water Island behind it.

for military use in the early 1800s, tops a 267-foot hill. Eventually converted into a signal station, Cowell Battery provided information for boats entering the harbor until the 1960s and today is frequently referred to as "Signal Hill." The southernmost tip of Hassell Island is known as Cowell Point.

Fort Willoughby, constructed by the Danes in 1779 and called Prince Frederik Battery, was taken over by the British during the Napoleonic Wars (1801-2) and renamed Fort Willoughby. Now in ruins, visitors can still identify a guardhouse, storage rooms, gun platform, and sleeping quarters.

Not far from Fort Willoughby along the shore is Garrison House, a ruin with pillared dignity, erected during the 1807–1815 British Occupation.

North of Garrison House on the shore is Palm Grove, an inviting old Indian camp site. The Park Service plans to put a picnic area in this idyllic spot for tourist and local "powwows."

Careening Cove is the next historic spot as one continues in the direction of Charlotte Amalie. A Danish and Virgin Island venture, Broensted and Company, bought the cove area in the 1870s and built a coaling wharf, warehouses, and offices. They operated there until 1907, when the St. Thomas Dock, Engineering and Coaling Company acquired the business and kept it until after World War I. At the cove's entrance on the left are what once were armed forces barracks. Around two dozen private residents who depend on their own boats for transportation live along the shore of the cove and sometimes occupy parts of the barracks.

Across the cove to the right are shells of two washed-out buildings left over from the Hamburg-American Line's coaling station. The company managed the station after they started a St. Thomas business in 1873 and built warehouses and offices at Careening Cove. Ruins of the warehouses and railway remain.

Beyond Careening Cove are a couple of sizable private homes before the modern Royal Mail Inn—closed in the 1970s—comes into view. The name came from the Royal Mail Steam Packet Company that ran between Europe and the Caribbean and opened a steamship transfer station there in 1841. The company built rain catchments, cisterns, wharves, offices, and warehouses and functioned on the island until 1865.

Shipley's Guardhouse and Battery, constructed in 1802 on the 202-foot hill above Creque's Marine Railway Complex, is one of few Napoleonic forts built on U.S. territory.

Our present day West Indian Company began life in 1903 on Hassel Island as the East Asiatic Company and added a coaling station in 1905. Later they started the Danish West Indian Company in Havensight, but eventually dropped "Danish" from their name. The beautiful pristine-white building on the hill behind Havensight Mall dates back to colonial times and is the company's headquarters.

Besides its rich historical interest, an extra bonus in visiting Hassel Island is the magnificent view of Charlotte Amalie. You might even see a prehistoric-looking iguana. They are protected there. Check with the Park Service on public transportation to Hassel Island. It might be available when you next visit St. Thomas.

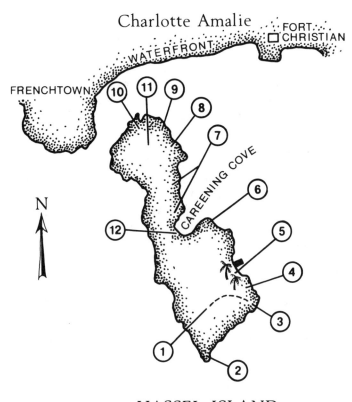

HASSEL ISLAND

Legend — Hassel Island

1. Cowell Battery — elevation 267 feet
2. Cowell Point
3. Fort Willoughby
4. Garrison House
5. Palm Grove
6. Careening Cove armed forces barracks from the past
7. Ruins of two Hamburg-American Line buildings
8. East Asiatic Company, today the West Indian Company
9. Royal Mail Inn
10. Creque's Marine Railway Complex
11. Shipley's Guardhouse and Battery — elevation 202 feet
12. Broensted and Company Coaling Station, later
    St. Thomas Dock, Engineering and Coaling Company

PART THREE: INSIDE INFORMATION

CHAPTER 14

ACTION IN THE GREEN BARN

After a gun search, a rafter-ringing rendition of "God Save the Queen"—the British National Anthem—opened the January 1985 session of our 16th Unicameral Virgin Islands Legislature.

The National Black Anthem followed and gave way to the Virgin Islands Anthem, all sung by the Charlotte Amalie High School choir. The Anthems ended with "The Star-Spangled Banner," played by the Charlotte Amalie High School Band. Al and I wondered if the islands had seceded during the night. Enlightenment came eventually. The presence of an official from Tortola, our closest British island neighbor, sparked the British National Anthem. The Anthem order afterwards still puzzles me and other citizens of the American Virgin Islands.

The Legislature's "operetta" opening session in the Senate Building—frequently called "The Green Barn," since the conduct of the august body began to deteriorate in the 70s—took place the same day The Daily News used their large editorial box to convey their "Good Riddance" evaluation of the 15th Legislature. They didn't think much of the goings on in the 16th or the 17th Legislatures either.

Our Virgin Islands are governed by a Governor and Lt. Governor, elected by popular vote and a unicameral legislature of 15 Senators. Seven Senators are from St. Thomas, seven from St. Croix, and one at large who must be a resident of St. John. The Governor appoints a commissioner to head each service department. These appointments are subject to approval by the Legislature, as are the Governor's budgets.

Funds that the government needs are raised by property taxes, income tax, and excise taxes on some items. Virgin Islanders pay regular USA income taxes at the same rates as other USA citizens, but all of these income taxes are remanded to the Virgin Islands government. There is no additional income tax levied by the Virgin Islands government. Tourists like our duty-free shopping. Deficits and capital improvements are financed by the sale of bonds. There is no constitutional requirement for a balanced budget.

The Governor's mansion and offices are located in the Government House described in Chapter 10. The Governor also has a residence and offices on St. Croix. The Legislature operates from the Green Barn, also described in Chapter 10.

The American Virgin Islands are a Territory of the United States. We elect one delegate to Congress, currently Ron de Lugo. He serves on congressional committees, but has no vote on bills before the House of Representatives. We cannot vote in national elections for President and Vice

President. The Virgin Islands does have voting representation at both the Republican and Democratic national conventions.

On occasion, there has been praiseworthy excellence in our Senate. One example was Senate President Ruby Rouss from St. Croix, once a Sergeant in the U.S. Army, who was elected to her office at the start of the 17th Legislature. After only two months in office, she was deposed by the defection of two senators to the seven-member minority. This transformed the minority into a nine-member majority that immediately ousted Senator Rouss from the Presidency.

The Daily News was highly critical of this disputable maneuver. In an editorial defending her, the newspaper said:

"Senate President Ruby Rouss can be quarrelsome and contentious. But she also can be charming and witty. She can be a sharp-tongued master sergeant or she can coat her gracious and well-chosen words with honey. But there are some constants about Ruby Rouss. She is a person of integrity, morality, and honor. She is a no-nonsense administrator. She does not condone fraud or waste, and she draws the line on frivolous spending."

The editorial went on to say:

"It may be in their selfish interest to switch allegiances. By bolting, they may get the fancy cars, extra employees, questionable contracts and costly rental space that Rouss has refused—and correctly so—to approve for them. But it is not in the best interest of the people of these islands to have an upheaval in our Legislature . . . to have a new Senate president two

"Green Barn," home of the Virgin Islands Legislature. See also photo on page 67

145

months into the 17th Legislature's term of office . . . to have Senators switch committee chairmanships and offices and assignments. This is a time for stability, progress and common sense . . ."

The action of the two renegade Senators really "tore up the pea patch." Fusillades of condemnation exploded like July 4th fireworks from all sides.

Unfortunately, Senator Rouss had a stroke in the fall of 1987 and was hospitalized until she died in May of 1988. The death of this feisty woman caused both friends and enemies to mourn. She had a unique place in the community. No one will ever be able to replace her. Senator Alicia "Chucky" Hansen offered a resolution to honor her and "her passionate drive to help the 'little' man, to give a boost to those in need." The resolution passed unanimously.

Our delegate to congress, Ron de Lugo, is trying to devise a plan to eliminate such upheavals in future Legislatures; perhaps by letting the people choose the Senate President in general elections. He said the current system in which senators use their support for a Senate President as a bargaining tool to wrangle committees and perks "leaves the people of the territory at the mercy of the scoundrels in the Legislature."

A bill our present Governor Alexander Farrelly intends to send to the Legislature will "Limit government holidays to those recognized by the Federal Government," a reduction from 23 to 10. It has as much chance getting off the ground as a 10-ton boulder. We can hardly wait to hear the pussy-footing around that one when it reaches the Senate floor.

Another of Farrelly's bills that has little chance is: "Impose a uniform pay scale throughout government."

One out of three Virgin Islanders works for the government—a higher percentage than any of the 50 States.

The Legislature's "goings on" are a never-ending source of amazement—and amusement. Linda Smith Palmer, a resident of St. John, created a Daily News cartoon strip called "Max." A mischievous mongoose, Max angers, shocks, or delights with bull's-eye remarks that only a mongoose would dare voice. In 1987, when the Senate discussed raising salaries from $35,000 to $55,000 a year, Max's mongoose friend asked:

"Should the government pay our Senators $55,000 a year?"

"Who else would pay them that much?" Max asked.

After the bill finally passed, Max said: "Our senators will be getting $55,000 a year."

"I just read Bill Cosby makes $57 million a year," his friend said.

The next panel showed Bill Cosby with a speech balloon over his head saying: "Yeah . . .but you can turn me **off!**"

"But the stuff **you** do isn't **funny** as our Legislature," Max said.

That pulls back the curtain on an average session of our Legislature during these times. Some sessions are more rambunctious; some quieter—but not much. At least now you know how government works "Inside Paradise." The same way it works in Washington and some states—only mini-sized.

Senator Lilliana Belardo de O'Neal from St. Croix ranked as our most glamorous senator. In 1983, as she recovered in the St. Thomas Hospital from automobile accident injuries, flowers and "get well" wishes inundated her. A Daily News photos showed her—with neck brace—as Lt. Governor Julio Brady presented her a large bouquet of flowers. The copy underneath read:

". . . The Senator also was visited by a singing band of her fellow Senators, including Elmo Roebuck, Cleone Maynard, Hugo Dennis, Virdin Brown, Kenneth Mapp, Milton Frett, Ruby Simmons and Adelbert Bryant."

Although still hospitalized when an important vote came up in the Senate, Senator de O'Neal managed to vote. Dramatic as Cleopatra and her entourage on a Nile barge, attendants wheeled the Senator into the Legislative chambers on a movable stretcher, and she cast her vote. She also looked quite fetching.

So it goes. Never a snoozy day in our Legislature. Anyone who wants some **action** in St. Thomas should visit The Green Barn. You will be highly entertained and learn more about our Virgin Islands than you really want to know. Legislature sessions are open to the public, whether they are Virgin Island residents or visitors.

Young people "limin" (hanging out) in Emancipation Park

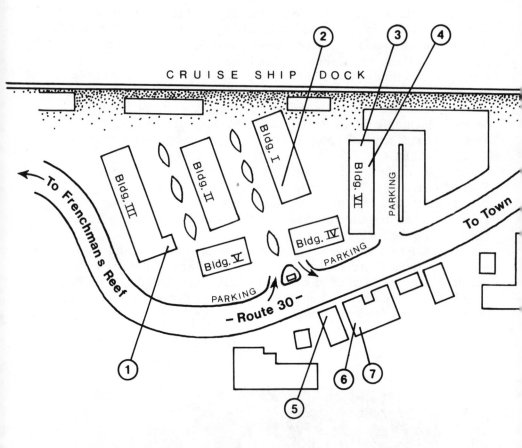

HAVENSIGHT SHOPPING MALL

Legend - Havensight Mall

1. **Delly Deck — Restaurant**
2. **Blazing Photos — Films developed in one hour**
3. **Havensight Café — Restaurant**
4. **Atlantis Submarine Office**
5. **Car Rental**
6. **Tropic Tours**
7. **American Express Travel Representatives**

CHAPTER 15

WATER, WATER . . . EVERYWHERE

Water, water . . . everywhere, and not a drop to drink!

All the water around us—and it stretches to the horizon on all sides—is salty sea water. Only a complicated desalinization process, not unlike a magician turning smoke into pigeons, makes our water drinkable.

Potable water is always a problem and comes to us countryside residents from the heavens via cisterns. Only large families and long droughts force us to buy water.

Children grow up thinking all big tank trucks—forever on our narrow, winding roads slowing up traffic—carry water. One friend, for the first time, took her young son to the States for a vacation. The boy appeared more interested in highway traffic than anything else. After several quiet hours on the road, he finally spoke. "Gee, Mom, I've never seen so many water trucks. People sure use a lot of water here." She laughed and explained they were gasoline trucks, but realized he thought tank trucks carried only water. Over the years, and without any coaching from her, he had become aware of the importance of fresh water and the big round-shaped trucks that hauled it.

Blessing of the Sea

Since the sea is an ever-present part of our lives and we cannot leave St. Thomas unless we fly over it, or cross it by boat, we have many reasons for "blessing the sea."

For well over 50 years, the St. Thomas Anglicans have kept faith with their "Blessing of the Sea." The ceremony, a tradition of prayer for those "who go down to the sea in ships," takes place the February Sunday evening closest to "The Feast of the Purification."

Services begin with the Solemn Evensong in the Charlotte Amalie Cathedral Church of All Saints. Afterwards the congregation forms a procession. Preceded by the St. Thomas Community Band, or another marching band, playing a slow hymn, the marchers move orderly and unhurriedly toward the Charlotte Amalie waterfront opposite Emancipation Garden. Priests and acolytes walk behind a young thurifer swinging the thurible. A crucifer goes in front of the bishop, resplendent in his ecclesiastical cape and miter. Another acolyte carries a large Cross of white flowers.

With lighted candles in hand, dozens of devout men, women, and children, black and white, follow. The band music and religious singing entice swarms of spectators from homes, stores, and restaurants along the way. They line the streets to watch the worshipers and sometimes join their singing. After the procession reaches the waterfront, more hymns are sung and prayers are offered, requesting protection for ships, sailors, fishermen, and all others who use the sea or travel on it. God's mercy is then asked for those who have lost their lives at sea.

The solemn waterfront rite comes to a climax when the bishop invokes this prayer: "Almighty God, who rulest the raging of the sea, stretch forth Thine Almighty arm to bless our waters and all those whose livelihood comes therefrom." The prayer is said for our stout-hearted French fishermen. Some lose their lives every year pursuing their vocation. Afterward, to commemorate those lost at sea, the bishop tosses the Cross of white flowers on the water, ending the harbor service. Singing hymns, the candlelight parade returns to the Cathedral for the final Solemn Benediction.

The exact date The Blessing of the Sea began is unclear. Older residents remember it from childhood and speculated it could have started in the last century, going back to the time when the Church of England's clergy were in port during February and performed the service. Since all islanders' lives are tied to the sea, the public ritual has meaning for all of us, regardless of religion, and offers each person an opportunity to unite in prayer to benefit everyone.

Such a community ceremony also reminds us of our dependence on the sea. Most everything we eat, wear, sit and sleep on, or drive for island transportation, comes by sea, aboard cargo ships, or huge barges from Puerto Rico.

Harbor Traffic

Our Charlotte Amalie harbor abounds with seacraft of every description: inter-island cargo vessels, small sailboats, large schooners, catamarans, power boats and 250-foot yachts.

Every day people-loaded cruise ships also dock along our waterfront, or moor in the harbor. We average four or five a day. Sometimes we have as many as ten or twelve. Those days I hide in the oven. Yet our economy depends on the currency cruise passengers (a million a year) scatter among the merchants on Main Street and the waterfront.

Charlotte Amalie's waterfront is busy with ferries and excursion boats

Sightseeing bus along the waterfront. Across the street are street vendors catering to tourists. See also photo page 59

Frequently naval ships, including aircraft carriers, dawdle several days for crew R&R. Port traffic, along with inter-island ferries and shuttle seaplanes taking off and landing downtown on the waterfront, makes our harbor look as if it belongs to New York City.

One of St. Thomas' most welcomed vessels is the Danish training ship "Danmark." In 1987, its annual visit coincided with the 70th "Transfer Day," the day our Virgin Islands were transferred from Denmark to the United States in 1917. On that Sunday, Captain Ole Peter Nielsen invited St. Thomas residents to inspect the ship from 2:30 to 4:30 p.m. at the West Indian Company dock. Young people especially look forward to this yearly treat during the Danmark's sojourn.

Jacques Cousteau and his working crew also come occasionally on a scientific expedition to plumb the wonders of our waters.

Private yachts, sleek and elegant as English swans, engender the greatest curiosity among us inhabitants. A large portion of the world's most glamorous yachts cruise our waters and pause in St. Thomas to shop, wine, and dine.

Editor's Note: St. Thomas is an excellent supply port and a frequent stopping-off place for sailors cruising south from USA, Bermuda, or Canada to the Leewards or Windward Islands. It's on the route south. They also stop at St. Thomas on the way north. You'll always see transient sailboats in the harbor, flying many different flags.

During the 60s, the *Atlantis*, owned by the Greek shipping magnate Stavros Niarchos, visited here often. Members of the Iranian royal family were among his guests (before the Ayatollah rose to power). Aristotle Onassis' yacht "*Christina*" came yearly with such glamorous visitors as Maria Callas, and later, Jacqueline Kennedy, Elizabeth Taylor and Richard Burton. In those days, celebrities walked among us without creating a stir.

Today, owners of private yachts are more reclusive. One, *Cedar Sea II*, remains a mystery vessel. The non-committal crew describes its owner, who wants anonymity, as "very private," thus fanning curiosity. The yacht, built in Holland and launched there in 1985, is well over two hundred feet long. Based in Monte Carlo, she holds British registry.

The chief officer told a Daily News reporter that the yacht was so well stabilized you could leave a glass of wine on a table and never spill a drop. The streamlined craft, with its multi-racial, hand-picked crew, carefully screened for security, took only nine days to cross the ocean. Amenities aboard include a helicopter pad, indoor swimming pool, and a Range Rover—British built four-wheel drive vehicle. *Cedar Sea II* is not rowboat transportation.

One year, Adnan Khashoggi's yacht *Nabila* graced our harbor off and on for several months. Al and I looked at that splendid creation from our gallery every morning while we ate breakfast. A lovely sight!

The Nabila came to St. Thomas before Iran-gate and Khashoggi's sudden limelight appearances with Manucher Ghorbanifar that started when Barbara Walters interviewed Khashoggi aboard his private luxury airplane palace.

Monsieur Khashoggi's "high-flying" days appeared to terminate with Iran-gate. Afterwards, his many-million-dollar flying palace sold at a bargain price, and his yacht *Nabila* went to Donald Trump for half-price: thirty million dollars—enough to keep Khashoggi in caviar and champagne.

Water Sports

Let's take a peek at water activities in Paradise.

The variety of sea sports makes these islands a seventh heaven for people who like to snorkel, scuba dive, deep sea fish, sail, power boat cruise,

Portion of American Yacht Harbor, Red Hook Bay, St. Thomas' largest marina

**Beach at Magen's Bay on St. Thomas' north shore
has been called one of the world's 10 lovliest**

and participate in races. We even have April Fool's and Halloween Regattas for sailboats.

A plethora of underwater fairylands exists for snorkelers and scuba divers. Several Charlotte Amalie dive shops rent equipment and offer day trips with knowledgeable guides.

For those who want to venture forth on their own, Secret Harbour is accessible and rewarding for snorkelers. Goatfish, spotted drums, assorted grunts and wrasses are among the array of water creatures found in the bay, and Aqua Action is there if you need guidance.

An adventurous scuba diver might head for Fortuna Bay to investigate its underwater wrecked plane, wrecked boat, and generous varieties of fish and coral. It is not easy to get there. You need a rented jeep and your own or rented equipment. The shore is rocky, but divers say the bay is protected and getting into the water no problem.

Once there, they add, you will agree the underwater sights are out-of-this-world. Well worth any inconvenience.

For Hi-Hos (Hook-In and Hold-On board sailors) there is the Annual Johnnie Walker Hi-Ho event. The 100-mile course offers contestants a thrilling challenge. A sizable group of Hi-Hos ride the waves around St. Thomas.

Sailing aficionados will not find a safer nor more beautiful sailing area in the world than the Sir Francis Drake Channel east of St. Thomas to Virgin Gorda in the British Virgins. Sailing the well-protected Channel is a great first Caribbean cruise. Many sailors enjoy the American and British Virgin Islands so well that they come back to charter every year.

Sailors, well protected from adverse winds or weather, enjoy gentle tradewinds; whereas in the Leeward or Windward Islands to our south, inter-island passages can be rough. Besides, the green-peak and sandy-beach beauty of the islands you glide past—Tortola, St. John, Peter Island, Norman Island, Virgin Gorda—will, like an exquisite painting in an art exhibit, remain engraved forever in your memory.

American Yacht Harbor at Red Hook, originally started by Johnny Harms, is our largest marina. Power boats, sailboats and sport fishing boats—*No Problem* is one—are available. Smaller marinas: Yacht Haven Hotel Marina and Sapphire Beach Resorts Marina are also popular. Avid deep-sea fishermen will find the 46-foot *Phoenix* and its Captain Spike Herbert, with 24 years of experience in Caribbean sportfishing, at Sapphire. Al Petrosky, also a long-time island veteran of game fishing, operates from East End Lagoon. His boat, *Fish Hawk*, can be found at the Fish Hawk Marina.

Crewed Charters

Editor's Note: There are about 140 bareboats for charter at St. Thomas and over 200 crewed charter boats. Many are based at Yacht Haven in Charlotte Amalie Harbor, some farther west along the waterfront and the others at Red Hook Bay and other harbors at the east end of St. Thomas.

Charterboat cruising with a captain and crew seems to me the most satisfying and carefree transportation for a sea vacation, and St. Thomas ranks high among the world's boat chartering centers.

Select a sailboat, schooner, sloop, catamaran, or power boat, and turn over all responsibility to a captain who knows his boat, the charted waters, and the best overnight spots to anchor.

Aboard, during the day, you can loll on deck to daydream or search the scudding clouds for hairy dogs, old men with beards, and angel faces. You can watch diving pelicans, fish breaking the water, or the panorama of foliaged islands with sugar mill ruins, or a giant statue of Christ. You may prefer to swim in a secluded cove, or an intriguing cave gouged out of sea cliffs.

Some charter boat passengers like to try a hand at fishing, or snorkel above coral gardens alive with neon-hued tropical fish. Others enjoy ex-

Coral World is a popular tourist attraction. It features this domed tower 100 feet offshore. This puts viewers in "people bowls" to observe fish in their natural sea world, and also in the world's largest circular reef-tank

Entrance to Building VI in Havensight Mall. The many fine shops in several buildings cater to cruise ship passengers. *Sovereign of the Seas* **is the cruise ship docked in the background. See map at the beginning of this chapter**

ploring lazy island ports, or favorite sailor hangouts such as casual Marina Cay and plush Peter Island.

Everyone is fascinated by Virgin Gorda's "Baths"—huge boulders looking as if a giant carelessly tossed them along the sand-packed beach. Passageways between these house-high rocks lead to hidden pools for private bathing or exploring.

Late in the afternoon, the captain drops anchor. It is "happy hour." Stretched out on a deck bench or chair with a rum punch in hand, guests watch an unforgettable Caribbean sunset—a burst of red, purple, and gold that sweeps the horizon and the sky above it like a sunset watercolor gone beserk.

If you're lucky you might see the "green flash." This phenomenon happens only when the horizon is cloudless but has a gossamer haze. The flash appears at the exact instant the sun slips into the sea. If you blink at that moment, you miss it. We have seen it a couple dozen times in our twenty-five years here.

Your strenuous "adjustment hour" activity is rewarded with a delicious gourmet dinner, followed by relaxed conversation, singing, or guitar music. Gradually, as the water laps softly against the hull, the sandman does his work. Off you go to a comfortable bed to be rocked to sleep by the boat's gentle movement. Can you think of a better way to unwind?

Do not be surprised, if you charter a boat, to find a female captain. St. Thomas has more professional women captains than anyplace else in the world, and often score higher on license tests than men. Over a hundred women are licensed, with about twenty full-time charter captains. Their safety records are excellent, and they have become highly respected and admired for their knowledge and competency. Besides, they are prettier than male captains!

Game Fishing

Game fishing charters are another hamper of fish. No relaxing time.

Strenous, white-knuckled, exciting, game fishing is the ultimate for fishermen, rather like pilots going into outer space.

In 1968, the largest blue marlin ever caught up to that time was brought "to keel" by St. Thomas businessman and sportsman Eliott Fishman. Fishman hooked his marlin aboard Captain Johnny Harms' charter boat *Savana Bay*. After the marlin took the bait, Fishman waited, counted to ten for the fish to swallow it—and struck him. "The water exploded," he said. The marlin leaped, tail-walked, then streaked off for the North Atlantic, reel screeching and slightly smoking as the "megafish" tore the line from it. Fishman battled the 845-pound marlin on an 80-pound line for three hours and twenty-five minutes before bringing it to the boat. Whew!

Laurance Rockefeller introduced Harms to the Virgin Islands. In fifteen years, the Captain's deep-sea fishing expertise helped fishermen aboard his game fishing boats win eighteen world records. Fishman and Harms co-founded the Virgin Islands Game Fishing Club and were active in the annual St. Thomas Blue Marlin Tournament in July. Although game fishing is excellent all year, experts tap June through October as best months for marlin, with spring, fall and winter best for sailfish.

After Fishman's catch, serious fishpersons—women, too—have made record catches. These include Gloria Applegate's 705-pound blue marlin, the women's world record in the late 70s. Fishermen now come from great distances to try their luck.

Game fishermen find fishing from St. Thomas especially advantageous, because the banks are nearby and eliminate a long, tiresome run before lines can be put out. Tournament records vouch for the abundance of fish. So, if you are fantasizing over a big game fish, the waters around Paradise might net you one that will not get away.

In 1987, Virgin Islands Game Fishing Tournament fishermen for the first time in the Tournament's history, released hooked marlin. The Fish and Wildlife Division of the Department of Planning and Natural Resources Management, trying to protect the marlin, required ones under two hundred pounds be tagged and released. Besides preservation, their release gives the Department a chance to study the fish when hooked again.

Marlin caught become the property of the Virgin Islands Game Fishing Club. They are sold and proceeds go toward scholarships for Antilles School. Do not despair, fishermen. As proof of your gamefishing skill, you can keep your marlin's exterior and have him properly mounted for display on a family room wall.

Tours and Short Cruises

For passengers on cruise ships, or tourists interested in short boat trips, the *Kon-Tiki*—a sturdy, sizable "South Pacific" thatch-roofed raft with refreshments and music—presents a pleasant "harbor seeing" tour. A great success with cruise passengers for many years, the Kon-Tiki also has other short trips available for tourists and islanders.

Day-sail boats range from those that carry less than ten passengers, such as the old-time favorite *True Love*, to an elegant sixty-five-foot schooner. In between are catamarans, trimarans, yawls, sloops, cutters, and clippers—so I am told. Nevertheless, they all seek secluded coves for swimming and lunch, and are preferred by boating vacationers who do not want to charter.

Catamarans, with the *Ho-Ti* probably the oldest, are popular for sunset cruises.

New underwater ventures started in 1987 with the submarine *Atlantis*. The 65-foot sub accommodates forty-eight passengers and makes daily two-hour excursions from St. Thomas. Included is an underwater cruise around Buck Island to depths of one hundred and fifty feet for observing fanciful reefs and marine life through large viewing windows. Owner Sub Aquatics of Vancouver, British Columbia, also operates in the Cayman Islands and Barbados.

•

Several hundred boats of every description moor in our Charlotte Amalie harbor and serve as homes for over two thousand boat people. Like a Caribbean Aberdeen (where Chinese fishermen live on junks in Hong Kong's harbor), the floating community is a world unto itself. Aberdeen people stay put for generations, but our boat people frequently take off to far places for a year or more.

A nucleus of these seafarers have formed an association. As good citizens,

Bolongo Bay Beach & Tennis Club has beautiful landscaping behind their beach

they support community affairs, join local organizations, and have responsible jobs. They vote, and their purchases and income taxes contribute substantially to the island's financial welfare. Even when clobbered by treacherous tropical storms like Hugo, they remain the invincible fleet.

•

The Daily News at one time published a supplement for boat people called "Marine Scene." It covered everything from spearfishing competitions and International Rolex Cup Regattas to Diving Association banquets and Christmas Wind Tournaments. "Christmas Winds" usually arrive in December and brew gales with 747-jet take-off intensity. Fortunately, these maverick winds last only a few days.

•

Boats going around the world, or starting from St. Thomas on a long voyage, anchor in our harbor, creating curiosity, excitement, and envy.

•

Every holiday weekend, the "Puerto Rican Navy" invades us temporarily. High-speed power boats whisk over the water's surface; sport-fishing boats roar behind; slower trawlers tag along; and lastly, sailboats tack their way more slowly. The prevailing winds are east. They go predominately northeast during winter months, and frequently southeast during summer. Calms are rare.

Although the Puerto Rican flotilla only pauses briefly in St. Thomas on its way to Sir Francis Drake Channel islands, it leaves a bundle of greenbacks in its wake when it shoves off. Freeport prices for fuel, booze, cigarettes, and designer merchandise is the magnet—and a great boon to our economy.

These fun-and-sea-loving Puerto Rican yachtsmen are avid boat enthusiasts who enjoy spending their money for a good time. Hard-working, hard playing, Puerto Ricans enjoy life more than any group of people I know.

•

Amphibian Aircraft

"Gooses" and "Mallards" used to land in our harbor, but they were amphibian seaplanes, not birds. Used by Antilles Air Boats—founded by Captain Charles Blair, former Air Force Brigadier General, famous pioneer North Pole pilot, and recipient of the Distinguished Flying Cross—they shuttled between Caribbean islands. Later, "Virgin Islands Seaplane Shuttle" flew them but Hurricane Hugo destroyed four of their six planes. Now negotiations are going on for their return. When a Senior Pan Am pilot, Captain Blair met and married actress Maureen O'Hara. During the 50s, they moved to St. Croix and started Antilles Air Boats.

In the 70s, Blair bought Australia's last two huge double-decker Sandringhams, British flying boats with four American Pratt & Whitney engines. Civilian versions of the famous wartime Sunderlands, the aircraft were originally used by the Allies for coastal patrol and anti-submarine work during World War II. Although capable of carrying forty-two passengers, they could not duck-waddle ashore like Gooses and Mallards, so were water-bound.

Accompanied by his glamorous wife, Blair piloted one Sandringham himself, halfway around the world, to the Virgin Islands. With two such celebrities involved, the daring adventure received considerable publicity.

Blair planned to use the planes, named *Excalibur VIII* and *Southern Cross*, for travel to nearby islands and "Flight-Seeing Cruises," available on no other airline or place in the world. The Flight-Seeing Cruise brochure was enticing. Flying south from St. Croix to St. Lucia, the Sandringham would work back, stopping at Martinique, Antigua, and St. Martin. They only made two trips. Al and I were on their second (and last) trip, and Captain Blair was our pilot and Maureen O'Hara the stewardess. Though none of the 28 passengers complained, rough, rainy weather upset the "Flight-seeing Cruise" schedule and made it a financial disaster. The Southern Cross, last of its kind, lay idle for two years, until a group of "flying boat" buffs raised money to buy and repair her. They couldn't bear to see such an important piece of aviation history rot away. Now in England's National Trust Museum, she is an historic treasure preserved for future generations.

•

Last, but certainly not the least of St. Thomas water attractions, is Coral World at Coki Beach, with a Marine Park and the only underwater observatory in the Western Hemisphere.

A three-story tower rises from the sea one hundred feet off shore and puts viewers in a "people bowl" for observing the fish. On the bottom lev-

Street vendors cater to tourists along Veterans Drive,
across the street from the waterfront

el you are eye-to-eye with the sea underworld, so fish ogle people while people ogle fish. Fair exchange.

On the second level everything from sting rays and barracuda to huge turtles and sharks swim inside a circular reef-tank, the world's largest, that surrounds viewers. Once, at the 11 a.m. feeding, as we watched the commotion created by a diver tossing out chunks of food for the fish to gulp down, a woman asked what was going on.

"They feed a tourist to the fish every day at eleven o'clock," a man replied.

The tower's top level, a geodesic dome, along with refreshment and shops, offers a magnificent view of St. John and the British Virgins.

A nearby domed Marine Garden captures natural seascapes in aquarium tanks: living coral, sponges, sea stars, and sea urchins. Some coral displays look like bouquets of flowers in rainbow colors.

Besides ocean life, a park area exhibits tropical birds, peacocks, flamingos, iguanas, turtles, and our perky mongooses (these feisty little creatures from India keep our island free of snakes). Coral World is a capsule of captivating aquatic life and island wildlife, but mostly it makes us appreciate the wondrous world of water all around us. Enjoy!

An appropriate ending for this chapter comes from these few lines of "America The Beautiful"—slightly altered:
"St. Thomas! St. Thomas!
God shed His grace on thee
And crown they good with brotherhood
From sea to shining sea!"

Frenchman's Reef's Morning Star Beach

CHAPTER 16

REVELATIONS

This chapter relates humorous happenings as well as interesting aspects of island life, unknown to outsiders.

Just Kidding (Goat Behavior) (See photo page 131)

In 1977, Al turned in his old Datsun for a sporty new yellow Chevette. As he signed the final papers, a stray goat started to nibble a potted palm at the car agency's entrance.

Al and Peggy Creque, who had the Chevrolet franchise at the time, took off after the goat. Not about to give up his tasty free meal, he tried to butt them. Only sprightly ballet footwork (a *pas de trois*) and "no kidding" tactics by Al and Peggy finally convinced the goat to give up the battle for the potted palm.

"As the goat moved off, his look wasn't friendly," Al reported.

Settling down again, Al and Peggy finished signing the papers, and Al drove away. Another normal day in Paradise.

We are accustomed to goats. They munch grass along our roadsides and wander where whimsy leads them. Even impatient cars stop to let bearded goat patriarchs convoy their spouses and offspring across the road. We cherish our goats—except when they devour our Hibiscus hedges.

One night Mary Gleason had an ill cat she took to the vet during night hours. As she opened the door to the office, a goat dashed out of the darkness and charged full speed past her into the lighted waiting room. When the young assistant appeared, Mary apologized for letting the goat inside.

"Oh, that's all right," the girl said. "He's afraid of the dark."

Young goats sometimes forage for food in schoolyards. Not long ago we saw a group lying down in a grade school's playground. "What are they doing **there**?" I asked Al.

"Just resting while they wait for the other kids to come out and play," he said.

This notice appeared in the November 30, 1989 St. Thomas/St. John Hospital Facilities publication, "The Payday Post," published twice a month on hospital paydays, given to me at a meeting Saturday, Dec. 2nd of EAST—Environmental Association of St. Thomas. The heading is:

Goats and Stray Animals Beware

The Board of Trustees announced at their November 17, 1989 monthly meeting that any stray goats and animals on the grounds of the St. Thomas Hospital must be removed by their owners immediately. If they are not removed, the Board will be forced to call the Humane Society and have them removed.

Our goats create a sensation among tourists. Not many places let them roam unattended as we do. So—when you drive in St. Thomas (on the left side, of course) remember not to be a "scrapegoat!"

Sometimes Life Is No Phone

Island phone problems are notorious. From time to time, nasty letters to-the-editor lambaste the telephone company (VITELCO). Here is a new approach to a phone problem in a 1982 "Notices" column of The Daily News:

GREETINGS

To all our friends, acquaintances, elderly relatives, pregnant daughter, son in the Air Force, ailing grandchild, business associates, trust officer, doctor, veterinarian and the I.R.S. This is to let you know that our phone is out of order and has been out of order for most of a month. There went the Christmas Greetings, the good wishes for the New Year, the consummated business deals, the family news, and the dinner invitations. Nevertheless, we want you to know that we rejoice for you that you got the raise, got married, recovered from Dengue Fever, fell in love, had the baby, shot par, had a Happy Birthday and sold all the puppies. We are so sorry that you lost your wife, your life, your temper, your boat, your jewelry, your job, and 100 balls in one day. Please know that we think of you and miss talking to you!

Sally and Bob Harkness

The "Notice" gave the Harknesses' friends a good chuckle, and the phone was fixed in short order. Sally, who has a great sense of humor, says the idea came to her in its entirety one night when she was desperate to hear a familiar voice in her telephone receiver. She immediately sat down, typed it up, and sent it off.

Humor often succeeds when all else fails—even with the telephone company. A sense of humor in Paradise not only goes a long way, it is a necessity.

Superstitions and Folklore

Many island superstitions came from African origins and have intermingled with Stateside folklore. St. Thomas children once believed the light in the Jack-o'-lantern man's head could kill if it shined into someone's eyes. Supposedly, this creature haunted the front of their house at night, disappeared during the day, and lived in a dilapidated old cemetery. They also believed salt thrown on him could kill him, and though no one could see him, he could see everyone.

I do not remember Hallowe'en being that spooky when I grew up in the

Tourists shopping on Main Street, downtown Charlotte Amalie

States. We went out in repulsive masks and costumes—mostly sheets— and hustled neighbors for apples and candy.

Another frightening island superstition, the "cowfoot woman," was believed to have a chest like a dog and to wear a horseshoe on her right foot. She removed it to sneak up to bite your neck and drink your blood. Only something shiny could drive her away, and when she died, she howled like a dog. To be safe from the cowfoot woman, people in the past closed their doors and windows at night.

Some Caribbean women wore hats indoors and out to ward off head colds. Others closed doors and windows to keep out night air and illness. I know people who believe black cats forecast bad luck if they cross your path. Others will not walk under a ladder.

Quaint customs and beliefs have always been part of people's heritage, whether they lived in an African veldt, or in the wooded lumberjack area of Wisconsin, where tall tales about Paul Bunyon abound.

Island tall tales for children center around Anansi, who can take the form of man or spider, a traditional wily character found in many cultures. Tricky, clever, greedy, he usually overcomes great obstacles solely by his wits, which makes him appealing to the underprivileged.

Lezmore Emanuel has two collections of these stories, "The Bull and the Golden Calabash" and "Broo 'Nansi—A Selection of Anansi Stories." Children love them. Emanuel, like Arona Petersen, is helping preserve island folk stories and customs.

In 1977, however, it was President Ford's signature on legislation authorizing a national folk life center in the Library of Congress that has, during the past decade, made folklore, once belittled and ridiculed, respectable. Myths, legends, folk tales, and ballads are taught in college folklore courses along with folk art, crafts, dances, costumes, even food, to preserve ethnic cultures in all parts of the world.

Well-educated people no longer ignore, nor laugh at folklore. When travelling, they buy animal woodcarvings in Africa, native Haitian paintings, Peruvian pottery, Eskimo stone carvings and New Guinea tribal masks. They proudly display their "finds" and carefully preserve them.

Other tourists fascinated by Bhutanese dances and tribal rituals of South American Indians, videotape them. Collectors seek out exotic Balinese musical instruments they sometimes learn to play. If a Stateside person discovers—tucked away in a great-granny's Bible—a spring tonic recipe composed of molasses and secret ingredients, it is concocted promptly.

Museums worldwide are filled with folk art, crafts, costumes, and history. I like that. It makes us aware and appreciative of each other's culture, and keeps world society from becoming one huge bowl of Pablum.

Change of attitude has also come to our islands. Only a few years ago young people rejected folklore medicine. Then world medical researchers learned that plants carry better cures for many diseases than ones created in a laboratory. Now children talk eagerly to grandparents and soak up medicinal folklore. They try the old remedies and find them effective.

Reality and superstitution sometimes are not easily separated. Folk remedies here include drinking soursop juice and rum for an aphrodisiac, making poultices from sweetsop to stop infections, and picking a soursop to "bust it open and grab a bite" for a hangover. If it works, is it superstition?

At present, scholars are making an effort to collect, categorize, and analyze the rich variety of West Indian medicinal plants for medical science. Caribbean young people now respond proudly to this heritage.

Island proverbs, expressive language, dances, music, and art offer appealing cultural interest for tourists. Visitors enjoy listening to our Calypso singers and buy the late Bill LaMotta's addictive record "Come Back to the Virgin Islands" by the dozens.

Bill LaMotta, widely known composer and musician, was our island "Music Man" and his wife, Joyce, our island "Guitar Lady." They inspired many young musicians. Their son, Leroy, is carrying on the family's musical tradition.

Calypso, the indigenous Caribbean folksong, cleverly improvised on the spot, combines the qualities of entertainer, composer, poet, philosopher, and social critic.

Lord Superior once said:

"A Calypsonian in his songs should touch on the problems of the people, speak out about them, and by so doing, change society."

During our Calypso Tents at Carnival time, they do just that, but between the West Indian vernacular and the subtle, meaningful phrases, an outsider gets lost. Just enjoy. Do not try to interpret. Like burlesque, body language tells a lot.

The spontaneous compositions of Calypso are true folk music and song. Besides being the most obvious example of island folklore, Calypso is also the most enjoyed by native and visitor alike.

Even though Calypso sometimes endures on recordings, usually its existence is fleeting, mostly sung to entertain tourists in hotel dining rooms or cocktail lounges. The Calypsonian composes light, humorous songs on-the-spot, tailored for each receptive man or woman. His ability to improvise and rhyme amazes, amuses, charms—part of island magic.

Harry Belafonte put Caribbean music and Calypso on the map. With a "map" like his, it was easy. Even without Harry Belafonte, Calypso is an island sound that gets to you.

Don't Stop the Style Show!

The early 1960s brought two momentous events. Ralph Paiewonsky was the first "bahn heh" businessman appointed governor of the U.S. Virgin Islands. And Cavanagh's moved their chic apparel and home furnishings store—filled with exotic imports from all over the world: India, Thailand, Japan, Philippines—from west Main Street to a larger and better middle Main Street location.

A style show, part of Cavanagh's official opening ceremony, took place right smack in the middle of the elegant new store. Lovely models in skimpy bathing suits and fashionable clothes—accompanied by the witty patter of Master of Ceremonies Elliott Wasson—strutted up and down the broad stairway leading to the second floor. A well-groomed St. Thomas audience, including Governor Paiewonsky and his party, responded with warm enthusiasm.

In the middle of this Country Club atmosphere, a stout tourist, attired in a flowered dress and sturdy oxfords, wandered into the store. Expression non-committal, she looked around at the mass of people before she passed

Marie Lopez is a stunning woman, always dressed in the latest fashion. She manages Aperiton, a chic European tourist shop with find jewelry and furs

in front of the Governor's group and other seated dignitaries and headed for the stairs, entirely oblivious to what was going on.

Slowly, as if ascending into heaven, she climbed the steps and disappeared into the upper regions. Elliott kept up his style show chatter and never missed a beat as the models moved on cue.

A few minutes later, the woman sauntered back down the stairs, face still expressionless as she again surveyed the crowd of people below her.

Watching her with head cocked and a twinkle in his eyes, Wasson suddenly deviated from his script and described her attire in the glowing terms he used for the models. The audience laughed hilariously and waited for her to discover her gaffe.

She regarded Elliott at the microphone and the seated audience as if she were looking at a picture on a poster. Finished with the stairs, she ambled down the center aisle that separated the seated audience, and without a backward glance, left the building for the street. After a moment of the kind of silence that follows a prayer, came thunderous applause. Wasson cleared his throat and bowed. The style show continued without any further distractions.

The vignette is as clear in my memory as it was that day. I have never before or since seen such complete, impenetrable concentration. There was nothing wrong with that tourist. She was quite normal in every respect. She simply did not know what was going on. What do you suppose she told her friends when she got back home?

Fed Up!

In the late 70s, an acquaintance, after having lived here many years, became thoroughly fed up with the island. He was fed up with all the new people moving to St. Thomas, with crime, litter, and with looking out and seeing water and boats in every direction. He longed for great sweeps of hilly, rolling land covered by vegetation that changed with the seasons.

Finally one day he said he was actually leaving.

"But where are you going?" another friend asked.

"I'm going to start across the country carrying an oar, and when someone says, 'What's that thing you're carrying?' I'm going to settle there. Nowhere near water.

That is exactly what he did. He is now ensconced on a farm in the middle southern States. He looks out on the kind of terrain he sought and is happy as a lark.

Moral: Paradise is not for everyone. Sometimes people get "fed up" with Paradise.

Let Us Bee!

In April 1986, men remodeling a building tried to rid it of swarms of bees, but ended up destroying the entire wooden section. For many years, the house was Laura Moorehead's "Mampoo Kitchen," where she sold honey and delicious homemade jams, guavaberry specialties, and other island treats.

When the bees became a nuisance as well as a threat, the construction workers decided upon smoke to rout them and accidentally started the fire. When all the smoke cleared away, the only part of the building left standing was the concrete rear. None of the men hired for construction work were injured, and through the efforts of four fire trucks, the conflagration was brought under control within 10 minutes. By this time more fireman than bees flitted around.

Now the men had nothing to remodel. A unique way of becoming unemployed. All the bees really wanted to do was make honey. They must have been burned up about being smoked out.

Foiled Again

An island visitor, staying at the downtown Windward Passage Hotel a few years ago, decided one evening to take a walk along the waterfront. After he left the hotel, he heard a voice order him against a wall and became aware of two black males approaching him with a gun.

They told him to do something he could not understand. Not even one word. They kept trying. He kept shaking his head, saying "I don't understand. I don't know what you want." Not angrily, just perplexed.

Before long the two would-be robbers conversed in low tones. A few moments later, shrugging their shoulders, they walked away, leaving the man to enjoy the night air. He reported the incident to the police before he left, but also said he had an excellent vacation and "enjoyed it very much."

Sometimes not being able to understand islanders can be an advantage. In St. Thomas anyway.

Thou Art

Our cartoon artist-in-residence, Linda Smith Palmer, creator of the daily comic strip "Max" in The Daily News (see Chapter 4) lives on St. John, but she knows exactly what goes on in St. Thomas and St. Croix. A lot of grapes hang on her grapevine.

Almost every day, Max, the witty, observant mongoose, and his mongoose pal, poke fun at politicans or stuffed shirts (not always the same), taxi

Windward Passage Hotel is on Veterans Drive across the street from the waterfront

drivers or WAPA (Water and Power Authority), VITELCO or the current controversial subject. Sometimes Max steps lightly on toes; other times he brutally "mahshes" them. Occasionally (about as frequently as one might win our lottery twice), Max praises someone in his own inimitable way. Such was the case when Max held up a painting of Van Gogh's "Yellow Flowers" in the first panel and said: "That little Van Gogh painting sold for 39 million dollars!"

In the next panel, he held a piece of a wall mural and said: "Can you imagine what Austin Petersen's murals are worth!!!"

That was Max's way of saying he liked Austin Petersen's murals. This talented young man's imaginative murals depict the past, present, and African heritage of "bahn heh" island inhabitants.

In 1979, Petersen, leader of a group of indigenous young artists (Wayne Rhymer, Allan Petersen, Mitch Davis, and Adolph Potter), fathered an effort to decorate all unsightly retaining walls with island subjects and scenes. They started with the Nadir bus stop shelter.

A later mural on the filling station wall at Four Winds Plaza Shopping Center in Estate Tutu offers a course in local horticulture with its festive paintings of St. Thomas flora. The sizable flowers are identified, so visitors can learn the names of the beautiful blossoms they see along our roads. The group painted students in graduation attire—black caps and gowns, marching one after the other—on one retaining wall at the Eudora Kean High School. On grade school walls, they used alphabet letters, children's building blocks, and other grade school items in bright designs.

Retaining walls and the large wooden doors of several buildings in downtown Estate Thomas are covered with the young men's murals. The artists do not ask for payment, only help in buying paint. When they work on a mural, passing motorists often stop to give them a few dollars.

The colorful paintings, even though not Sistine Chapel quality, are arresting. My favorite is beside the Weymouth Rhymer Highway near the Ft. Mylner Shopping Center. Portraits of prominent black island citizens,

Austin Petersen mural on Weymouth Rhymer Highway
near Ft. Mylner Shopping Center

past and present, and island scenes share honors with a section that portrays an African heritage in Masai-like huts and tribal costumes.

The mural on a low wall in front of the St. Thomas Hospital is quite explicit. Hospital items are on a lavender background, syringes to intravenous feeding equipment. A newborn baby and human organs; heart, lungs, liver, kidneys, graphically identify the building. Not my favorite.

A recent 100-foot mural on a retaining wall several blocks beyond the Nisky Moravian Church, on the way to the Cyril E. King Airport, has attracted the attention of tourist photographers as well as St. Thomians. Petersen thought about the theme for two years before deciding where to put the mural. Although his main purpose is beautification, this one, along with several others, carries a message. As usual, he features the past, present, and future of the islands, with the youth trying to hang onto the past values. I hope Austin Petersen and his group of artists realize there are some of us "oldies," both black and white, also trying to cling to past values. It is not easy.

He portrays the past with tranquil scenes of flowers and sea. It was like this when we first came in 1960 and had not changed much when we moved here in 1965. The present shows youth struggling to keep the values of the past. For the future, skyscrapers, pollution, and drugs, problems now, are catastrophic. It gives your conscience a wallop. I am grateful for these murals. We are lucky to have young men painting murals instead of graffiti on unattractive concrete walls.

Carnival vignettes, fishing boats, peaceful town and country island scenes were trademarks of the late Albert E. Daniel, artist and sculptor. Self-taught, this native St. Thomian was a familiar and beloved island personage.

Historian Magda Smith, in 1987, compiled an exhibit of 70 Daniel paintings and sculptures dating back to the 1930s and up to his death in 1981, for the Fort Christian Museum. She called the exhibit—partly funded by a grant from the Virgin Islands Humanities Council, "When Time Passed Softly By." She described Daniel as a folk artist and an important cultural figure in the Virgin Islands who tried to give a continual sense of history. He succeeded.

I treasured Albert Daniel's friendship. In his later years it was difficult for him to get around, and sometimes I drove him home when I saw him downtown or at a civic gathering. He always invited me into his small cottage. We would sit among his artistic creations and talk about art, music, and "the good old days." He never lost interest in what was going on in the world.

Native born, nationally acclaimed painter, sculptor, and graphic artist, Ademola Olugebefola was the featured attraction for Tillett's "Arts Alive" summer fair in 1986. The occasion celebrated their 25 years in island visual arts. An extremely talented man, Ademola spent three years on a touring exhibit sponsored by the Smithsonian Institution. In museums all over the world, his works stress African textiles and sculpture. We have our share of outstanding native artists, and the list grows each year.

Since 1965 we have become acquainted with several gifted artists who found special inspiration here, adopted the island, and painted its beauty.

Jim Tillett and Ira Smith were the first of these artists and were residents long before we were. They sell their work personally, through local exhibits. Jim also sells at his Tillett Gardens Gallery. Fred Morrison, who has lived on St. Thomas since 1965, and James Perigord, here since the early 1980s, sell their work mostly through agents in the United States and Europe and through exhibits arranged by agents.

Eljay combines the two. A bundle of energy with a prodigious output, she uses local galleries, but has frequent exhibits here and in Europe where she is at present. She feels personal contact with prospective buyers is important. Her long list of people, local and international, who own her charming watercolors, certifies this reasoning.

Some artists have come and gone, finding more profitable markets

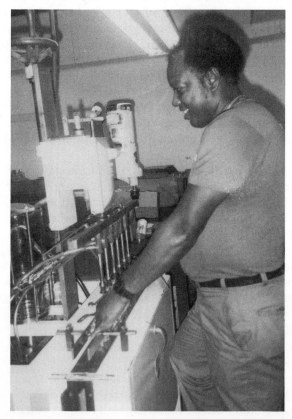

West Indies Bay Company makes St. John's Bay Rum at their Havensight Mall Factory in St. Thomas. They use bayberry tree leaves from St. John. Here's Alvin Gomez filling bottles

elsewhere. One was watercolorist Larry Gluck, extremely popular here in the 60s. Another was Russian-born Israeli artist Yankel Ginsburg, part-time resident of St. Thomas as well as part-owner of the Gallery Virgin Isle at Market Square in the early 1980s.

We bought our Larry Gluck watercolor in 1961, before we moved here. As I lolled in a beach chair in the shade of the Island Beachcomber's seagrape trees, Gluck came to display his watercolors on a Sunday afternoon, with permission from owner Lorette Resch. My eye went immediately to one of a cargo sailboat with a bright red hull, moored along the Charlotte Amalie waterfront. Still damp, the watercolor, fresh and clean of line, stood out as one of the most well-executed I had ever seen. I bought it at once. For years that boat came regularly to Charlotte Amalie, but I have not seen it lately. Consequently, the watercolor and its subject matter become more precious with the years. Its beauty still stirs me and others.

In the late 60s, Yankel Ginsburg was honored with a one man show at the Washington Gallery of Art sponsored by the Ambassador of Israel and Lynda Bird Johnson, and in 1975 was selected for "Who's Who of American Art." Still sitting in for the women's radio show when he opened his gallery in St. Thomas, I had the pleasure of interviewing him. Because of his dedication to peace between Israel and Egypt, Ginsburg became a good friend of the late Egyptian president, Anwar Sadat, and was the first Israeli to have an official government sponsored exhibit of his paintings in Cairo. A highly intelligent and gifted man, he ranked among my *crème-de-la-crème* interviews.

When we first came to St. Thomas, an amateur art group of residents had a permanent exhibit in the Grand Hotel lobby. Talented Britisher Doris Winckler had the most paintings stolen. A questionable compliment.

Many good artists are here now, but with the great influx of new arrivals, it is not possible to know people as we used to.

Caribbean Witchcraft

A few years ago, the International Seafarers Union in our neighbor island, Puerto Rico, claimed the Del Monte Tuna Company in Puerto Rico used witchcraft to swing a union election.

In a news conference, the union executive secretary said a complaint would be filed with the National Labor Relations Board in San Juan. He insisted a witch, employed by the company, and "rare lizards" brought in from Haiti, the home of voodoo in the Caribbean, influenced the election. He also asserted that police failed to stop the "irregular tactics."

The witch cast the spell at the polling box, he maintained. Using seven colored scarfs and a series of exotic necklaces, the witch took each voter by the hand and said, "Turn around three times so that all of your negative thoughts will leave your head." The union leader added: "And then they voted against the union."

In Tune With Past Times

In the 60s and early 70s, during the winter, Hugh Shannon, the first supper-club singer in St. Thomas, appeared nightly at various piano-bars, including Contant's old sugar mill in The Mill Restaurant's gardens. Called one of America's four "consummate" cabaret singers in a New Yorker Profile in 1977, Shannon was less known than the others: Mabel Messer, Bobby Short, and Blossom Dearie, because he spent most of his career in Capri, Paris, Rome, and the Virgin Islands. Author Whitney Balliett described Shannon's singing as "cheerful and full of bonhomie." I cannot improve on that. We only knew him in the late 60s when Laslo Zenda, former movie director of Italian, Austrian, and French films, and his beautiful Haitian wife, Marie-Thérsè, were host and hostess of The Mill Restaurant on Crown Mountain Road. Now it is the Old Mill Restaurant and the owners have recently opened a museum in the 200-year-old sugar mill for the enjoyment of patrons. Photos, tools, and printed information tell the story of how sugar mills produced sugar in colonial days. The Old Mill is the only St. Thomas sugar mill open to the public.

In the Hugh Shannon days, the mill was where he held court around the piano-bar. After a gourmet European dinner, diners strolled through the gardens and headed for the sugar mill. The conviviality around the piano-bar was contagious, and the catalyst was Shannon. Handsome, debonair, always friendly and smiling, he had a devoted St. Thomas following. His repertoire included classic old favorites: "I Get A Kick Out of You," "Poor Butterfly," "Send in The Clowns," "As Time Goes By," I never heard anyone play and sing them better. International playmates and followers of Hugh Shannon included Billie Holiday, Marlon Brando, Julius Monk, Faye Emerson, Truman Capote, Tallulah Bankhead, Joan Bennett, Joan Crawford, Doris Duke, Prince Michael, and the Duke and Duchess of Windsor—to name a few. I do not believe any of them came to St. Thomas to hear him, but if he was anywhere in Europe or in New York, they did. He brought our little island a sizable chunk of savior-faire. Shannon's death in the 80s was a great loss to all who knew him.

Nat Blake, Stateside and around since 1970, also has a large piano-bar following. For fourteen years he held his own kind of piano court at Bluebeard's Castle Hotel. Now at the "grand" Stouffer Grand Beach Resort, he blends sophistication and laid-back island geniality in a manner that pleases both tourists and residents.

Let's Hear It For Rum!

A good excuse for drinking Caribbean Rum is its Vitamin C content. In a Daily News article, Gail Shulterbrandt-Rivera, Licensed Dietition and member of the American Dietetic Association, divulged her "rum" research.

When our islands belonged to Denmark, rum was king (1777-1820). Called by several names: Rhum, Rum Bullion, and Rum Booze, the name was believed to come from Latin "saccarum" meaning sugar. Rum was a highly profitable by-product of the industry during the "Golden Age of Sugar."

Shulterbrandt-Rivera says Florence Lewisohn, in her book "St. Croix Under Seven Flags," explains that rum production needed some form of acid. According to the planter's taste, local limes, tamarinds, saltpeter, or Seville oranges were added, all good sources of Vitamin C.

In those days, rum supported the notorious "Triangle Trade," running from Boston to North Africa, to the Virgin Islands, and back to Boston. After the sugar was converted into molasses in the Virgin Islands, it was shipped to New England and distilled into rum. The rum was then transported to Africa and traded for slaves—the cheap sugar plantation labor that fueled the vicious "triangle."

In 1745, Caribbean rum played a vital part in the cure for scurvy, a vitamin deficiency disease. British Admiral Edward Vernon, desperately seeking a solution to a scurvy outbreak that disabled his crew, gave them daily rations of rum instead of the usual beer—probably by accident. Voilà! The disease cleared up. Rum from then on replaced the daily beer rations. So, if anyone chides you for drinking Caribbean rum, tell them you are warding off scurvy.

A man forced to ship his automobile north one winter could not find anti-freeze on the island, so filled the radiator with rum. Upon its arrival

Paul Guerrard working on production line making St. John's Bay Rum

in New York, its headlights must have looked like the eyes of cartoon drunks.

Filmflammed

When launched in 1975 by promoter J. Hunter Todd, the first Virgin Islands International Film Festival engendered more fanfare than the launching of the second *Queen Elizabeth* cruise ship, known as the *QE II*.

Publicity flowed like rum during Carnival. With a potential attendance of five hundred film makers in every category—educational and experimental films, documentaries and television movies—a rush of celebrities was assured: film stars, directors and writers.

The Film Festival had been held in Atlanta for eight years and was not a financial success. The move to the Virgin Islands seemed, to some people involved with its transfer, to offer "more picturesque and attractive surroundings" and "lend a more truly international flavor to the festival."

Limousines, spotlight beams playing across the sky, parties, dinners, and movie actors added up to a gala that brought the islands a star-studded treasure chest of glamorous publicity. All a bit overwhelming even for our jaded little island, well-accustomed to celebrities and "Big Events."

Another Big Event was the 1967 "Governor's Conference," our most spectacular success, to commemorate our 50th anniversary under the U.S. flag.

The International Film Festival Big Event went off triumphantly. Almost everyone who was supposed to show up, did. Even a deluge of rain did not dampen events nor spirits.

We attended a large party at "Villa Riviera," the home of Virgil Tsuluca and Fred Morrison, with Roberta Flack, Roy Scheider of "Jaws", Peter Graves, and Jason Miller, star of "The Exorcist." We didn't manage any intimate conversations in the milling crowd, but it was fun to rub "Hellos" with them.

The Festivals lasted two more years and remained a glamour event by producing an impressive celebrity list: among them, Cicely Tyson, Catherine Deneuve, Silvia Sydney, Burgess Meredith, Otto Preminger, and John Dykstra. The year Telly Savalas came he stole the show, even from the porno queens. After three years, the government was neither inclined, nor financially able, to give the Festival a $75,000 subsidy. Disagreements between Todd and the private and government sectors hit high C, and the Festival, like a burst dirigible, came to an ignominious finale. A large number of people were not unhappy to see Todd toddle off to other cinematic playgrounds.

The dark-glasses-and-weird-clothes brigade no longer sauntered up and down Main Street each November either, though many celebrities visit St. Thomas. The Festivals did let us play Hollywood and gave our V.I. Film Production Department, under Win de Lugo's and Eric Mathews' capable wings, connections and exposure. The Virgin Islands are now a priority place for shooting commercials to full length movies. So why complain about being "filmflammed"?

We shared a British Virgin Islands Big Event when the Queen of England came to the British Virgin Islands in 1966 to dedicate a bridge connecting Tortola and Beef Island. The local British subject who had the key to the bridge lost it, somewhat altering the ceremony.

Another Big Event, a visit from Her Royal Majesty Queen Margrethe II of Denmark and His Royal Highness Prince Henrik in 1976, also turned out well. Except for the tense moments when the gangplank of the Royal Yacht *Danneborg* and the men on the pier scurrying back and forth with the red carpet failed to mesh so the Queen could step ashore. The Yacht's captain and the men entrusted with the red carpet were out of "sync" from the beginning when the gangplank and carpet ended up several feet apart. Each one immediately hastened to solve the error. By moving simultaneously, they finished in the same position as before. After the third try, it took on the aspect of a comedy *pas de deux*. The officials managed straight faces, and on the next try, the participants accomplished a successful mating of red carpet and gangplank.

Other Notable Island Personages

For such a tiny island, we are home and/or birthplace of an inordinate amount of notable people. Known far beyond the shores of our little dots of Caribbean islands are **Terence Alphonse Todman**, former Ambassador to Spain and Denmark, and now U.S. Ambassador to Argentina, who recently received the rank of Career Ambassador to the White House, the highest honor that can be bestowed upon a career diplomat and held by only five people at a time, and **Henry Kimelman**, Democratic activist and former Ambassador to Haiti.

In the local political milieu, the late **Cyril E. King** was the man I admired most. If Governor King had lived, these islands would be different today. During his shortened regime, this unselfish, incorruptible, and dedicated man always appeared on the scene when tragedy or disaster struck.

The first black aide to a U.S. senator (Hubert Humphrey), King's gentle hand rested permanently on the public pulse. His main goal was to improve life for every Virgin Islander, and especially the underprivileged. Unfortunately, cancer defeated him halfway into his first term. He died January 1978.

Notable St. Thomian, the late **Alton A. Adams, Sr.**, born in 1889, was the first black U.S. Navy Bandmaster. He grew up well-trained in music and became a flute and piccolo virtuoso and composer. His band, considered by some the Navy's best, travelled throughout the U.S. and Canada performing concerts, radio shows, and a command performance for President Wilson.

After World War I, Adams returned home. Appointed music supervisor for St. Thomas public schools, he helped organize the first music department. He held the post until 1931. Among his friends were music greats such as W.C. Handy, Eubie Blake, and John Phillip Sousa. A tireless composer, his "Virgin Island March" is the territory's anthem. Adams also edited and wrote articles on musical subjects for newspapers and magazines (including Life and Time), pioneered and actively supported island tourism.

In 1947, Adams retired to devote his energies to preserving island folklore and writing his memoirs. He died in 1987. Fortunately, Geraldo Guirty, Isidor Paiewonsky, Arona Petersen, and Dana Orie remain to record island history and folklore.

The late **Alfred "Nazo" Hughes**, a modest, self-effacing man, deserves a place among "island notables." When Hughes died in 1982, veterinarian Andy Williamson considered himself a better person for having had Nazo as a friend.

"He represented the finest Virgin Islander qualities: honesty, industriousness, loyalty, and concern for neighbors and friends," Williamson said. Hughes' love for animals touched Williamson deeply. He called Nazo a truly "gentle man" representing the best standards of "the old and noble profession of veterinarian medicine." A huge compliment for a self-taught animal doctor from a highly trained one. Before St. Thomas had caring Andy Williamson, Nazo filled in as veterinarian.

Hughes gained his knowledge as a young man, studying animal anatomy at the slaughter house, reading about animal care, and questioning doctors and pharmacists. Before long, word spread of his knack with sick pets. His nickname came from an old horse, Nazarene, that he rode at the Sugar Estate race track. Despite his efforts and the crowd's encouragement, the horse ran last, and "Nazarene" shortened to "Nazo" became Hughes' sobriquet.

With time, Nazo learned electrical work, plumbing, mechanics, even the principals of refrigeration, and became a jack-of-all-trades for Berne's ice plant. He also became a jockey, boxer, tennis player, and long-distance swimmer, but nothing took precedent over his love and concern for animals. In 1958, he began to work part-time for the Government's Veterinary Service, and his competency soon earned him a full-time job.

After Nazo died in 1982, a Daily News editorial said: "His life should be an inspiration to all, particularly to those concerned about the erosion of V.I. culture and traditions." I had the good fortune to interview this unpretentious man. I wish the island had more Nazos.

Other "notables" include **Dr. Alfred O. Heath**, doctor, surgeon, singer, and musician; **Ex-Governor Ralph M. Paiewonsky**, founder of our University of the Virgin Islands and still its benefactor; and **Irwin "Brownie" Brown** of radio station WSTA. Brownie, who received Rotary's 1988 "Man of the Year" award, became an island celebrity for his witty and often hilarious radio commentary and for acting as Master of Ceremonies at many worthwhile community functions. A dozen more men are eligible, but this list proves St. Thomas can be proud of men from all walks of life.

On the female side of notables, **Irene Bayne**, who came to the islands in the 40s, played "mother hen" to St. Thomas social service groups. A fireball of energy, she was honored at a Partners for Health Gala Ball in 1985 for her gargantuan efforts in raising several hundred thousand dollars for major equipment needed for our new St. Thomas Hospital.

Irene, a petite woman with upswept blonde hair and soft bangs, first became involved in volunteer work at the old Knud Hansen Hospital serving meals to patients. When the fresh fish did not smell right, she demanded the hospital kitchen buy only frozen fish. Everything was out front with Irene. If she did not like something, she came on like a battalion of crack riflemen. Quick as a shot, everything was under control.

In 1946, with **Elsa Linqvist** and **Elizabeth Connor**, Irene founded the Women's League to supply volunteer workers for the hospital. The League, unquestionably Irene's greatest gift to our community, was her way of softening the blow of losing her son in World War II. Instead of giving her life to grieving, she gave it to relieving, helping others.

Bertha C. Boschulte of the Women's Club, organized in 1941 as a church group of All Saints Anglican Church, backed a successful move to join forces with the Women's League, thereby mustering a formidable body for community service. Under **Lucinda Millin's** direction, one of the first projects was to organize a committee to visit shut-ins and the aged.

Made up of women from every area of St. Thomas, the League went on to tackle social problems.

Edna Christensen was a primary supporter for the Girls' Home, operated by Social Welfare, and the League played an active role in the Home's management. This worked so well that League member **Rita Christmas** and the Child Welfare Division joined hands to fund and establish Day Care Centers for children of working mothers.

After day care legislation passed, the League sought other projects including the Lucinda Millin Home for the Aged, a Detention Center for Youth, anti-litter efforts, and many more.

Besides the Women's League, community service **orchid** bouquets go to The League of Women Voters, Business and Professional Women's Club, and other clubs of lesser strength.

Along with her League activities, Irene Bayne opened Main Street's first gift shop, The Bolero, in 1948 (the year she was named "Man of the Year" for her volunteer programs). In 1950, she and her husband, Ben, and the Sidney Kesslers, anticipating tourism growth, built the Virgin Isle Hotel. In 1952, she was the first woman to run for the Legislature. Defeated, she dropped out of politics, but she never dropped out of community service.

Always well-groomed, Irene was, before crime came to the island, famous for her beautiful jewelry. I have seen her walking Main Street on her way to a luncheon wearing a fortune in diamonds, rubies, or emeralds. She kept alive the Golden Age of Hollywood Glamour Queens for all of us. Irene died at 88 in June 1989. Daily News columnist Barbara

Pryor expressed everyone's thoughts best: "The pain is deep . . . on the passing of our beloved Irene Bayne. The community will never forget this gracious lady. She leaves a legacy of love."

Among native female notables is **Judge Eileen Petersen**. Because we were friends, I was able to interview this attractive and articulate young woman shortly after her appointment as Judge of the Municipal Court of the United States in November 1971. Since she was the first woman so honored in the U.S. Virgin Islands, and probably in the entire West Indies, I commented that Women's Lib in the West Indies took a "giant step" forward.

Judge Petersen explained, however, that West Indian women had been liberated since a courageous Crucian woman confronted the Danish slave system by burning the St. Croix town of Fredericksted. Consequently, the Judge considered herself a woman first, and next, a West Indian.

Born and schooled in St. Croix, Judge Petersen attended Hampton Institute, receiving a B.A. in English and M.A. in Education. She taught in St. Croix schools before becoming a legal secretary and going to Howard University for a law degree. Returning to the Islands, she worked up to Assistant Attorney in the Attorney General's office before being appointed a judge.

Concerned with youth, Petersen believes in working closely with them to develop creative abilities and offer wholesome recreation. Active in legal and civic affairs, she is an outstanding judge, caring and compassionate, but stern with those who flout the law. In 1972, she married Ellie and Jacques Ellison under Hidden Hill's big Saman tree, lending a warm island blessing.

Marie Joseph packing St. John's Bay Rum. Attractive packaging has helped make this a popular tourist item. St. John's Bay Rum is sold at 250 Caribbean locations, and over 1000 on mainland USA

Agatha Canfield, orginator of the Toneskolen School of Music (a non-profit cultural organization), has been the guardian angel to more St. Thomian musically inclined children than any other single force. You might expect a buxom diva type, but Agatha is small and gentle. Yet she has a King Kong-sized iron will to give the island's musically talented young people a chance for success.

Annually, for years, she sent outstanding students for advanced training to Interlochen, Michigan's National Music Camp. She developed Summer Youth Bands, Handbell Choirs, and Piano Lab programs.

Like **Kay Atcheson** with her St. Thomas School of Dance, Agatha has made it possible for St. Thomas children with limited financial means to pursue careers in the Arts. Her students perform for many local functions. The Virgin Islands Council on the Arts and the National Endowment on the Arts in Washington approved and financially supported these programs.

Nightlife Nostalgia

Recently Daily News columnist, Dana Orie listed night spots he frequented during the 60s (his maturing years). Some we did not know, but we also like **The Luau**, a great steel band, but no grass skirts, and the **Fallen Angel**, sophisticated Stateside singers.

Black Patch, one we liked, Orie called "sleazy." With walls painted black or red and padded banquettes in small, intimate rooms opening onto each other, to us it exuded island charm: combos, local singers, diverse clients. "Sleazy" never entered our minds.

Tourists never know which night clubs residents consider taboo. It might be wise to find out.

Orie did not mention **Trade Winds** that looked out to sea from a hilltop. Now the Harvey Student Center, it belongs to The University of the Virgin Islands. In the 60s, Trade Winds was a popular restaurant and night club with an outstanding dance combo.

The first time there, we were guests of Virginia and Jere Cavanagh, owners of Cavanagh's in San Juan, St. Croix, and St. Thomas. As we came in, the band saw Jere. They stopped playing and marched from the room.

Strange.

A few minutes later they hurried back, laughing, and wearing white shirts with black drawings of tropical flowers, plants, donkeys, and Cavanagh stores, originally designed by Jere. After bowing formally to him, they sat down and began to play again.

No longer strange.

In the mid-60s, Julie and John McLeod operated **The Gate**, once an elegant early 18th century townhouse at the foot of Synagogue Hill. With three-hundred-year old stone walls, a three-story fiddle leaf tree in its middle, and a colorful history, it was a popular guest house and restaurant.

Named for its attractive iron gateway, The Gate was best known for its night club. The casual dining terrace transmogrified into a midnight to dawn night owl retreat for merengue and what-have-you-dancers. A steel band, Calypsonian Mighty Zebra, and Spaghetti and His Meatballs—a scratch band using a pennywhistle and washtub—were regularly featured. Everyone always had fun in this relaxed and romantic setting. Another past era.

In those days, Katie's dominated Market Square. In a small, unimposing wooden shack, noisy and crowded, Katie played the piano, and I once played the "gut-bucket" while Jerry White sang. Two stars that were never born. No one listened.

The chic **St. Thomas Club (now Villa Blanca Hotel)**, with pianist Dilson Petry, sparkled atop Raphune Hill at that time. Jim Bridgeman's lively waterfront restaurant, **Sebastian's,** under a thatched roof held up by bamboo posts and beams, offered South Sea island atmosphere and gourmet food.

After a ruinous fire in the early 60s, Sebastian's was rebuilt with fireproof materials. It lost its grass shack Tahiti charm, but remained a favorite until it closed in the mid-80s, **The Caribbean Beach Club** featured Limbo dances—and still does, one of the few places to remain popular since the 60s.

Latifah Chinnery-Nadir offers St. Thomas children the best in education aids
in her Education Station Ltd. in Nisky Shopping Center. Visit her, she's fascinating

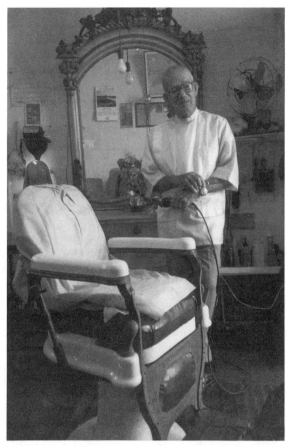

If you need a haircut, you're in for a real treat. Eric Perkins' barber shop is in the Grand Hotel. He has trimmed the hair of many celebrities

Past Perfect

In the late 60s, Mr. Petersen, who lived two-thirds of the way up Crown Mountain Road, rode one of his two donkeys into town almost every day. He saved his sleekest one for Sundays.

Mr. Petersen could very well afford a car, but as an older man, he preferred safe and sane transportation. As he jogged along with great dignity, I found special pleasure waving at him, sharing the pastoralism of a tranquil time I suspected even then would vanish.

Sometimes I gave Mrs. Petersen a lift to town. Only her husband rode the donkeys. We enjoyed each other's company and conversation came easily. She always repaid me soon afterward with a dozen fresh eggs. I expected nothing. In the 60s, we offered rides to anyone walking to town.

I stopped the practice in the 70s after Gussie Jouett, wife of renowned Air Force Colonel John Jouett of Chenault's Flying Tiger-Chiang Kai-shek days, picked up a young schoolboy who put a knife to her throat and demanded her purse.

Stopping the car, she ordered him out. A small, commanding woman, she spoke with E.F. Hutton authority and everyone listened. The boy got out.

I do not have that kind of presence. Fear subjects me to rigor mortis. I would end up with my throat cut.

Mr. Petersen is gone. Though I talk to Mrs. Petersen sometimes by phone, I rarely travel Crown Mountain Road. When I do, I remember Mr. Petersen on his donkey trotting along happily to town, and I wish our island had not changed so quickly. Platitudes about "progress" do not comfort me.

Street Steps

The most famous of Charlotte Amalie's historic "street steps" is "99 steps." (See photo page 101.)

They lead to privately owned Crown House, one of few remaining authentic Danish mansions. Beyond is The Mark St. Thomas and Blackbeard's Castle for dining and panoramic views of town and sea. Sunday Brunchers loll beside Blackbeard's pool to read the Sunday New York Times ($7.95).

Built around the middle of the 1760s by Danish Civil Engineers, step streets were not planned by the Copenhagen architects who never visited St. Thomas. They had no conception of the town's steep terrain as they drew up plans for expansion, using grid patterns for residential streets.

The men assigned to fulfill the drawings, fearing the King's ire, did not question the layout. If the terrain was too steep for a road, they built steps of Danish brick to the next "real" street. There was a good supply of brick, used as ballast in Danish supply vessels.

Here, ignorance was a blessing. No quaint stairs would now take us from one street to another had the architects known what they were doing.

It's In The Bag

Sometimes in St. Thomas, you can close your eyes and make believe you are in the Scottish Highlands.

That is when Pipe Major Willie Cochran, bagpipe player for Dewar's White Label Scotch, visits the Virgin Islands. In dress uniform, a towering chin-strapped shako, and colorful plaid kilts, this internationally known entertainer merrily bagpipes his way along roads and down streets into bars and restaurants from one end of the island to the other.

Cochran pipes for locals and tourists from plush seaside Frenchman's Reef and Limetree Hotels to Crown Mountain's popular Club Z, The Old Mill Restaurant, and Sib's. He leaves no bar or restaurant "un-tuned."

When I first saw him, I did a double-take, but will not forget him. Good advertising. No signs, no hyp, only pleasant bagpiping.

Island Tele

"Do you have television?" we have been asked.

Remembering the same question about electricity in the 60s, I try to be patient. I explain that for a small island, St. Thomas has remarkably good TV coverage from our commercial and PBS stations. They bring us the latest world news and momentous events as well as important community activities, from Carnival and Caribbean Chorale concerts to sessions of the Legislature.

Even cable TV is available, but Al and I don't have it. We live on top of a mountain and receive good reception from St. Croix and a half-dozen Puerto Rican stations. Shocked that we were among the underprivileged, a friend said to me, "You don't have cable TV! How can you get along without news every hour on the hour?"

"Very nicely," I said. "News once a day is enough to warn me when we're approaching Armageddon."

Our PBS channel keeps us daily abreast of crucial social and political world happenings with the McNeil-Lehrer News Hour, and brings us opera, ballet, symphony orchestras, and White House concerts by satellite. Local PBS personalities, Addie Ottley and Marielu Burnett, keep us up-to-date by interviewing a cross-section of newsworthy people in the community and from abroad. So don't call us provincial. PBS even gives us French lessons through "French In Action." C'est Bon!

An "Inside" Glimpse of Contented Islanders

St. Thomas is still a place that offers the individual, through initiative and hard work, a decent living doing what he or she wants to do. The small cross-section of contented islanders I'll tell you about have something in common. They like people and enjoy meeting new ones.

An example is Latifah Chinnery-Nadir, poet, educational consultant, and former University of Virgin Islands professor. She dreamed of owning an establishment that offered island children the best educational aids. Her Education Station, Ltd. in Nisky Shopping Center does that. She stocks the latest books, games, cassettes—anything that stretches children's minds and educates them for a competitive world. She wants all Virgin Island children to "shine" here and abroad and helps teachers and parents achieve that goal. She loves what she does and is a fulfilled educator.

•

For 75 years Eric Perkins has done what he enjoys most—barbering. He sheared Danish royalty before our islands belonged to the U.S. and has shorn celebrities' locks ever since. When Laurance Rockefeller opened Caneel Bay, he asked Perkins to operate the barber shop. He did so for 25 years. Though offered barber shops at the Virgin Isle Hotel and Bluebeard's, he declined. "The Proud and Profane," filmed on St. Thomas in the 50s, starred Deborah Kerr and Bill Holden. Perkins handled the cast's barbering, but turned down Holden's invitation to accompany them to California. This "tonsorial artist" has trimmed the hair of Hubert Humphrey, Ted Kennedy, Navy officers, five generations of the A.H. Lockhart family, and Al Brown. Antiques surround an ancient barber chair in Perkin's old style Grand Hotel barber shop. These include a large rococo Italian mirror and locally handmade mahogany hat rack, table and rocker. Conversation is encouraged, but bad language is not allowed. At 90, Perkins is his own man and happy.

•

Norma Jackson-Burke's four St. Thomas florist shops include Ft. Mylner's 19-year-old "Jackson's Florist" and new "Basket of Flowers" at Havensight's Buccaneer Mall. Active in the St. Thomas Orchid Society, she teaches math and science at Seventh Day Adventist School and has time for her four chidren. Always a gardener and flower lover, she says, "Gardeners are happy people," and expresses her pleasure over the delighted faces of people who receive her flowers. Valentine's Day is her biggest day now. Mother's Day once was. "Thanksgiving and Easter are no longer important days," she adds, "because high food costs have changed peoples' lifestyles." Her smile when she holds up a prize orchid tells you that tender loving care of plants and flowers is the joy of Norma's life.

•

On the other hand, Frenchman Jean Aubin, once an island professional landscape gardener, dreamed of operating a tourist shop. His "Caribbean Market Place," in Havensight Shopping Mall, is that dream come true. Caribbean hot sauces, teas, herbs, spices, St. John's Bay Rum, down-island

Jean Aubin at entrance to his Caribbean Market Place in Havensight Shopping Mall, Building 3. St. John's Bay Rum is prominently displayed

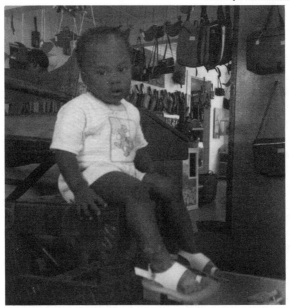

Zora, the sandalmaker, has sizes to fit everyone. See also photo on page 83

batiks, clothes, and accessories entice tourists to buy tropical items that will warm them with Caribbean sunshine even when they are home and knee-deep in Stateside snow. "It's hard work and long hours," Jean says, "but I enjoy meeting tourists and helping them learn about the many things our islands have to offer." I am sure they enjoy it too, because a man who takes pleasure in his work makes friends—and sales.

•

Because of a small upstairs factory hidden away in Havensight Mall, men worldwide smell better. Over 40 years ago, West Indies Bay Company started producing St. John's Bay Rum—an after-shave and all-purpose lotion. Made in St. Thomas with the world's finest sweet-scented bayberry tree leaves from St. John, the lotion languished until the early 50s when it was repackaged in a square bottle covered with a glamorous French fishpot weave of palm fronds. Shortly, better stores throughout the U.S. carried it with great success. Then sold and resold several times, the West Indies Bay Company suffered setbacks until retailer Jerry Woodhouse, a devotee of St. John's Bay Rum, could not stock the lotion for his customers. He visited St. Thomas, found the remnants of the company, and bought it in 1978. Innovative retailing and distribution placed the product with 250 Caribbean distributors and 1,000 on the mainland. Bottles encased in the handwoven palm are wrapped and labeled by hand in the factory's fragrant, cheerful work place. Thanks to the dedicated production employees and the enthusiasm of Jerry Woodhouse, St. John's Bay

Rum is once again a "hot item." Woodhouse enjoys the challenge of his successful lotion and offers factory tours on request. Future plans include being on the tourists' "things to do" list and giving away small samples.

•

A sandalmaker who has played the French horn in symphony orchestras raises disbelieving eyebrows. But it's true. Since 1962, French-horn player "Zora the Sandalmaker" has made our island feet more comfortable with her selection of over 25 styles of made-to-measure leather sandals. She is as meticulous with their fit as with her music, so tourists and locals keep coming back. Zora first opened her shop in a tiny cubbyhole, long since gone, on Main Street near Roosevelt Park. She later took over Camille Pissarro Building's second floor and added Oriental rugs that she personally selected in Iran, India, and Afghanistan. The addition of handmade canvas items necessitated more room. In 1980, she moved to another historic Danish building on Main Street. Across from Roosevelt Park and near her original location, it housed the American Consulate after Transfer Day in March 1917 when the United States bought the Virgin Islands from Denmark for $25,000,000. A sign displaying a large red footprint with "Zora of St. Thomas" beneath identifies the building, often used by the police as a landmark for traffic directions: "Go to Zora's and turn left." Indomitable, Zora loves what she does, and except when her French horn is contrary, or the sandal leather she ordered is not perfect, is contented with island life.

•

St. Thomas taxi drivers are a law unto themselves. As a whole, though, they are accommodating, entertaining, knowledgeable, and good ambassadors. Unfortunately, a handful are scoundrels who alienate local residents and tourists. They overcharge tourists and pass up locals who don't tip as much as our visitors. The Taxi Association, using a program similar to

Taxi driver Rachel Brown operates out of Frenchmen's Reef Hotel and has a contagious smile

186

"Miami Nice," is making a sincere effort to ferret out bad apples. I wish them luck.

Here are two taxi drivers I vouch for: they are representative of the majority. Rachel Brown, one of only a few women drivers, came from Nevis to St. Thomas in 1964. She always wanted to drive a taxi for tourists, but at first, to make a living, settled for housework, then became a courier for a prestigious law firm and saved her money until she could buy her own taxi van five years ago. "I like to meet people, and I like to talk," she says, laughing, "This is the best way to do both, and I love my independence." She finds no resentment from men drivers. If her van breaks down, they go overboard to help her. Brown operates out of Frenchmen's Reef Hotel and sometimes is busier than she wants to be, but she never complains. "The dollars from those days put money in the bank for lean days," she says. Is she happy? "Of course. I'm doing what I like most to do." Her contagious smile verifies that.

The independence of driving his own taxi also appeals to Holman Harley. "I work only the hours I want to," he says. He doesn't have a van. Instead he drives a sleek passenger-car taxi, and because he enjoys talking to local residents, caters mostly to them. He transports children too young to drive to parties, elders too old to drive, carless residents, or people who don't want to drive at night. He occasionally takes tourists sightseeing, but unlike most taxi drivers, does not meet cruise ships. It brings in more money, but means waiting long hours in the taxi line at the cruise ship dock for one's turn and a fare. Harley's base is the Windward Hotel on Veterans Drive. A quiet, dignified man, he was born on St. John. He came to St. Thomas forty years ago to work at the West Indies Company, then at A.H. Riise's Liquor and Drug Store for tourists, and finally served as a male orderly for almost 25 years at the Knud-Hansen Hospital. During all that time, he drove a taxi on his days off and sometimes at night, but the last ten years have been devoted entirely to driving a taxi—to being completely his own boss—and that makes him another Virgin Islander well-satisfied with his life.

•

Each of these St. Thomians would agree with Sidney A. Weltmer who said: "Work should be a joy—and it would be if we regarded it in the light of being a labor of love."

CHAPTER 17

BITS AND PIECES

PIECES

Signs of Our Times

Recently seen bumper sticker: "I'm in no hurry. I'm on my way to work."
St. Thomas is an island of bumper stickers. "Animals Have Rights Too," "Save Our Harbor," and "Think Before You Drink" are popular, but my top choice is a recent one: "If You Can Read This, Thank Your Teacher."

Dana Orie, stuck in traffic one day before an election for a heated gubernatorial race, spent the time counting bumper stickers and related various observations in his column.

He reported on which type of carrier—trucks, Mazdas, BMWs, and Jeeps to Mercedes Benz—supported different candidates. His vehicular sociological study revealed much about each candidate's voter appeal. He also mentioned a rumor about a well-known female candidate's bumper sticker having been seen on a hearse.

Orie continued his survey counting the "Abolish Apartheid" stickers along with "sanctified bumpers":

"Know The Lord or go to Hell." This bumper turned left without signaling. "Jesus Saves." This one swerved into Orie's lane.

He commented that "only Jesus saved me from driving over the waterfront to a salty grave. But that's all right, I've got guaranteed rust-proofing."

Dana Orie, author of "People of Passion," a collection of his newspaper columns effectively illustrated by local artist Myron Jackson, makes us laugh while he tweaks our conscience.

Paradise Tales

When Nat Norris was building his Oriental house "Kaleidoscope" and worrying with plumbing problems, the Postmaster told him about how happy his own family had been when a flush toilet was finally installed in the house.

The children were so happy, they invited all their friends in to use it one day when their parents were not home. The children "used it" until the cistern ran dry. The fate of the children was not discussed.

Nat also tells a story about a frustrating important telephone call from New York one morning. It begins with his contentedly eating a luscious papaya for breakfast on an open gallery. When the phone rang, he had to get up to answer it, because the extension cord did not quite reach the table.

Nat stood talking only a minute before a Trashy bird from the surrounding forest swooped down and pecked at the papaya. While trying to concentrate on the call, Nat took a swipe at him. The bird, just out of reach, did not budge and kept pecking away. Trashy birds love papaya.

Nat continued to lash out threateningly, so the bird tried to lift the papaya and carry it off to his tree condominum. It proved too big and plopped back on the plate.

A moment later, another Trashy bird flew in and they struggled together. Despite Nat's dancing about in rage and shouting at them (hand over receiver), they managed to fly off with his papaya, beady eyes triumphant and diabolical as a Lucifer. Two Trashy birds after a papaya are worse than one cackling in the bush.

Weekend Frenzy

You have a good idea of what we do daily, but you do not know what we do weekends. Here is a typical Daily News column on "Things to do This Weekend":

(1) Cake Sale in front of Woolworth's for the benefit of the Youth Multi-Service Center.

(2) "Historical Elections" for election of officers and Board of Directors of St. Thomas Historical Trust and lecture on J. Antonio Jarvis by Addelita Cancryn for opening of exhibit of his art works at the Fort Christian Museum.

(3) "Bazaar" Pre-Christmas on the Nisky Church grounds—music, games, popcorn, a flea market.

(4) "Salassie Celebration" cultural celebration honoring Haile Salassie at Paul M. Pearson Gardens.

(5) "Steel Band Concert" by St. Thomas Rising Stars Steel Band in the College of the Virgin Islands cafeteria.

(6) "Lioness Dinner" awards dinner/dance at Mahogany Run with music by Eddie and the Movements.

(7) "Voters Rally" the United Caribbean Association conducting voter registration at housing projects.

(8) "Fun and Games" by the 1956 class of Charlotte Amalie High School at Tau's Club House.

(9) "Movements Jam" Eddie and the Movements performing live at Lindbergh Bay Beach Club sponsored by their Fan Club.

With such a broad spectrum of activities, you can see why we never have time to lie on the beach under a palm tree.

October Sunday

The people of St. Thomas are always dreaming up ways to have fun. Jeep rallies raise money for good causes, and special regattas such as April Fool's Regatta are popular with sailors. So was Pirate's Day, but it didn't last. Not so with October Sunday that started out as Octoberfest at Sib's Mountain Bar, but outgrew their facilities.

After Barnacle Bill's restaurateur, Bill Grogan, took over the event, it moved to the Crown Bay landfill Sub Base, near the new cruise ship docking area. Under the tutelage of attorney Fred Watts, coordinator of entertainment, this "musicfest" celebrated its 13th Anniversary on a rainy overcast Sunday, October 29th, 1989.

Several thousand fans of traditional-folk and down-island music were on hand. Some sat contentedly in a big tent and listened to a stream of live music from musicians who included Nicky "Mighty Whitey" Russell, Calypsonian and WVWI-Radio One personality, and a wide variety of other entertainers from New Sage Mountain Boys to Family and Friends.

The more intrepid patrons sloshed around in the water-soaked grass, sampled an enticing array of food and drink, chatted with friends, played the few games that were offered, and gyrated or toe-tapped to the catchy tunes. Despite the weather, it was evident that October Sunday has become a traditional St. Thomas "happening" for the whole family. Proceeds always go to charitable organizations and a large portion was designated for Hurricane Hugo relief funds in 1989.

BITS

Names of St. Thomas restaurants, past and present: Pink Mongoose, For The Birds, Crazy Cow, The Oar House, Squirrel Cage, Royal Rum Barrel, Fat City, Bus Stop, Three Virgins' Restaurant, Walter's Living Room, The Sweet Pot, and Lord Rumbottom's. Paradise is imaginative.

•

When you see our spectacular red flamboyant trees in unlikely places on St. Thomas, thank Ariel Melchoir, Sr. In 1950, he ran ads in his Daily News to buy flamboyant seeds at ten cents a pound. When he felt he had a sufficient amount, Pilot Jack Monsanto flew him over St. Thomas, and the newspaper man tossed out the seeds in hard-to-reach areas so the beautiful trees would flourish on our island. Doesn't that make him a Johnny Flamboyantseed?

Rain didn't stop the crowds at October Sunday

An "Appreciation Day Parade" on December 3rd, 1989, honored WSTA-Lucky 13 for public service during and for 10 days after Hurricane Hugo. A Carnival atmosphere prevailed as hundreds of people lined a mile of Veterans Drive to see the 21 entries that included Miss Virgin Islands, ROTC and High School marching bands, steel bands, Girl and Boy Scouts, Sebastian Majorettes, Junior Firefighters, and The Parrott Gang Boys' Club.

Following the parade, the Day's ceremony to honor the WSTA staff took place at Emancipation Garden with the presentation of an impressive plaque and the announcement that a monument would be constructed to honor these "Hugo Heroes".

•

On the police blotter (Dec. 4, 1989): "A Cruz Bay man reported a disturbance 'between him, a mule and his girlfriend at Fort Christian parking lot.' " Yes, yes, go on . . . These kinds of teasers are frequently in the newspaper, and we never hear anymore about them.

•

From Tom Lawrence's Dec. 4, 1989 "Business File" column in The Daily News: "OOPS! James Michener's hit selling novel, 'Caribbean,' displays a map of the Lesser and Greater Antilles. Seems someone failed to indicate where the island of St. Thomas is located. St. Croix and St. John are easily spotted. Maybe that is why he canceled his speaking engagement at UVI. Guess he couldn't find us."

•

The West Indian way of expressing things is catching. You do not "arrive" at a place, you "reach" it, as in "I reached her house at one o'clock."

When a store item is no longer available, "It's finish."

Something unimportant is, "No big t'ing," and cars in accidents get "mahshed up."

Those of us who have been here a long time, fall naturally into the vernacular, because we hear it so often and also because we find it more colorful and expressive than standard English.

•

KATS on our islands stands for our recent Kids and the Sea Skills program. Besides basic sea skills such as safety, rowing, and handling someone overboard, KATS teaches children to swim. Strangely many children do not grow up learning to swim, even though we are surrounded by water.

MORE PIECES

Traffic Jamming

The Daily News regularly carries police notices of traffic changes for upcoming events. By the time we figure them out, there are other notices, and we must start all over again.

Here are some examples covering traffic flow for the Carnival Calypso Tent held at Lionel Roberts Stadium:

"From today through April 25, starting at 6:30 p.m. each night, traffic to and around the stadium will be converted into a one-way flow.

"Traffic entering from Veterans Drive on Hospital Gade may flow north and west or east on Norre Gade. Traffic can also flow into Seventh Day Street and Prindsen Gade because they are both one-way going east.

"Traffic flow will be allowed to make a left turn into Pollyberg or continue onto Kongens Gade. Traffic coming out of Kongens Gade will be allowed to make a left or right turn onto Hospital Gade.

"Traffic on Pollyberg Hill will not be allowed to travel into Madamberg at the crest of the Hill . . . "

Had enough? We usually have had after the first paragraph.

These are only four excerpts from eleven changes for that five-day period. We decided it was easier to stay home.

The gobbledegook of traffic directions and signs in Paradise is confusing. Except for the "One Way" sign that used to be beside the cemetery road!

Inn Trouble

If you ever thought about running an inn on a tropical island, think again.

First, read Herman Wouk's "Don't Stop The Carnival," and take it as gospel truth. He humorously exposes the interminable problems: electrical outages, telephone snafus, appliances that do not work, shopping for food, getting and keeping good help—especially chefs, running out of water, coping with unreal happenings and difficult guests.

We became acutely aware of the pitfalls of running an inn after we adopted a young couple, Sue and Jay Houston, when they became part owners of the Inn at Mandahl.

We frequented the Inn for many years before their arrival. We liked to indulge in banana pancakes, the house specialty for Sunday Brunch. The eight-room hotel, built in 1963 and called Bali Hai, first operated under owners Kay and Bill Strasser. With an impressive view of islands skirting Sir Francis Drake Channel, its restaurant ranked among St. Thomas' most popular, despite the horrendous road leading to it. You felt you were jolting over a mountain-goat trail. Many roads then fell into that category. Now most are more or less paved, but potholes the size of moon craters still thrive on several main roads.

The Houstons became Bali Hai's managers in 1978 and renamed it "Inn at Mandahl." Because whales cavort in the nearby ocean from January to March, a whale became their logo.

Since we went every Sunday for banana pancakes and once a week for lunch, we became involved in the joys and frustrations of running an island inn. Frustrations came out far ahead.

The Houstons soon acquired two Great Danes, Max and Val (for Valentine), from a friend, and from the Humane Society's Animal Shelter, a donkey named Ginger that needed a home.

The animals contributed their share of problems. Ginger liked to check out the breakfast baskets on the front doors of the eight rooms. If guests did not get there quickly enough, the donkey filched the banana bread.

Ginger also wandered off occasionally, and Sue would set out after her. When she found the animal, she rode the donkey home. Bobbing along on her pseudo-steed caused much hilarity among friends and acquaintances who honked and waved, shouting: "Sue, get your ass out of the middle of the road." The lovely lassie on **that** chassis was not classy. Sue found it amazing the same comment came from everybody, each one considering it highly original and uproarious. Another donkey, Cinderella, later joined the menagerie (now including a parakeet and cat), adding to the problems.

When the Inn was not lively enough for the donkeys, they trotted off and usually headed for Sib's Mountain Bar. This was where they had the most fun with Mafolie Frenchies on holidays like Octoberfest Day. They enjoyed having children climb aboard for rides, and charges for the rides were collected for a "good cause." So the Houstons endured these naughty excursions and did not tether the animals.

Susie, an amateur artist, routed an Inn "Donkey Crossing" sign (with donkey) out of wood. It became a tourist photographer's delight. Like many clever island signs, however, it was stolen.

The donkeys were a great asset to the Inn, entertaining and lovable—sort of. Unhappily, after one of their outings, they never returned. Rumor

If you can find taximan Holman Harley, hire him.
He enjoys his work and you'll enjoy your trip. See page 187

193

had it they "went Hollywood" and joined the bougainvillea bedecked donkey brigade at Drake's Seat, where tourists sit on their backs for a fee to have pictures taken. Since the donkeys seemed well cared for and provided young men a way to make a living, the Houstons did not press for their return.

Jay received his initiation into island labor vagaries when he added a swimming pool to adjoin the Inn's restaurant. He also planned and executed several remodeling projects: moving the bar to a more convenient location and roofing over an open terrace to be used as the Inn's reception room. Jay had an uncanny eye for such improvements and the ability to see them through. Here, that is akin to running a sixty-day tricycle race—a bicycle goes too fast. Workmen and supplies rarely appear at the same time.

It is "the St. Thomas law" that no one ever embarks on a construction job who does not consider murder or suicide before it is finished—weeks, months, even years later than expected.

"Room Number Two" also became an unending headache. Items not nailed down disappeared or were broken, and domestic scenes of trouble flared up with disconcerting regularity. For example, a single woman rented Room Two one afternoon, and later in the night, the Houstons heard a loud commotion, glass breaking, raised voices. They rushed to the scene. The estranged husband of the woman, who turned out to be local, had found her and a fist fight ensued. Result: a glass-jalousied door shattered and a room in shambles.

Jay called the police. By the time they arrived, the couple had reconciled their quarrel. The roughed-up woman said Jay tried to rape her and refused to pay for the room. It was enough to make the Houstons want to sell out the next day. Fortunately, the police did not believe the woman.

So it went with Room Two. Other marital disturbances resulted in overturned furniture or a disarrayed room. No other room gave them trouble, but Room Two never let up. I think it would have been a neat idea to board up Room Two.

Chefs, the Houstons next biggest problem, use the restaurant circuit like a revolving door, going from one to another and often returning to the first one to start over again. If a restaurateur whose chef has just walked out finds himself facing a cocktail or dinner party for fifty or a hundred people, he hires the first live one he can find via the "cookvine."

In such predicaments, Jay and Sue, using other available help and any visiting family, retreated to the kitchen. In an amazingly short time canapés and hors d'oeuvres, or more substantial fare appeared, and the party went off as if all were well. Some restaurateur-managers are not so versatile.

The Houstons even had a chef who became angry at another chef, not at the Houstons. In his fit of anger, he so devastated the Inn's kitchen it had to close for three days. Then he asked to be taken back.

Chefs are invariably models of efficiency and good behavior the first few weeks or months. Then truth will out. Some fight with dining room help; others are as tempermental as old-time prima donnas. Those with a penchant for the bottle—seemingly the biggest problem—start nipping surreptitiously. Little by little it builds up until they cannot find the kitchen. A really good chef without bad habits is worth his weight in gold, and since his salary is usually weighed that way, he remains at a big luxury hotel. Some reliable ones open their own restaurants, which solves *their* chef problem.

Despite the difficulties, the Inn under the Houstons' management was a delightful place to stay—good food, hospitable, a spectacular view. Guests never knew the superman legerdemain involved to keep it that way.

Being young and energetic, the Houstons quickly became part of the community by participating in the Carnival parade and joining such events as the Jeep Rally to raise money for civic causes.

Other dividends came when celebrities like Victor Borge stopped by for dinner and Jack Nelson of "Washington Week In Review" and his author wife Barbara Matusow became Inn "Time Share" owners. All was not grief. Unhappily, the Inn at Mandahl no longer exists. It floundered for sometime after the Houstons gave up, then Hurricane Hugo destroyed it.

If you are day-dreaming about a cozy, worry-free little Caribbean inn and restaurant, do not rush in where the "burned" fear to tread. It is significant that such small hotels are not under the same management long. The turnover would delight a department store—if it were merchandise. Caveat emptor!

MORE BITS

One morning in the early 80s after our traffic increased drastically, the policeman giving radio-traffic information said:

"We're going to have to move the lady selling papers on Raphune Hill. She's messing up traffic."

•

Several times lately I have seen a man with a perky dachshund draped over one shoulder. The dog wears a stylish, loosely knit sweater, a rakish knitted cap with front turned up, white-framed harlequin sunglasses, and observes the world contentedly from her vantage point. Named "Chi-Chi," the dog belongs to Louis Villegas. In Paradise, you never know what you're going to see next. It keeps you on your toes.

•

During the construction of the airport, when airport signs were first put up to mark the way to the airport, the airplanes on the signs were upside down. St. Thomas' expanded airport opened December 1990.

•

When workers were constructing a new water main—on the opposite side of Charlotte Amalie from the airport—large orange signs from the airport project were used by Public Works to direct traffic, especially to the Main Post Office inside a high link fence. One day at the entrance gate to the Post Office was a huge orange sign with "Airport" on it in large black letters. An equally large arrow pointed inside the link fence.

"I see we have a new short cut to the airport," Al said.

Again, we understood how it happened to be there, but we chuckled over what a tourist's reaction might be. Signs are often bewildering in Paradise.

•

In 1986, The Golden Hind, a replica of Sir Francis Drake's famous ship, brought a nautical museum to St. Thomas and offered a cocktail hour tour and dinner hosted by a "reincarnated" Sir Francis Drake. He moved on to happier hunting grounds. Paradise has many unusual attractions.

LAST PIECES

Colorful Island Personalities

From the 30s to the early 50s, a number of "colorful personalities" moved to St. Thomas or spent half the year here. Only a few remained through the 60s. Al and I were fortunate to become acquainted with several.

The late **Aileen Winslow Powell ("Petsey")** came in 1949, and at first spent her half-year residency with several other people in Louisenhoj Castle. Later, she rented a wonderful old Danish townhouse in Charlotte Amalie and stayed there until it was sold. She then finished building her own house of long standing in Bakkeroe.

In 1955, Petsey started the Grand Hotel's Grand Gallery Restaurant. Its "Round Table" (borrowed from New York's Algonquin Hotel) was a luncheon "must" for Continentals who wanted to keep up with St. Thomas gossip.

Active in the St. Thomas Friends of Denmark Society, she hosted the yearly events aboard the *Danmark* when the Danish naval training vessel was in our port. A sailor and horsewoman of note, she sponsored junior sailing events as well as St. Thomas Pony Club activities, and her love of animals kept her busy at the Humane Society's Animal Shelter.

Although Petsey also had a home in Washington, D.C., she travelled extensively when not here. Once when we were in Majorca and met Faye Emerson, she asked if we knew Petsey. It did not surprise us. Petsey's outgoing personality and insatiable interest in everyone drew people to her like a magnet.

Full of fun and humorous stories, she was an inveterate party-giver and loved a Bohemian mixture of people. Among her party guests might be Prince Georg and Princess Anne of Denmark, Burgess Meredith, Countess d'Amecourt, a coterie of Continentals who had adopted the island,

and a sprinkling of charming vagabonds. The St. Thomas Continental social scene gathered momentum when Petsey arrived after Christmas. Life was always more fun when she was around. Her untimely death in January, 1981 distressed everyone who knew her.

•

Jane and Brooks Pratt, also colorful Continental islanders, lived in India for twelve years during the 20s and early 30s, before they came to St. Thomas. Their years in India taught them to live as English colonials did in those days, with plenty of household help and English formality.

They brought with them the English custom of "elevensies," before-lunch drinks, usually champagne, starting at eleven o'clock. The custom still prevailed when we arrived in 1965 and continued until the retired group of Continentals of that era moved or passed away.

Brooks Pratt died in 1967, and afterwards, as long as Jane lived, she was "at home" to her friends every afternoon at 4:00 p.m. She loved laughter and lively conversation and was a master storyteller of her days in India and early days in St. Thomas.

Dubbed "Mrs. St. Thomas" by her circle of retired Continental friends because of her long residency here, she offered genial relaxation and stimulating conversation at those daily gatherings.

As Jane grew older and more reclusive, her friends arranged to come on different days so someone was always there to keep her company until dinner was served at six o'clock. Jane's late afternoon drink was a "pink gin"—gin with a drop or two of bitters, left over from her days in India when the drink was popular. She was straight out of "The Jewel in the Crown," but never English stuffy. We would never have called her "Jane," however, until she asked us to.

Replica of our U.S. Liberty Bell in Emancipation Park

Ever since her years in India, Jane Pratt supported Dr. Graham's Homes, a Scottish Missionary school in Kalimpong, started in 1900 with six orphan boys of European descent.

Jane had told me a great deal about the school after I booked a trip to the Kalimpong and Himalayan kingdom area a couple of years before she died. She wanted me to visit Dr. Graham's Homes and give her a report. Unfortunately, that tour was cancelled. Jane died soon after and left the school a substantial bequest.

In 1983, following her death, I set up another trip that was not cancelled, but we arrived at Kalimpong behind schedule. Even though Jane was dead, I still wanted to visit the school. However, it appeared impossible.

Then a series of unexpected occurences, including a bus driver's strike that affected our driver, lengthened our stay. Afterward, several coincidences made it possible for me to go to the school. You may laugh at me for saying I felt a singular, unexplainable force behind all this—a very strange feeling, and I am usually not sensitive to this kind of Shirley MacLaine experience.

Jane Pratt was probably the last person in St. Thomas to use finger bowls regularly at dinner. When Stateside cousins visited her with their children, Jane, by custom, seated the children apart from adults at dinner. The children were not unhappy with this arrangement, but when the finger bowls arrived, one little girl sidled up to the adult table and sotto voce said into her mother's ear:

"Mother, what do we do with the water?"

Jane delighted in telling the story, which always brought laughter. Sometimes at dinner when the finger bowls arrived, we would say:

"Jane, what do we do with the water?"

Her robust laugh rang out.

She loved jokes on herself such as the one she told about the time she endlessly fussed over Brooks when he was very sick and confined to bed.

Finally one day he said, "Jane, don't you have any errands to do in town?"

That ended the fussing.

Jane's friends celebrated her late August birthday every year with champagne and cake. Always a festive occasion. When she died at ninety-seven in 1981 another era ended.

Little by little over the years, we have left behind bits and pieces of that past, so tranquil and uncomplicated compared to today, but we try not to fall into a crevice of memories that keeps us from enjoying the present.

LAST BITS

Fairchild Park, one of St. Thomas' best kept secrets, is near Mountain Top—famous for banana daiquiris.

A lovely little knoll of grass, plants, and trees effectively set amid boulders, it is visited by few people. Yet, cool and shaded, the fenced-in area offers strollers serenity, peace, and panoramic views.

The Park is another Arthur Fairchild gift to St. Thomas. Part of the past that belonged to Arthur Fairchild and Jane Pratt visit it.

•

A U.S. Virgin Islands bobsled team? Are you kidding?

Realtor and longtime resident John Foster was not. Still I suspect he organized it because the idea pinged his funny bone. He is like that. (As a yachtsman, Foster represented the Virgin Islands three times at the Olympics.)

The bobsled bug bit John in February 1986, and in March he and auto racer Chris Sharpless went to Calgary, Alberta, 1988 Winter Olympics site, and passed their first bobsled course.

In 1987, Foster, Sharpless, Harvey Hook, and John Reeve (all in their 40s) competed at Innsbruck. Only one one-tenth second behind the U.S. team, they outdid Japan, Holland, and Great Britain. The impressed International Bobsled and Toboggan Federation recommended the V.I. Committee support a bobsled team.

Foster believed the team equaled any competition and could win a bobsledding medal in the '88 Games. Unfortunately, they did not, but Virgin Islands bobsledding remains a laughter-getting conversation piece.

Paradise Chuckles

One week some years ago when Al and I went grocery shopping at our Pueblo Supermarket, a sizable quantity of big bags of dry dog food were neatly stacked on top of each other near the checkout counter. A large hand-lettered card on top of the stack said:

"Do not sit on the dry dog food."

The following week, the dog food was still there, but a new sign read:

"Do not sit **at all** on the dry dog food."

The next week brought another sign:

"Do not sit **positively** on the dry dog food."

The fourth week the dog food was gone.

•

A prominent St. Thomas hostess in the 60s put "black tie" on her dinner party invitations. All the men came and wore black ties—along with slacks, shorts, sandals, and tennis shoes.

Another St. Thomas hostess once requested "dinner jackets." The gentlemen again obliged. But some wore jackets green with mold, other were badly faded, and all the jackets were out of style. Our men used to prefer to leave their jackets in the closet, except for a funeral. With our population explosion, however, and the numerous big public social events, our attire for evening parties is more formal.

At one time we had a seafood shop in the Wheatley Shopping Center called "The Fishery" that kept us chuckling over their window signs. Here is a sampling:

"Don't stand too close to showcase. Our fish are fresh."

"Bouillabaisse today. Now isn't that a fine kettle of fish?"

"Come in. We like the smell of people."

"Make a cow happy, eat fish tonight."

"Great products. Great service. We offer a lot to get fed up with."

"Please have some shrimp or scallops over for dinner tonight. They've had some chilling experiences here."

•

A young man from Michigan lived next door to us at Hidden Hill for a year. He taught school at St. Peter and Paul School and was beloved by his students. On his time off around his house and wooded grounds, he usually wore sandals and the kind of sarong men wear in the South Seas, acquired before he came to St. Thomas.

One day when a sightseeing safari bus came by, he was out on the road at his mail box getting his mail. A woman shouted "Stop!" to the driver, and the next thing David knew, the woman had jumped down from the bus, snapped his picture, and hopped back on. We speculated a long time about what she would tell her friends back home.

•

In the late 60s, Art and Judi Witty occupied a temporary residence with phone problems in Fortuna while they built their home in Mafolie. One night at a party a friend said to Judi, "I thought I saw you in the rain yesterday half-way up that telephone pole, and it looked as if you were wearing galoshes."

Judi laughed. "You did see me," she said. "I was replacing the fuse. It has to be done every time we have a hard rain."

Even a glamourous movie gal can't always be glamourous in Paradise.

Barbara Battles had an opposite telephone problem. In one residence she had to water her telephone line when we needed rain. The telephone only worked when the line was wet.

•

After a stranger called and found out our number was not the one he thought he had dialed, he related a couple of his telephone frustrations, then said, "Are the telephones here always this goofy?"

Another day I lifted up the phone and it was making a funny noise. "It doesn't make sense, the phone is pinging. There isn't any dial tone," I said.

"You know nothing makes sense if you live here. You just have to live with it." Al said.

•

For my birthday one year, young Robert Murphy, for whom I had done some favors, brought me a bouquet of flowers from a florist. I unwrapped them from their green tissue paper, put them in a vase, and pulled the card out of its envelope. The printing on the card said, "welcome to your new baby girl" and featured a cute baby girl in a corner. Written on the card was "Many thanks—Happy Birthday!" It was signed "Robert." I began to laugh.

Robert grinned, "I was hoping you wouldn't notice. It was the only card the florist had," he said.

Such things are always happening in St. Thomas. Marion Van Dyck picked up her birthday cake for a party she was having to celebrate a special birthday. When she reached home, she opened the cake box to look inside. "Happy Birthday Lauren" was written across the cake. Marion rushed to the phone to alert the bakery of the error.

"We were behind and hadn't made yours yet, and we didn't want to disappoint you," the baker said. "It'll be easy to change the name."

Marion, who has lived here since the 50s, laughed and did just that. "At least the last letter didn't have to be changed," she said.

•

I love West Indian first names. You know they have been given careful thought and carry sentimental significance. Girls names are: Cynthelia, Christalia, Oxlena, Sepheria, Oraletta, and for boys, Obel, Oswin, Egaltine, Autwin and Evermond. I suspect the names are composed of letters from beloved family members. "Mary" and "John" are nice, but bland. Wouldn't it be exciting to find a name to make your child feel special? Think about it.

•

Ninety-year-old Blanche Sasso, teacher, educator, and descendant of Indian tribes who were the first people to settle the Virgin Islands, went through the devastating 1916 hurricane and said it is difficult to compare

Refreshment stand at a corner of Main Street does a brisk business
on warm afternoons

201

to Hugo because life was so different then. Electric power and television did not exist and water was dipped from wells. She said the 1916 hurricane hit fifty years after a major ravaging one, so people then also took warnings lightly. Her family house lost its roof and rain poured in all night. After the storm they had nothing left but the clothes on their backs and had to stay with friends until they could find another house. "It was terrifying," she said.

A week-long November 1989 cultural exchange program "Pow Wow in Paradise" was a great success in St. Thomas. North American Indians of the Six Nations of the Iroquois and West Indian Caribs from Dominica participated. Originally from the Amazon River Valley and Guiana lowlands, the Caribs migrated to the Caribbean in 1300 A.D. Today 3200 live on a 5.5-square-mile preserve in Dominica. Basket weaving and boat building are important aspects of their culture and their colorful dances portray legends. Irving Auguiste, the Carib leader at present, and his people work with U.S. Peace Corps volunteers as one way to preserve their culture. Their colorful dress and dances attracted favorable attention and support from everyone who came in contact with them during the "Pow Wow in Paradise." Blanche Sasso was honored at the Pow Wow as a Carib Elder.

HURRICANE HUGO

Since this century's most devastating Caribbean hurricane also touched the United States and was an experience one must undergo to appreciate, I will take you through Hurricane Hugo, first-hand, with Al and me. Fasten your seat belts! It's a rough ride.

Full of scowling clouds, the sky loomed dark and heavy on Sunday, September 17th, 1989. The ominous atmosphere warned of Hugo's approach. Al and I took precautions: lowered the hurricane shutters; secured windows and doors; stowed valuables, paintings, bric-a-brac in closets and went to bed uneasy.

Not long after midnight, we awakened abruptly to the roar of a dozen train engines from wind that shook the house with earthquake intensity. The prediction had been right. Hugo, classed a "killer'" hurricane, had walloped us full force.

The following hours became an endless nightmare of noise: crashing, banging, breaking glass; of merciless rain and thundering wind. We learned later that gusts reached more than 200 miles an hour. Trees danced like crazed spirits. Water-saturated ceilings collapsed. The storm's fury broke the mechanism of our guest room awning widows, and the glass partitions swung with pendulum freedom in their twisting frames, helpless as we were against the battering onslaught. Wind forced rain through every opening, every crevice. We fought back with pails, plastic ice cream cartons, towels, blankets, even small rugs, and watched the deluge shred the draperies and water ooze across the tile floor like terror-movie goo. To save family antiques, we pushed furniture against walls and used thick bedspreads for protection. We shoved smaller endangered treasures into already crowded closets and bathrooms, and clutched at anything, including shower curtains, to stem the flood.

After six hours, the hurricane shutters on the gallery overlooking Charlotte Amalie suddenly splintered as easily as toothpicks, and the sliding glass doors they protected began to curve out like potbellies. One door finally burst in, but landed, unshattered, on a couch. It pulled down a 20-foot rod of draperies, pierced a screen door, then lodged itself against the other glass door and kept that one from smashing in. It was a lucky Rube Goldberg happenstance that saved our living room and furniture and left us with only minor ceiling damage.

Hugo's rampage lasted more than twenty hours. Hurricanes usually pass in six or eight hours. The attack stripped trees of leaves and small branches; plants sprawled flat, entangled, drained of color, as if dead. Miles of utility poles enwreathed with power lines lay along the roads like matches carelessly tossed from a giant's matchbox. Numerous poles had snapped in the middle; others resembled Towers of Pisa as they leaned precariously across highways and festooned wires an inch above car roofs, offering a game of Russian Roulette for drivers.

Hundreds of houses gaped roofless; many lost porches or walls; others suffered complete destruction. Thousands of windows gave up their glass to Hugo; huge sections of corrugated steel roofing, casual as newspaper pages blown from a car, found resting places everywhere on streets and hillsides. One man saw a complete roof and later a dumpster fly through the air when the hurricane was at its height. With wreckage far and wide, the countryside desolate, our beautiful island could have been bombed-out Viet Nam.

Through that terrible time immediately after Hugo when recovery seemed impossible, our spirits, courage, and sanity were kept alive by radio station WSTA, Lucky 13. Lee Carle, Addie Ottley, and Brownie spearheaded the station's pledge to stay on the air day and night to relay emergencies to the hospital and power company. Through their message center, they assured listeners that friends and relatives were still alive and safe. They told the homeless where to go for food, shelter, and aid. They gave sensible advice to the stunned and frightened. Hurricane Hugo demolished all other radio and TV stations, but WSTA operated under its own emergency equipment.

For days, Lucky 13 was our only contact with the outside world, a lone voice of hope, as Al and I struggled to adapt to life without electricity, telephone, running water, and, at first, isolation because of a huge fallen tree across our driveway. The station made us feel someone cared, that if we didn't panic and held on, everything would be all right soon. Gleanings indicated that sheer will power and ingenuity kept the station on the air, that they literally held wires and antennae by hand to keep broadcasting. They even dispensed with their commercials and the revenue to serve the public during this critical time. The people of these islands will never forget the station's unselfish efforts in our behalf.

Miraculously, casualties were few, but Hugo's swath of destruction deprived thousands of people of electricity, telephone, and running water. Although some residents were better off, many were homeless and had to find public shelters and emergency kitchens for food. As one man put it: "Paradise is in a helluva mess."

Before long, though, islanders thanked God for survival and began to build anew. People opened their battered doors to the homeless, helped neighbors they didn't know, reached out to unknown victims of the disaster and gave food, clothing, and moral support. As in Charleston, South Carolina, heartless looters did their dirty work in the first few hours of the hurricane, then greed satisfied, or afraid of being shot, they halted their evildoing against their stricken fellow men. Nature cooperated by sending out small green shoots on trees and plants within ten days. Power crews came from Florida, Georgia, Alabama, Texas, Tennessee, Massachusetts, and even Guam, with their own equipment to help restore electricity. They worked in shifts around the clock. Still it took weeks, for some households months, before utilities were functioning.

Since Al and I live in the country, we had to endure five weeks without electricity and running water and seven weeks without telephone. I learned to scramble eggs and make "cook-whatever-you-have-left-soup" on Sterno, to take a "Bird bath" in a quart of water, to save every drop of used water, including dishwater, to flush toilets, and to pail water from the cistern under the gallery floor on my hands and knees. Friends finally eased our electrical deficiency with portable generators.

We groped around at night in the insecure light of candles, flashlights, and battery-operated and oil lamps. The light seemed never enough, like spelunking with a handful of matches. We felt fortunate, though, to be alive, and to have a roof over our heads. Weeks after Hugo, hundreds of people remained homeless, and St. Croix was still a heartbreaking wasteland. Such terrifying experiences make you think about things you have not thought of before.

Ray Smith summed it up well in a letter-to-the-editor: "This devastating experience has shown us how less important material things are compared to how valuable a living soul is to all of us. Thank God for life—we survived Hurricane Hugo. Now it is time to pick ourselves up, dust ourselves off and start all over again—for better and not for worse."

After the first shock, anguish, and despair over Hugo passed, like a Shakespeare tragedy, light moments flickered. The following vignettes are significant of the formidable spirit of Virgin Islanders:

(1) Ten days after Hugo, as I drove along Skyline Drive, I saw a friend sitting at the side of the road talking over a telephone with a 20-foot line that came from her roofless house and completely cleaned out second story behind her. She waved and smiled as if this were a normal scene.

(2) The Daily News ran a picture and story about a sizeable horse that

walked into a laundromat and refused to leave. Was he ready to "come clean?"

(3) The spunk of this ad appeals to me. It appeared under "Notices": Tom Lorey-Pianos. Roof, phone are gone. Living and working now at Tillett Gardens. "I can fix your piano."

(4) After Hugo, Susie Houston, an American Airline flight attendant categoried "homeless" by the airline, couldn't get direct transportation from San Juan to St. Thomas when she finished her flight duties. For days, she and her husband, Jay, had been incommunicado. Worried about him and their house, she flew on a tiny plane to Beef Island, Tortola, in the British Virgin Islands. There, she persuaded the plane's ground mechanic, who also drove a taxi, to take her clear across Tortola to West End Dock to catch the ferry to Red Hook, St. Thomas. The 45-minute bumpy ride cost her $25. Unknown to Sue, Hugo left their home uninhabitable, and Jay was staying on a friend's boat at Red Hook. As luck would have it, Jay saw Sue get off the ferry, and he rushed by tender to intercept her before she found a ride to their wrecked house. He made it. A Hugo story with a happy ending—sort of.

(5) After Hurricane Hugo, airline employees were asked to come and help clean up Cyril E. King Airport terminal. Several times this announcement came over the radio: "All American Airline employees report to the airport terminal wearing only your American Airline shirts."

Aren't you glad you didn't go through all this? Adieu, Hugo.

Photo by susan Houston

Hurricane Hugo denuded most trees in the Virgin Islands. Those that weren't uprooted, came back. This photo, taken shortly after the hurricane, shows one of St. Thomas' two ancient African Baobab trees in Roosevelt Park, leaves gone. Baobab trees can grow to 30 -ft. diameter, but St. Thomas' are only 4-ft. diameter. Baobab trees can hold from 200 to several thousand gallons of water in their hollow trunks making them valuable in dry areas. They are also used for making rope and glue

CHAPTER 18

EXODUS

Highs and Lows in Paradise

It is a perfect day in Paradise.

Your telephone is on duty. Public works has just fixed "with licorice and spit," as a friend said, the year-old pothole near your driveway. The one that could garage a VW and you never seemed able to straddle. You sip your breakfast coffee contentedly on your gallery and look out on the peaceful Charlotte Amalie Harbor and Caribbean Sea.

Morning sunbeams dance on the turquoise water as you watch luxury cruise ships maneuver into their dock "nests" for the day. Small sailboats bob at anchor, or unfurl canvas and move like bits of drifting white paper toward open sea. Bananaquits nibble from the sugar tray, then shake their feathers with delight as they shower in the bird bath. Nearby a lizard performs his morning push-ups and pauses to lap up an unwary insect. All is right with the world. Ah, Paradise...

Look out! Tomorrow will be a hellion.

A barge will knock out power lines crossing a section of harbor (as happened recently) and leave the entire island without electricity for several hours. A snafu in the telephone company's new digital switching system may zap the island's complete telephone service for an entire afternoon. The man will not show up to abracadabra the swimming pool's murky greenness into crystal clear water, and the gardener will come down with chicken pox. Finally, when you rush out to your car, late for a dental appointment, you find a flat tire.

Mahogany Run Golf Course and Condos. Clubhouse is visible upper center below road. As could be expected in mountainous terrain like St. Thomas, this course is challenging

Secret Harbor Beach

That is life "inside" Paradise. Like a giant roller-coaster, it awards you a "high" one minute, but the next, plunges you into an abyss of the damned. You live constantly in the fast lane—skirting one catastrophe by a hair and the next one by a half-hair.

Yet, usually by each day's end, everything comes together, more or less. The phone rings, electricity whirs the meter, the roof leak is fixed, and the post office found your lost package. You decide you have not done badly, even if the bank has not straightened out your account, your car is not repaired as promised, and the Stateside stove parts you ordered are the wrong size.

Exodus from Paradise?

Probably never. Most of us old-timers feel about the island as Leo Buscaglia's mother did when she referred to her husband of many years: "Murder often. Divorce never!"

Every long-time Continental I know has at one time or another exclaimed:

"Why do I stay on this crazy little island—it's a disaster area!"

Those are the days you should have stood in bed. Nothing—and I mean **nothing** goes right. Like a hangover, such days pass. Before long you read about blizzards in Michigan and people freezing to death. On TV you see the warlike havoc of an Iowa cyclone, or watch half-drowned houses buffeted by turbid waters in a flooded Pennsylvania valley. You say to yourself:

"Thank goodness, I live on an island in the sun!"

Island People

This comes from being an "Island Person." You is, or you ain't. Al has been physically unable to travel for over ten years. During that time, Mary Gleason and I have traveled together. After several trips, we realized we always headed for islands. Find us an island and we will go there.

People who suffer from claustrophobia, however, and newcomers who get restless as caged cheetahs in a short time, should forget Paradise.

They are not Island People. True Island People never feel confined. We look out every day at a grand expanse of cloud-dappled blue sky, the sea stretching to every horizon, graceful sweeps of mountains, lush trees and exotic flowers. We feel we can throw our arms out wide and not hit a wall. It is a condominium on the tenth floor of a high-rise building in flat Florida that would turn me into a caged cheetah. To each his own.

Most of us feel the need to get away from time to time. It has nothing to do with the island's mountains and beaches being squashed into a 32-square-mile area. Simply the need for a change.

Culture in Paradise

We harbor no illusions about St. Thomas being Shangri-La. It is not even a "rich and famous" island. Yet, for a vacation, it is as close as you can get to Paradise. We plan to take advantage of that sometime.

Besides beaches, water sports, horse races, tennis, and Mahogany Run Golf Course, St. Thomas has a credible amount of "culture." Lovers of the dance (all St. Thomians) enjoy St. Thomas School of Dance revues, V.I. Folkloric Dancers, The Mungo Niles Cultural Dancers, and the Odomadakoma Asawfo Dance Company.

Music lovers are impressed by the Caribbean Chorale, V.I. University concert groups, Music in Motion, our V.I. Jazz Festival, first sponsored by the V.I. Council of the Arts in 1987. The Festival featured such jazz greats as Richie Cole, Dizzie Gillespie, Bobby Hutcherson and Gary Bartz. For

West Indies Inn in Frenchtown. Replaces Villa Olga Hotel where Gilligan's Garden Café and Crosby were located. Caters to scuba divers. See page 122-124. Do not confuse with the Chart House which replaced Villa Olga. Villa Olga and Villa Olga Hotel were two different places

October Sunday. See also photo page 190

theater buffs, we have The Point, Sunshine Theater and Coral World's Dinner Theater by the Sea. Art shows flourish: Reichhold Center, A.H. Riise's Art Gallery, Fort Christian Museum, hotels, restaurants and shops.

"Arts Alive" Fairs at Tillett Gardens have escalated into extravaganzas. Categories include oil paintings, watercolors, acrylics, sculpture, photography, jewelry, needlecraft, graphics, woodworks, ceramics, and novelties.

For entertainment, Mocko Jumbies stilt-dance, acrobats execute fantastic gymnastics, bands oompah, choruses trill and dancers leap. The three-day event, given three times a year, has grown like Jack's beanstalk and attracts enthusiastic crowds. People come from other Caribbean islands, the United States and Europe.

We also have cultural events from the sea. Confused? I am not talking about singing porpoises or performing sharks, but about entertainment that comes via ships.

Navy bands from U.S. naval vessels frequently perform in Emancipation Garden, and chorus groups and musicians from cruise ships use the Park bandstand to give locals and tourists musical treats.

A few years ago, fifty Canadian bagpipers, complete with kilts and accompanying drums, aboard the *Victoria*, marched down the waterfront to Emancipation Garden and gave a rousing concert. No one said "Pipe down!"

Paradise Organized

With the passing years, St. Thomas has become an island of organizations.

The list of their meetings takes up almost a whole column in The Daily News. Groups range from women's civic clubs to Alcoholics Anonymous and a chef's group called The Virgin Islands Culinary Association. We have Rotary and Lion Clubs, The American Association of Retired Persons, The Caribbean Executive Women's Network, beauty pageants that include the selection of Miss American Virgin Islands and our Carnival Queen. Sometimes I think we have more organizations than people.

Youth in Paradise

In the past few years, I have noticed a new pride among Virgin Islanders, such as the fathering of a successful "Savan Day Celebration." Savan became a deteriorating town area, but a group of residents decided to change that. Cleanups, refurbishing, and a street of new shops owned and operated by Savan people was the result and will surely inspire others.

I am gratified also to see native St. Thomians winners in the yearly Daily News "Best Contest" that covers 30 categories from "Best Dressed Woman" and "Best Dressed Man" to "Best Bartender" and "Best Kallaloo."

I commend, too, groups of caring local and Continental businessmen, educators, marine people, and others who organize programs to bring deprived young people into private enterprise. One, V.I. Private Industry Council, conscientiously seeks applicants for their employee training program. Anyone 16 or older is eligible. Directors include a banker, the island's owner of McDonald's, personnel from the University of the Virgin Islands and the Vocational Education Advisory Council.

The FBLA (Future Business Leaders of America) also provides youths with "a positive forum for learning the rewards of entrepreneurship and its value to the community." By developing competent, aggressive business leadership and building each student's confidence in himself, the group creates an interest and understanding of American enterprise. The Multi-Purpose Youth Center, supported by a wide range of civic organi-

Coral Bay General Store, St. John, after Hurricane Hugo.
This is the back of the store and refreshment area being repaired.
Though damage was severe, they kept going as best they could. See Chapter 17

Friend with Jerry the parrot at the Green Parrot Bar at Magens Point Resort Hotel

zations, including Rotary, does an excellent job preparing school dropouts for a second chance. Hope is never lost for our deprived youth.

Our privileged young people do not need help. They shine wherever they go and are frequently tapped for honor societies, Rhodes scholars, and by publications that list outstanding college students. Many excel in sports and are winners of gold and silver Olympic medals. Our Julian Jackson is the World Boxing Association's middleweight champion.

Celebrities in Paradise

Although much has changed negatively in St. Thomas during the past twenty-five years, some things have not. One is our celebrity visitors. As a resort area, our sun, sand, surf, and spectacular scenery has always attracted them for vacations.

During our early years on St. Thomas, movie greats came: Elizabeth Taylor, Richard Burton, Ginger Rogers, Leslie Caron, Burgess Meredith; yearly royalty included Prince Georg and Princess Anne of Denmark; political royalty: Jackie Kennedy, Ladybird Johnson and the Henry Kissingers (regulars at Caneel Bay on St. John); and the rich Aristotle Onassis.

Now our celebrities are Rosalynn and Jimmy Carter and their secret service agents; PBS star reporter Charlayne Hunter-Gault; columnist Art Buchwald; authors James Michener and Robert Ludlum; comedian Flip Wilson; Major League Baseball's all-time home run king, Hank Aaron, and his wife Billye. Aaron wants to help develop the islands' baseball talent. Popular radio and TV commentator Charles Osgood; and soap opera stars often stretch out on our beaches.

John Patrick, Pulitzer Prize playwright, who wrote the eternally popular play, "Teahouse of the August Moon," came and stayed. He resides now on a charming old sugar mill estate in Fortuna. Long-time St. Thomas resident, novelist Eleanor Heckert, still writes her Caribbean novels here. Tony Brown vacations on the island regularly, and in May 1988 premiered his first film, "The White Girl," in St. Thomas.

All celebrities are welcome, and, for the most part, not pestered. Enchantment with the islands keeps bringing them back. If they remain tourists, that magic will never fade.

The magic has faded over the years for starry-eyed promoters with schemes ranging from island tourist films to a replica of the *Santa Maria* Columbus sailed to St. Croix. A Chinese junk from Hong Kong and a hydrofoil that skimmed the waves like a flying fish added panache for a few seasons. Twenty-five years ago a restaurant-ship dawdled in the harbor (unsuccessfully), and a couple of years ago, several backers were enthusiastic about a gambling ship. But nary a roulette wheel ever twirled. Talk of legal gambling always brings forth a gaggle-of-geese outcry from our citizenry. They know gambling on other islands has yet to deliver the promised pot of gold at the rainbow's end. So it goes. Never a dull moment in Paradise. You tend to keep a mental score, however, on the pluses and the minuses.

Minuses:

1. The discovery in April 1988 of a trailer of mail lost in Puerto Rico since November 1985. Almost all mail came through Puerto Rico then, and we often suffered from their indifference. At least, once the shipment arrived in St. Thomas, our post office dispatched its contents promptly.

2. People no longer reverently walk Main Street in funeral processions headed for the cemetery, nor do merchants respectfully close their doors as a cortege passes by.

3. Telephone linemen, high on their poles, no longer work under beach umbrellas, and bulldozers no longer decorate their fronts with huge bouquets of bougainvillea.

Tourists entering Coral World. See also photo page 154

Mongoose Junction (Cruz Bay Village shopping center, St. John, with tour buses

4. Hurricane Hugo. (Did you know "hurricane" comes from "hurrican," a Caribbean word that means "evil spirit?" I won't dispute the definition.)

Pluses:

1. Ed Bradley with his "60 Minutes" crew covered island Texans who came to St. Thomas after the Texas oil market slump. The coverage brought us publicity and put us "on the map," but spotlighted our defects.

2. Our St. Thomas Rotary Clubs admit women.

3. Six weeks after Hugo, sixty young Virgin Island musicians of the Territorial Court Rising Stars Steel Orchestra performed at New York's Lincoln Center to help rebuild the island's image. The group received high praise and remains our best ambassador.

4. St. Thomian Vanna Thomas, our 1989 Miss American Virgin Islands, who also won the regional Caribbean Queen title, placed in the top ten contestants at the Miss World Contest in Hong Kong.

5. Tour operator Roy Sheridan, despite lack of cooperation from government officials and the general public, persists in trying to keep our island litter free. In 1987, he and Eloise Mack, a legal assistant, organized Pride Day for islanders to show pride by cleaning up the roadsides. Around 35 groups participate, but roadside litter has not stopped. Still one heartening outcome is St. Peter and Paul School's "Radius Club." Members wear red T-shirts imprinted with the club name. Their original goal was to keep clean only a small "radius" around the school, but their success let them expand. The club encourages other schools to form clubs, and they speak to adult groups, using clever, well-executed posters to persuade people, young and old, to keep our island clean. Bravo! Radius Club.

6. A recent group, VISSA (Virgin Islands Social Singles Association)

organized to bring together single people of all races for social events not involved in cruising bars and night clubs. Members do not expect romance, only companionship. Teachers, an accountant, a doctor and a lawyer are among its members, ranging in age from 25 to 60 and equally divided between sexes. For meetings, they have toured the harbor, hiked, enjoyed potluck suppers, dances and guest speakers. VISSA seems to me a splendid idea for getting lonely singles together.

•

I "exodus," leaving each reader this wish: May all your future days be as happy and idyllic—wherever you live—as you have heretofore imagined American Paradise. God bless!

Author June Brown at doorstep of her Harbor Ridge East townhouse condominium

CAPSULE GLANCE AT ST. THOMAS
by the Editor

If you've read all through June's book, you've learned a great deal about St. Thomas, its people, how it works, what makes it tick, and how it got to be the way you see it. What follows is a brief descriptive summary of "American Paradise" today.

Population—1990 census, 50,000; 1987 local estimates, 52,000. People who live on St. Thomas believe that both these figures are grossly undercounted. They believe the correct figure to be approximately 70,000. The difference could be in illegal immigrants who hide from census takers. St. Thomas has had an influx of these from the Dominican Republic and from Puerto Rico. To the extent that it exists, this undercounting is similar to what happened in many parts of mainland USA.

Climate—Tropical. Palm trees. Winter temperatures an average daily high in the low 80s F, dropping to an average low 70s at night. Easterly breezes make it pleasant almost the year round, though summers are hot. There's only about 8° or 10° F temperature difference summer and winter. Water temperatures stay warm and swimmable year round. Water colors are indescribably beautiful shades of blue, green and turquoise. Sunshine is brilliant, requiring sunglasses and skin protection. To stay in the USA, and be guaranteed the excellent winter weather enjoyed by eastern Caribbean isles, you have to go to the U.S. Virgin Islands or to Hawaii. Other parts of the USA are subject to continental weather patterns.

Average annual rainfall is about 40 inches, but like the rest of the Caribbean, there is a wet season and a dry season. I'll never forget our first Caribbean cruise out of St. Thomas in February. We never had winds less than 15 knots, nor more than 25. It rained only once in three weeks, a 20-minute squall off Tortola. The dry season extends from mid-December to early June. It rains a little at first, then more often in July, and too much in August. In September comes the deluge, and it doesn't taper off much in October. November is like July, early December like mid-June. Before Christmas, the rain shuts off. The island is beautifully green into early spring, but becomes parched and dry by May. Really, 40 inches is not excessive rain, about what we get in the northeast USA, but St. Thomas' rain is concentrated in summer and fall.

Caribbean trade winds prevail in St. Thomas. Strong northeast to east winds start in mid-December and last well into January, coinciding with the onset of the dry season. These are called "Christmas Winds," and they can blow 30 to 35 knots for days at a time. This moderates mid-January to 20 to 25 knots, still strong. During February you'll have mostly 15 to 20 knots, pleasant sailing, and winds will become lighter during spring, but still pleasant, 10 to 18 knots. During summer there's increasing frequency of winds below 10 knots, and a few calms.

The basic wind direction is east. Many days during the winter, winds will be northeast, and it will swing south of east during many summer days. These southeast winds will usually be lighter and the days will be hot.

Hurricane season is from August to mid-November, most common in the Caribbean during September and October. Some island resorts close down after Labor Day and open again Thanksgiving. Read Chapter 17 for June's graphic description of Hurricane Hugo.

Land area of St. Thomas is only 32 square miles. As you can see from our map on pages 12 and 13, the island is long and mostly narrow. St. Thomas is volcanic in origin, and is craggy. The population is accommodated only because they've built on every hill and atop mountains. Roads are mostly narrow, following contours. There are approximately 22,000 registered vehicles!

Language is English though you'll hear Spanish, and see some Spanish labels in supermarkets. Many local people also speak Creole, some having immigrated from other Caribbean isles.

Religion—As in the USA, every major and most minor religions are represented, including Bahai, Hindu, Jehovah's Witness, Moravian, Moslem, and Seventh Day Adventist.

Government—The U.S. Virgin Islands are an unincorporated territory of the United States. The capital of St. Thomas and the territorial capital is Charlotte Amalie (pronounced am-ahl'-yah). Voters elect a non-voting delegate to the U.S. House of Representatives. There are three branches of government—executive, legislative, and judicial. The governor is elected for a four-year term. Fifteen senators are elected every two years. There are local and district courts. June describes this more fully in Chapter 14.

Hotels—At this writing, there are about 4000 hotel rooms in the U.S. Virgin Islands, more than ⅔ between St. Thomas and St. John. Occupancy during the last two years has been mostly below 70 percent. There is room for you! Tourism is the mainstay of St. Thomas' economy. There's a 7½ percent tax on hotel rooms.

Cruise Ships—There were 648 cruise ship visits to St. Thomas during the first six months of 1990, with more than 616,000 passengers, making St. Thomas the Caribbean's most popular cruise ship stop. This keeps Havensight Mall and downtown Charlotte Amalie very crowded. You've never seen such traffic jams.

Following is a list of cruise lines currently calling at St. Thomas. Nearly all of them have several ships. Rather than list all the ships and their amenities, we're giving you addresses and phone numbers so you can get sailing dates, prices, etc. These change continuously, and more ships are coming into service every year. There's room for you!

A few of these lines also call at St. John. We have noted this. At present, Paquet French Cruises calls at St. John, but not at St. Thomas. This also is noted.

Admiral Cruises (also stops at St. John)
1050 Caribbean Way
Miami, FL 33132
(305) 374-1611 or (800) 327-6700
Carnival Cruise Lines
3655 N.W. 87th Avenue
Miami, FL 33178
(305) 599-2600
Celebrity Cruises (see also Chandris below)
900 Third Avenue
New York, NY 10022
(212) 223-3003 or (800) 621-2100 or (800) 432-4132
Chandris Fantasy Cruises
Same address as Celebrity Cruises above
For reservations, main office
5200 Blue Lagoon Drive
Miami, FL 33126
(800) 437-3111
Club Méditerranée
40 West 57th Street
New York, NY 10019
(212) 977-2170 or (800) 258-2633
Commodore Cruise Line (also stops at St. John)
800 Douglas Road
Coral Gables, FL 33134
(305) 529-3000 or (800) 237-5361
Costa Cruise Lines
World Trade Center
80 S.W. Eighth Street
Miami, FL 33130
(305) 358-7330 or (800) 462-6782
Cunard Line
555 Fifth Avenue
New York, NY 10017
(800) 221-4770; (800) 458-9000 for *Sea Goddess*
Dolphin Cruise Line (also stops at St. John)
901 South America Way
Miami, FL 33132
(305) 358-2111 or (800) 222-1003
Holland America Line
300 Elliott Avenue West
Seattle, WA 98119
(206) 281-3535 or (800) 426-0327
Norwegian Cruise Line (also stops at St. John)
95 Merrick Way
Coral Gables, FL 33134
(305) 447-9660 or (800) 327-7030

Paquet French Cruises (Ocean Cruise Lines) (only stops at St. John)
1510 S.E. 17th Street
Ft. Lauderdale, FL 33316
(305) 764-3500 or (800) 556-8850 outside Florida
Princess Cruises
10100 Santa Monica Boulevard
Los Angeles, CA 90067
(213) 553-1770 or (800) 421-0522 for reservations
Regency Cruises
260 Madison Avenue
New York, NY 10016
(212) 972-4774 or (800) 388-9090
Royal Caribbean Cruises
1050 Caribbean Way
Miami, FL 33132
(305) 379-2601 or (800) 327-6700
Epirotiki Lines
551 Fifth Avenue, Suite 605
New York, NY 10176
(212) 599-1750 or (800) 221-2470 outside NY State
International Cruise Center
250 Old Country Road
Mineola , NY 11501
(516) 747-8880 or (800) 221-3254
Sun Line Cruises
1 Rockefeller Plaza, Suite 315
New York, NY 10020
(212) 397-6400 or (800) 872-6400 outside New York City

Air Transportation—The Cyril E. King Airport near the waterfront west of Charlotte Amalie had nearly 300,000 air arrivals during the first six months of 1989, and about 270,000 during the first six months of 1990. They come on direct flights from New York, Dallas, Miami, Puerto Rico, Tortola and various Leeward Islands. Service is by American Airlines, Continental, LIAT, Pan American, Midway, and some smaller charter airlines. Many inter-island lines connect St. Thomas with other Caribbean islands, including Eastern Caribbean Airlines, Air Caribbean, Dorado Wings, All Island Airways, Air Mello, Virgin Air, Marshall's Air, Trans-Commuter Airlines, BVI and Vieques Airlink. A seaplane service was cancelled after Hurricane Hugo, but is about to resume. The new enlarged terminal at Cyril E. King Airport was opened December, 1990.

Car Rentals require a valid license. Prices are approximately $40 per day, mostly with unlimited mileage. Taxi service is very good except when several large cruise ships arrive at the same time. Driving is to the left, British style.

Activities and Sightseeing—For me, beaches and sailing are St. Thomas' main attractions. Beautiful palm-lined beaches are everywhere. There are no nude or topless beaches. Many of the hotels have their own beaches, and we've included photos of some. I like Magen's Bay best. It's public, and a mile long. Other popular beaches are Secret Harbour, Morningstar, Coki Beach, Brewer's Beach, and Stumpy Bay. As mentioned in Chapter 15, St. Thomas is a center for chartering, both bareboats and skippered boats, all sizes, many pretty luxurious. The Virgin Islands, British and American, are the most popular chartering areas in this hemisphere. Chartering a boat is easy. Look in the chartering advertising sections of boating magazines. St. Thomas is also a cruising destination. In Red Hook Bay and Charlotte Amalie Harbor, you'll meet cruising sailors from all over the world.

Other water sports include snorkeling, scuba diving, sport fishing (excellent!), board sailing, para sailing, and day sailing. There are rentals and/or charter boats for all these activities.

Shopping—The other major activity is shopping. Our maps delineate the downtown shopping areas and there are worthwhile stores in Havensight Mall, many described by June. Refer to list of maps on page 3. This is high grade, duty free, first class, industrial strength shopping! You'll recognize the names. Like many men, I try to stay out of stores, but my lady friends have all flipped over St. Thomas' stores. You can buy everything from diamonds and emeralds priced in six figures to more affordable souvenirs.

Are there bargains? Sure there are but I hesitate to spell them out in detail because duty-free shopping prices at any time depend on rates of exchange in countries of origin. Currently the U.S. dollar is depressed against the stronger currencies of most of our major trading partners. Nonetheless, I'll make a stab at present conditions. Shopping areas are delineated on the maps of Charlotte Amalie on page 102, West Charlotte Amalie and Frenchtown on page 104, and Havensight Mall on page 148.

Native handicrafts are excellent, and always a bargain, beautiful handwoven straws ranging from hats to handbags to baskets. For an excellent selection, try Coconut Republic in Royal Dane Mall, or the Straw Factory at Bakery Square. Street vendors offer more limited selections but the price is right. If you only want mementos, local handicrafts and T shirts won't break your budget.

Also always a bargain is liquor. You're allowed to bring home five litres per person if at least one liter is produced in the U.S. Virgin Islands. I think the Caribbean's best rums are produced in Barbados and Puerto Rico, but I'll take Cruzan rum anytime it's offered. You'll see plane returnees schlepping cartons of hooch, along with their other acquisitions. I've never done this, though most of my cruising companions do. I don't drink enough to make it worth the effort to get it home, but the savings will range up to 40 percent of mainland U.S. prices. I'll never forget my friend Earl Bragdon valiantly trying to manage his many carry-ons at Barbados. A bottle of 12-year old scotch fell through his bag's bottom, splintering against the asphalt as we walked out of the terminal to the plane. Earl just kept on walking as though nothing had happened. What else could he do? Sparky's Gifts and A. H. Riise Liquors will package them in a carrying case to try to prevent this, but you need a free hand to get liquor home intact.

Sometimes you'll find bargains on cameras, watches, perfume, china and crystal. If you need any of this, be sure to check your local stores before you visit St. Thomas, so you'll know a bargain when you see it.

I've never been able to buy cameras as economically at any duty-free port as I've bought in New York City's discount houses. Nonetheless, Boolchand's and A. H. Riise both have excellent selections of good camera and video recorder equipment, and you might like their prices.

A.H. Riise has a series of connected Main Street stores as well as facilities at Havensight Mall, more convenient for cruise ship passengers. Besides liquorand cameras, these stores sell watches perfume, crystal and china among other items. There are four locations of Little Switzerland stores, including one at Havensight Mall. They have lovely displays of expensive gift items. If you don't shop anywhere else, at least look into A. H. Riise's complex and Little Switzerland. These are old establishments. Nearly 30 years ago, our ladies were fascinated by Little Switzerland's display at Roadtown, Tortola, and A. H. Riise's busy store in Charlotte Amalie.

The English Shop at Market Square specializes in crystal and china. They have quality in all price ranges. Also look at The Crystal Shoppe in Royal Dane Mall. You'll see some very fine crystal in both stores.

H. Stern distributes Piaget watches and their own sapphire watches. Royal Caribbean on Main Street has Seiko, Swatch, and Pulsar watches. Columbian Emeralds International is famous for emeralds, but also has Omega, Calypso, and Tissot watches.

Perfume is available in bewildering profusion, good selections at the Perfume Palace, Bolero's, and Tropicanna Perfume Shoppes. Perfume is nearly always a bargain.

I have no patience for any of this, but if you want to make your ladies happy, turn them loose in these and other stores while you have fun in the other St. Thomas attractions.

•

June has mentioned much worthwhile sightseeing and these places are located on the maps we've made for you. The docks at Red Hook and Yacht Haven at Charlotte Amalie are a bustling nautical scene. Go to the Frenchtown shore to watch the activity when the fishermen bring their catch in and sell it. Have lunch and enjoy the view from Blackbeard's Castle. Sit on Drake's Seat and admire the view. You can go horseback riding, play tennis, play golf, visit Coral World underwater marine park, or go for a submarine ride. Walk "99 steps" to Crown House, an 18th Century mansion that was home to two past governors. Fort Christian, built in 1672, has a museum with old maps and early island artifacts. The synagogue is the second oldest in this hemisphere, and has a sandy floor. Visit one or another of the produce markets, a colorful scene in any Caribbean country. Visit the Legislature Building (the Green Barn!). Try to time your visit to the Reichold Center for the Arts when there's some cultural offering going on. There are many other interesting areas that June describes, including Emancipation Park, Fairchild Park, Tillet Gardens, and Palm Passage. Take this book with you, and use our maps. Read Chapter 10.

June describes the advantages and disadvantages of living in St. Thomas all through the book. These are summarized in Chapter 18.

Dining Out—As might be expected on an island where so many people visit, there are many excellent restaurants in American Paradise. Some are mentioned in this book. You can have every kind of cuisine you ever heard of, but indigenous to the island are Caribbean delicacies, and even the noted French cuisine has some island influence. Be sure you and the waiter reach an understanding on the meaning of "hot" (degree of spiciness)!

•

June has enjoyed many wonderful years living on St. Thomas. I have enjoyed visiting. Go see for yourself this truly unique part of the USA.

Produce market outside Lionel Roberts Stadium, St. Thomas

INDEX

224